M. VODOPYANOV

WINGS
over
THE ARCTIC

I0224749

Fredonia Books
Amsterdam, The Netherlands

Wings Over the Arctic

by
Mikhail Vodopyanov

ISBN: 1-58963-385-7

Copyright © 2001 by Fredonia Books

Reprinted from the original edition

Fredonia Books
Amsterdam, The Netherlands
http://www.fredoniabooks.com

CONTENTS

CONTENTS

PUBLISHER'S NOTE

Mikhail Vodopyanov is a well-known flyer whose life abounds in interesting events.

In 1919 he joined the Soviet Army where he fulfilled various duties until finally he developed into a first-class air-mechanic.

At the end of 1928 M. V. Vodopyanov obtained a pilot's certificate and six months later was detailed to the Far East where in extremely difficult conditions he opened an airline to Sakhalin. He worked on different air routes, flew the *Pravda* matrices to Leningrad and Kharkov and in 1932 reconnoitred seal in the Caspian Sea.

In 1934 M. V. Vodopyanov took part in the *Chelyuskin* rescue operations in the Chukchi Sea and was awarded the title of Hero of the Soviet Union, which was then only instituted.

From then on he devoted himself entirely to work in the Arctic, to the polar air service, participating in the great flights from Moscow to Cape Shmidt and to Rudolph Island.

In 1937 a great victory was won in the Arctic—on May 21 M. V. Vodopyanov, in charge of an air group, landed his flagship on an ice-floe at the North Pole where a drifting station was established.

During the war against the White Finns in 1939-1940 M. V. Vodopyanov took part in the air operations at the fronts, sharing his rich polar flying experience in severe frost with the combat pilots. During the Great Patriotic War against the nazi invaders he participated in many bombing missions. After the war he went back · the polar air service.

M. V. Vodopyanov is the author of a number of books and plays which have been staged by many theatres in different parts of the Soviet Union.

The book *Wings Over the Arctic* is a revised and supplemented edition of *Way of a Pilot* and is not only a story of arctic flights, but is actually a brief history of air conquest of the Arctic. The book tells about the tremendous work done in the Arctic by Soviet polar explorers, under the leadership of the Communist Party and the Soviet Government, their contribution to the development of the country's aviation and to cultural and economic construction in the northern regions of the Soviet Union.

ne flight of the polar regions, where aircraft are rare but welcome visitors, and the lure of the North for ever grips the pilot, calling him back again and again. He is no longer content to fly "from bush to bush" along the quiet, well-equipped airlines of the European part of the U.S.S.R. where unexpected snow-storms are rare and the country is dotted with inhabited localities and intermediate airfields. Such flying is dull when you have known the joy of flight over unexplored territory.

I shall never forget the first of December, 1929. On that day, when I had had little more than six months' flying practice, the director of the Civil Aviation Department sent for me.

"Comrade Vodopyanov," he said, "we want you to go to Khabarovsk to start a new passenger line to Sakhalin."

"Well, it sounds rather a difficult job for a young pilot," I said in surprise.

"That's just the point," he answered. "You're young and strong and that's the kind of men they want over there."

In those days even seasoned flyers regarded the North as a kind of bogey. The horrors told about arctic flights made one's hair stand on end. There was the story about the tragic end of the dirigible *Italia* on its return flight from the North Pole, about Eyelson, the U.S. pilot, who lost his life while evacuating furs from Olaf Swenson's schooner ice-bound off the coast of the Chukchi Sea, about the appalling hardships endured by the first Soviet polar pilots—Chukhnovsky, Babushkin and Slepnev—while rescuing foreign explorers. As I was then a mere novice who had never flown beyond the Ural Mountains, I hesitated about taking on the job, but afterwards I never regretted my decision.

Today I think with pride of that pioneering Sakhalin flight, which I was the first to make.

There, in the far-away northern outskirts of the U.S.S.R., I realized how superior was air travel over all other means of communication. In those days only the first steps had been taken to win the North, whose vast, untouched expanses spread under the wings of my plane. Its scanty populated localities, divided by hundreds of miles of impenetrable taiga, were isolated from the mainland for many long months and sometimes even years. You can imagine what it is like when a plane appears over such a locality. The inhabitants have never seen one before, but they know it brings them letters, newspapers, ammunition for their guns, medicine and everything else they need. Besides, the arrival of an aeroplane signifies regular communication with the outside world. That is why they are so overjoyed at sighting a visitor from the sky, why they make so much of the pilot. And the airman who has come there at the risk of his life, flying over places not to be found on any map, over virgin taiga and bleak rocky mountains, has a feeling of glorious achievement at having won his dangerous battle with the elements, and triumphed over all difficulties to bring happiness, and sometimes even salvation, to people. Therein lies the great attraction of the North.

Socialist construction, carried out on a grand scale throughout the Soviet Union had spread to the Far East—a place of exile and penal servitude in tsarist Russia. For economic development there, Sakhalin furs, oil, coal, timber and other materials were required and so a reliable and fast communication system had to be established between the island and the mainland.

At present there is a mail and passenger air service linking the island to Khabarovsk, Vladivostok and other towns. Things were different in 1929 when even the radio could not be relied on for regular communication, and the shipping of passengers, freight and mail across the turbulent Tatar Strait called for supreme effort. During the brief summer navigation the trip from Sakhalin to Khabarovsk took five or six, or sometimes even ten days. In winter there was actually no communication at all between the island and the mainland. Alexandrovsk-on-Sakhalin—the Far Eastern regional centre—could not be reached in under a month, and the difficulties were sometimes almost insurmountable. At that time of the year the Tatar Strait is a sea of jagged ice divided by turbulent channels difficult to negotiate.

When a local official had to go to Sakhalin he would fit himself out with furs—a sleeping-bag, fur suit, special headgear, etc. Then he would hire a cart to take him to Nikolaevsk-on-Amur. The more practical traveller would purchase horses and a sledge, drive to the Tatar Strait, and from there cover the rest of the way in a dog sledge. In about twenty-five to thirty-five days he would eventually reach his destination—uninjured, with any luck.

Economic development in the region proceeded at a rate which made this state of affairs intolerable. Therefore, arrangements were made with the Civil Aviation Department to start a regular air service between Khabarovsk and Sakhalin.

Working parties went to set up landing fields, fuel dumps and an aerodrome service at places designed to become junctions.

I was met at Khabarovsk railway station by Anikin, an air-mechanic, who had gone there with the plane that was to open the new air service.

It was thirty-five degrees below and I was numb with cold by the time we got to our department. "How am I going to fly in such weather?" I wondered. I was given little time to get used to the frost.

"We intend opening the Sakhalin air service early in January," said the director of the Far Eastern Civil Aviation Department. "Teams have already been dispatched to prepare winter airfields. There's a map: let me show you the route. We make our first landing at Verkhne-Tambovskoye and then go on to Mariinsk and Niko-laevsk-on-Amur. From there we set course for Sakhalin across the Tatar Strait to Okha. Then we keep to the eastern shores of Sakhalin as far as the River Tym, follow its course for a while, skim the mountains and head straight for Alexandrovsk.

"And now," concluded the director, "get the plane ready and try it out in the air."

Next day, my two mechanics and I drove to the aerodrome and made vain attempts to take off: all our efforts to start the engine in the bitter cold and strong wind were futile. We had little experience and none of us had ever worked in the North. We struggled unsuccessfully for ten days. Working under cover of a canvas, we tried warming up the engine with a torch, but to no purpose.

Meanwhile, a wireless message came from Sakhalin: "Landing fields ready along the whole route. Expecting you."

Then Anikin said he had thought of something that would start the engine. When I saw his apparatus I could not help laughing. It was in three parts: a felt boot minus the top, a rope, and a rubber cord to act as a shock absorber.

We immediately set to work. The felt boot, with a rope attached to it, was secured to one end of the airscrew. Then the rubber cord was passed through the loop and four men on each side began to pull. The other end of the screw was held by a mechanic so that the stress should fall on the propeller shaft. When, at the count of "three," he let go, the airscrew turned sharply and the shock absorber with the felt boot was torn from the propeller blade, falling with a hiss at our feet. We did not get the engine going but it sparked for the first time in ten days. That cheered us and we felt confident that we would eventually get it started.

"Say, comrade," shouted the mechanic to a fireman. "There's no need to guard your fire extinguisher; we can't get the engine started, so there's no danger of a fire! Come and lend a hand!"

A dozen more workers joined in and everyone pulled so zealously that one end of the rope snapped and the men fell, while the boot hit the luckless fireman straight in the face. When he rose from the snow we saw a black ring forming round his left eye.

"Catch me pulling that damned thing again!" Holding his bruised cheek, he added: "I could walk to Sakhalin quicker than you'll fly there in your machine."

But we worked on, warmed up the engine a second time, heated some petrol in a pailful of hot water and flooded the engine with it. Then we repeated the operation with our "starter" and got the engine running.

Next day we started the engine in the same way and tried out the machine in flight—all was shipshape. We had wasted twelve days trying to get it going. The fireman's remark about walking to Sakhalin had become a catchword at the aerodrome.

Soon we were able to start the engine at very low temperatures.

The take-off was fixed for January 10. I was to fly with the director and three passengers. We wore arctic clothing and I had a fine pair of high fur boots, which were not a very good fit, but did not hurt much. The first leg of our journey to Verkhne-Tambovskoye was 220 miles distant.

The ice-bound Amur presents a strange picture from an altitude of 1,600 feet. You see a broad valley stretching far into the distance with here and there yellowish dirty islets and white ribbons of channels; the narrower the ribbon the more intricate its windings. In the distance disappears the broad fairway.

Below us a pointed black spot caught the eye. What was it? Ice, swept clear of snow by the winds, or a belt of open water? Evidently water, for steam was rising from it.

On our left, through the mist, we could see a distant mountain range and on our right the rough thickly wooded Amur valley. And nowhere the slightest sign of life! The visibility was excellent and flying was unusually smooth so that the controls required very little attention and I could watch the ground carefully.

More than an hour had passed since the take-off from Khabarovsk and according to schedule we should now sight the village of Troitskoye. I peered out and began to glide to earth. Below stretched a smooth strip of river ice.

Fir-trees marked the four corners of the white field. In the centre was a black circle, also of firs. That was our landing-place.

In the distance on our left was Lake Bolen-Odjal. I recognized it from the map by the black islet in the middle. Beyond the lake towered the mountain range which explained its existence. The waters which used to flood the Amur valley were now blocked by the mountain chain. The main flow had cut a passage through the mountains near Malmyzh while the small tributaries had hollowed out a basin at the foot-hills on both sides of the river, forming on the left larger Lake Bolon-Odjal and on the right smaller lakes Zherun and Sharginskoye.

Our path lay across the mountain range which had once barred the way of the currents. We were flying at 1,600 feet, but now I began to climb. Fleecy white clouds raced past us. Trees looked like blades of grass, and an opening in the woods was like a white arrow.

The air was becoming bumpy. In the mountain passes it is apparently not as uniform as in the valleys. We had left the hills behind and were again over the river. Beneath us lay a village and beyond it a well-appointed landing field.

"Tambovskoye!" I shouted through the peep-hole. The first to greet us on alighting at Verkhne-Tambovskoye was a dog which had evidently rushed out with the villagers at the sight of the strange bird and reached the plane ahead of everybody else. In the dog's wake dashed the boys and then came the grown-ups. A few minutes later school children, headed by their teacher, and members of Osoaviakhim (a society designed to further the development of the chemical industries and aviation in the U.S.S.R.) arrived with red banners. In short, Verkhne-Tambovskoye gave us a grand reception.

My feet were numb with cold. Paying no attention to the salutations I hurried to the nearest cottage and, taking off my fur boots, pushed my feet into a small stove. Feeling better, I looked about me and saw that the people who lived there had been half-way through their midday meal, when they ran off to meet the plane. About a quarter of an hour later one of my passengers walked in.

"I saw you coming here... Anything wrong?"

"It's all right for you inside the cabin, but my feet are frozen. I can't fly in those boots any more."

"Here, try mine."

I put them on. They were large and I was able to wear two pairs of socks. The boots were old and not much to look at, but my feet did not freeze in them.

All the villagers wanted us to come and have a meal with them.

While enjoying their hospitality we kept the engine running. The mechanic, posted on the wing, filled the tanks with petrol, which peasants drew in buckets from a nearby drum. Nearly all the local people were gathered around the plane. I was told afterwards that many of them had come from villages twelve miles away.

They felt the wings, the tail and the undercarriage. The youngsters climbed the ladder on to the wing and from there inspected the cabin. The more daring ones had the thrill of sitting in the pilot's cockpit and mothers lifted smaller children so that they could peep inside the wonder bird.

Finally, when everything was ready, we took leave of our hospitable friends and set off.

We steered straight for Mariinsk. In about twenty minutes we encountered heavy cloud banks. The visibility was becoming bad and I felt uneasy, for I was not familiar with the layout of the country, that being my first flight in the area. Fearing to lose sight of the ground I planed down to 160 feet.

Gradually conditions improved and I was able to climb to my usual height, which was 1,600 feet. Here the Amur flows between steep banks, the valley is much narrower than it is between Khabarovsk and Malmyzh, and there are few islands.

Here and there, skirting the villages on the river-bank, were little black patches—watering-places with fir twigs piled around them.

There are no big populated localities between Verkhne-Tambovskoye and Mariinsk. The majority are native settlements with anything up to half a dozen tents.

By about two o'clock a mist had begun to crawl over the green river-banks. We climbed above the haze. To the right of us the bleak hills and summits of Sikhote-Alin disappeared in the distance.

At last we could see the broad snowy surface of Lake Kizi. Somewhere near was Mariinsk—our final destination for the day.

Here it was at last. We flew low, almost touching the roof-tops. I peered down looking for fires to indicate the direction of the wind. In a corner of the river puffs of smoke curled from a barge frozen in the ice. That gave me the direction of the wind and I circuited the field, looking for a landing-place. Having found what I wanted, I turned into the wind and came down, but not as smoothly as at Verkhne-Tambovskoye.

At Khabarovsk they had warned us that the airfield at Mariinsk was none too good, but we had not expected it to be so bad. The river here is open to the winds, which either sweep it clear of snow, baring the rugged surface, or pile up drifts, which are even a greater menace to aircraft.

We had enough fuel to take us to Nikolaevsk before nightfall, but we had to make a detailed survey of the countryside, for Mariinsk was to be a junction on the new airway. And so, it had been arranged that we should spend the night there.

Mariinsk gave us a cool reception compared with the one at Verkhne-Tambovskoye. There were many kulaks in the locality who looked upon aviation as a dangerous rival, which would rob them of their passengers and profits. There being no railway, people had to use horses and dogs for travel—but now the aeroplane had come.

At ten the following morning the air-mechanic overheated some oil which he poured into the tank, fusing the celluloid oil-gauge. As we had nothing to replace it with we had to seal the gap with tin plate, which took the best part of a day. It was then too late to start, and so we had to spend another night at Mariinsk.

This little misfortune caused quite a commotion at Nikolaevsk-on-Amur. People there had never seen an aeroplane and they all gathered at the airfield and waited... But the scheduled time passed, including allowances for "normal" delay, and still there was no sign of us. Only when our wire arrived did the troubled and frozen people return to their homes.

We spent the evening chatting with members of a railway survey expedition, who told us some interesting things. Their experience was that the best time for survey work in the taiga was winter. In summer it was practically impossible to do anything because of mosquitoes, which gave no peace day or night. The winter cold in the taiga, they said, was less severe than in open country. The dense forest gave good protection against wind, and frost without wind was bearable. Then there was the advantage of free movement in any direction without having to skirt marshes and slush. The weather was fine, whereas in summer there was frequent rain and fog. You could sleep in a tent with an iron stove without any risk of freezing.

"What kind of footwear do the natives use?" I asked. "Can it be that fish skin keeps the feet warm?"

"It's the vetosh, not the skin that warms you," explained a member of the expedition who was half-Gilyak, half-Russian.

"Vetosh" is a kind of grass which the Gilyaks use for stuffing boots. This grass has some very peculiar properties: unlike hay, for example, it is not reduced to powder when walking, and it does not clot like cotton wool, but turns into a soft silky fibre which preserves the warmth better than any felt boots. This "vetosh" evidently has some of the properties of cloth.

When, finally, we put out the paraffin lamp, an unusually bright moon shone. I went to the window and gazed spellbound at the river and distant mountains, lit by the full moon.

"We should have gone," I said bitterly. "I'd chance a landing anywhere in such light."

I just could not forgive myself for having broken our schedule and for keeping thousands out in the cold because of slight engine trouble.

"Tomorrow there'll be no one to meet us at Nikolaevsk," I thought.

But we had a fine reception, and banners with words of welcome were stretched across the main street.

Nikolaevsk delayed us for quite a while. For two days I gave "joy rides" to a score of the town's best shock-workers. The people expressed their appreciation by showing us around their heroic city, razed by the Japanese invaders and afterwards rebuilt.

No wonder the interventionists fought so stubbornly for Nikolaevsk. The surrounding taiga has huge reserves of high-grade coal, then untouched; gold is found on both banks of the river, and the area is rich in fur animals. The Amur River is well known for its fish, especially salmon.

We heard many a tale of the battles with Whiteguards from 1918 till 1922 and of present struggles to win the wealth of the area—as well as stories of hunting sable, polar fox, otter and marten.

On January 13 we took leave of our hosts and made for Sakhalin. We had been well warned about Sakhalin.

"You'll run into sudden hurricanes that can wreck a ship, let alone a plane," people had said. The Tatar Strait is rarely calm and ships have to wait in the rough seas for days before they can come near the shore.

"But that's in summer," I ventured.

"It's worse in winter. Snow falls and evenly covers the ground, then the wind blows and huge snow mounds arise. You'll not find a level strip of land anywhere."

The Tatar Strait which we crossed in the neighbourhood of the Sea of Okhotsk looked menacing but magnificent. Colossal ice blocks alternated with belts of open water. The thought of engine failure here was not inviting. But it persisted, for we were the first to cross the Tatar Strait by air.

The strait was left behind and beneath us lay Sakhalin, former prison island. We flew over fisheries and I saw some radio masts, chimneys and small houses. Socialist construction on the island was in full swing. The very fact that I had come here by air was an achievement of socialism.

The visibility ahead was worse. I flew on to the eastern shores of Sakhalin till I sighted oil reservoirs, which meant that the city was near, and then I struck out for Urkat Bay.

Suddenly I spotted the aerodrome signs. We had arrived! But there seemed to be no one to meet us. I circled a few times and saw someone start a fire. This must be the place! I landed and taxied up to a small shed. A mechanic ran up to meet us.

"We didn't know you were coming, we didn't get your radiogram."

"How far is the town?"

"Four miles from here."

"We must let them know we've come and have them send someone for us," I thought.

Seeing two Russian lads driving a dog team to Okha, we asked one to go to town and report our arrival. He willingly agreed while the other remained with us at the plane. We waited three hours, shivering in the cold.

Finally they came, took us to town, fed us, and invited us to the club where all the Okha workers had gathered.

Next morning I took twenty-five people for "joy rides." We went to the aerodrome in dog sledges. There was a good crowd there, despite the 36 degrees of frost; some people had come for a "ride," and others to look on.

We started the engine, warmed it up, but inadequately, as we were to learn later.

The aerodrome was large but uneven. I took five passengers, seating four in the cabin and one beside me in place of the air-mechanic. Having taxied down the landing ground into the wind I opened the throttle and began to climb. In front was a narrow-gauge railway and beyond it the taiga. And then at an altitude of 310 feet the engine failed and I began to lose height. Immediately ahead was the railway which I just managed to clear, but then I saw a telegraph-pole in the path of my right wing. I swung round and saw it rush past under the wing. Then followed two loud reports. I levelled out but pancaked and the machine raced on along the snow, heading for another pole.

I thought a smash was inevitable. But, fortunately, the pole, secured on one side with wire, stood on a small mound. The machine rolled up, hit the wire with the propeller hub and came to rest. I felt relieved. The passenger beside me, too frightened to move, was holding a camera above his head. I jumped out, frantically inspecting the machine; there was no damage apart from two big dents in the left wing.

Luckily, between the poles was a strip of level ground, covered with soft snow.

Many willing hands helped to haul the machine across the road. My passengers returned to their seats and we took off, this time successfully.

But why had the machine failed in the first instance? It was in good trim, but cold. And it is dangerous to go up with a cold engine for the petrol is sucked in without giving it time to evaporate, with the result that there is a falling off in engine revolutions. This lesson was firmly drilled into my mind and never again in the North did I take off without a good warm-up of the engine.

The "joy rides" over, we again took the air setting the course for Alexandrovsk. Near Alexandrovsk was a mountain range completely obscured by clouds, so that we were forced to climb to about 6,100 feet.

The sun was already sinking, but we still had 25 miles to cover over unfamiliar country. Unable to see my compass, I kept the sun's glow on my right. Below was a layer of clouds and beneath them were the mountain peaks. This was territory unexplored by man. I wondered if we were on the right course. The times I had promised myself never to set off with little time to spare, and here I was doing it once more, the deuce knows why!

When we passed the mountains the mist rose and I began to descend. There was ice in the Tatar Strait. I glided down to 600 feet and saw towering cliffs straight ahead. Should I steer to right or left? What if we landed in Japan? I turned leftwards. Five anxious minutes passed, dusk had gathered, but there was still no sign of Alexandrovsk. I decided to turn back and go northwards along the coast which would at least keep me on home territory.

A quarter of an hour later lights appeared ahead—too bright to be anything but electricity. This was good news for I had been told that only Alexandrovsk had electric light. Here we were at last. I saw houses wedged between the mountains but no aerodrome. Where were we? I circled round twice but could see no petrol flares. One passenger, who had a front seat in the cabin, had been to Alexandrovsk several times. I shouted to him:"What's that light?" He said it wasn't Alexandrovsk, but probably Due, eight miles from Alexandrovsk. In another five minutes I saw a brighter glow, which must be Alexandrovsk. Four huge bonfires marked the corners of the aerodrome. After one circuit I landed and taxiing up to the shed, switched off. We were greeted by music specially arranged for our benefit.

Presently, the chairman of the regional executive committee told me how they had expected us.

"We were informed from a neighbouring district that you had passed overhead. Of course, we got ready, keeping a close watch on the sky. You had twenty minutes to fly at most—only 25 miles. But thirty minutes passed, and then an hour, and still there was no sign of you. I announced that the first to sight the plane would get the first ride. Everybody looked in the direction where you were expected to appear, for we all wanted to see you first. But then we heard the drone of an engine from the opposite direction. Everyone spotted the plane at once. So you'll have to give us all a ride..."

On January 16, 1930, the Sakhalin airline was opened.

★ ★ ★

I made regular flights along this new air route, carrying passengers alternately to Okha and Alexandrovsk. And every trip was different.

In mid March I was returning from Alexandrovsk. It was not very cold—about 15 degrees below zero. We were using a mixture of petrol and toluene for fuel. Skirting the coastline of the Tatar Strait we reached Viakhta and then struck out across the strait, expecting to reach the mainland far to the right of De-Kastry Bay. About half-way we discovered that there was no flow of petrol from the main tanks to the upper tank which fed the engine. The fuel pump had failed. We tried the hand pump, but it did not work. The petrol-gauge indicated that the supply in the upper tank was rapidly diminishing. I wondered what to do. There was not enough fuel to take us back to Sakhalin and land at Viakhta and there was no landing-place anywhere nearer. Ahead was the mainland shore and it was out of the question to try to cross the taiga and mountains, to reach Lake Kizi. I looked down and saw ice floating in the strait. Some slabs were pretty large, but if I attempted to land I might smash the machine. But I had to do something!

Sighting near the shore a flat ice sheet about a hundred yards wide I decided to take the risk. I could not be too particular in my choice for our petrol was almost finished. When we got down we let the engine run and, unscrewing the petrol filter cap, pulled out the filter which we found clogged with snow—someone had accidentally or deliberately put snow in the tanks.

All this was easily righted. But how was I to take off? The skis were frozen fast in the ice. Someone had to rock the machine by the wings but there was no one to do it. The nearest place where help could be got was De-Kastry Bay—some 30 miles away. I tried to break loose on full engine power, but could not. Eventually, I turned to the passengers and said:

"Will someone near the door get out and rock the machine and then climb in as soon as I get started. I'll taxi slowly."

The youngest passenger got out and started rocking the wing. With great difficulty I got under way. The passenger ran for the cabin but was caught in the backwash. A strong gust of wind tore his hat off and he ran after it. I had to stop for I couldn't leave a passenger behind.

I said to Anikin, the air-mechanic:

"You'll have to see to it yourself. Not much good asking the passengers."

Anikin pulled off his fur coat, flung it on the seat beside me and, with only a sweater on, went to the wing. As I began to taxi he jumped on to the wing of the moving plane and climbed over the engine cowling. Before he had clambered into the cabin I throttled out and began to climb. With one hand on the controls, I helped him into his coat. It was a difficult job in the howling wind and crowded conditions but we managed somehow and reached Khabarovsk in safety.

In spring the ice melted from the shores and communication with Alexandrovsk by horse or dog sledge became impossible. Sakhalin could be reached only by air. I went to Alexandrovsk on my last flight of the winter season.

Two ships were anchored near Alexandrovsk: the ice-breaker *Dobrynia Nikitich* and a passenger boat which had on board 500 people, sent by the People's Commissariat of Railways to work on the construction of a new line.

Some of the men had high felt boots, and some ordinary leather shoes. They had to be provided with warm footwear, but high boots were unobtainable at Alexandrovsk. Each day of enforced idleness was costing the state a lot of money and holding up construction.

Inquiries were sent to every locality on Sakhalin Island and soon it was discovered that there were high boots in the village of Veresh-chagino, 220 miles from Alexandrovsk. But the problem was how to bring them when the slush had made the few existing foot-paths impassable? The sea route was closed: Vereshchagino, on the northern shore of Sakhalin Island, was still blocked by pack-ice.

I was asked to call at the executive committee's office, where I found several people.

"Good you're here, Comrade Vodopyanov," said the chairman. "We're in a terrible predicament. We want you to fly to Veresh-chagino for some boots."

"I can't, comrades."

One man smiled, thinking probably that I was joking.

"Why not?"

"I can't go without permission from the department chief. Wire to Khabarovsk and if he agrees I'll be only too pleased to help."

That same evening I was called back to read the reply from Khabarovsk: "Strictly forbid flight to Vereshchagino."

"That settles it," I said.

Meanwhile, a three-man committee had been set up. This "boot committee," as I called it, kept pressing me.

"We have the right to mobilize you for the flight," they said.

"Say what you like, I'm not going," I argued and walked out.

I was staying at the chairman's house and that evening he turned to me again:

"What are we going to do, Misha? The situation is pretty desperate. These boots must be got at all cost if we don't want the men to sit idle for six weeks."

I made no reply, but tried to think of some way of making the flight. Formally, it would be a breach of discipline on my part, but actually I would be doing a service to the country.

"I've found a way out," I said presently. "I set out tomorrow morning. You're going to mislead me..."

In the morning I was off.

Half the way all went well, the weather being fine, but then I ran into a heavy snow-fall and had great difficulty in locating the village, situated on the shore of the Tatar Strait. I circled round at low altitude looking for a place to land but visibility was wretched and I would find a suitable spot only to lose sight of it as I swung round. Then I would begin the search over again. This went on for about twenty minutes until, finally, I alighted. Wasting no time, I put the boots in the cabin, but decided to take no risks and postpone the return flight till the morning. I only asked my hosts to wire to Alexandrovsk: "Vodopyanov arrived. Weather bad, returning tomorrow." But as sometimes happens with urgent wires the message did not reach its destination. Alexandrovsk did not get the wire, which went instead to Khabarovsk! There it was immediately handed over to the head of the Air Department who sent an inquiry to Alexandrovsk. But this radiogram also failed to arrive.

Next morning, when I set out from Vereshchagino, I had the same bad luck. First the weather was fine, but midway heavy sleet began and ice formed on the wings. I could not keep close in to the coast because thick clouds almost hid it from view. It was also difficult to keep to the course over the sea, which was covered by a hazy mist. So I was compelled to use the winding coast as landmark and fly at a height of 15-18 feet over floating ice. As I approached Alexandrovsk the snow-storm became so much worse that I was afraid of hitting the shore with my wing.

The members of the "boot committee" kept watch at the Alexandrovsk aerodrome night and day, feeding the bonfires in the hope that I would return. But as the minutes passed they began to imagine the worst: that I had crashed, and the machine was wrecked, etc. The vigil continued throughout the night; at the first streaks of dawn the half-frozen people were still gathered round the fires, hopelessly watching the clouds. At noon a decision was taken to send out a search-party, when suddenly the roar of my engine was heard.

The "boot committee" was overjoyed. I had returned safely and brought three hundred and fifty pairs of boots.

Next day I got all my papers ready and set off for Khabarovsk, which I reached late in the evening. At the hostel I ran into the head of the department.

"Did you go to Vereshchagino?"

"I did. On your instructions."

"But I didn't give any such instructions."

"You did not? But that was what the chairman of the executive committee told me."

"It's a misunderstanding. They simply fooled you."

"Did they really?" I smiled.

"I got a wire from Vereshchagino. At first I thought something had happened, that you had lost your way or made a forced landing—I was terribly worried. Why did you take the risk, knowing there was no landing field at Vereshchagino?"

"Oh, I found a place, and it wasn't at all risky—only a matter of 220 miles. And it meant helping a whole expedition out of trouble."

* * *

In Moscow I was instructed to fly a one-engine plane to Khabarovsk. My air-mechanic, as far as Irkutsk, was Fyodor Groshev, who had given me my first lesson in engine overhauling. There he was replaced by Anikin, and we decided to fly non-stop to Khabarovsk—a distance of 1,900 miles.

The Baikal looked black and inhospitable. The thin ice, lined with cracks, would have collapsed under the weight of the machine. But I had nothing to fear for the engine was running smoothly.

Ahead, on a horizon broken by rocky mountains, a bright cloud gleamed. The sun was rising slowly, glinting into the pilot's cabin. Beneath stretched the thickly wooded taiga. Mist came up and soon a huge black cloud hovered over the mountain peaks.

We ran into a heavy squall, the raindrops streaming over the wing surface, and then sprinkling down.

The machine was tossed about like a play-ball. I tried to locate the approaches to Yablonovy Range, but could not penetrate the heavy cloud bank. I came in from the north and south, climbed in an attempt to fly over the peak, but the weather was against us.

Then, trying in vain to fly low over the railway, I was compelled to land. We waited for the mist to lift and then struck out for Chita, where we spent the night and next day flew on to Khabarovsk.

There I was greeted with the news that this was the last flight on wheels. The department chief had ordered the wheels to be replaced by floats and I was to qualify as a seaplane pilot without delay. This was necessitated by the absence of landing grounds.

I willingly began to train. After four flights with an instructor I went out on my own, and after three solo flights the instructor said:

"That'll do. You can fly to Sakhalin now."

Although I had made only a few take-offs from the Amur it was being suggested that I should fly solo and come down in the sea. The naval pilot whom I asked for advice said:

"If the sea is rough you'll have to alight in Viakhta Bay, about 55 miles from Alexandrovsk. In a calm sea it's best to land in the mouth of the River Alexandrovka. But even then a crash is possible if you come down in the dip instead of on the crest of a wave. That's all the advice I can give you."

This advice did nothing to reassure me and I decided to ask that experienced naval flyers be sent out ahead. The suggestion was adopted.

Early in June two seaplanes started out from the mainland, one making for Alexandrovsk and the other for Okha. I was impatiently waiting for the return of the plane from Alexandrovsk when a wire came instead:

"Returned to Mariinsk. Encountered dense fog in De-Kastry area."

In its wake a wire came from the other aviator:

"Piston broken. Please send another at once."

I was ordered to fly immediately to Mariinsk with the piston, pick up the passengers and take them to Alexandrovsk.

Thus, against my will, circumstances forced me to go first. I delivered the piston, collected the passengers and set out along the familiar route to Sakhalin.

An hour later we were over Alexandrovsk. On the roof of one building a red flag hung loosely. There was no wind, but the sea was choppy. Should I come down with the waves or across them? I turned to the air-mechanic:

"Would you say that was a big wave?"

"Don't ask me. I know very little about that sort of thing."

I asked the passengers.

"Have you been to sea? Would you consider that a big wave?"

The passengers merely looked at each other and shrugged their shoulders. Deciding to cheat fate I came down at an angle of 45 degrees—a middle course between alighting on and across the waves—softly touching the water. On closer examination there was only a slight swell, but I, seeing the sea for the first time, had thought it was a storm. Trying to appear imperturbed I began "taxiing" towards the shore, but when we were still 55 yards away we suddenly ran aground. We sat watching the commotion on shore until the tide began sweeping us back to sea. My passengers looked worried and I, too, was a bit ruffled, but then a boat appeared and towed us to safety.

When we were towed into the River Alexandrovka I was amazed at its size and wondered why I had not seen it from the air, but the director of the airport explained that the river is very small but gets bigger when the tide is in. That was why I had missed it.

We learn from our mistakes. This flight with all its misadventures taught me a lesson. I gained confidence with each flight and even began to set up records. Occasionally I would fly from Khabarovsk to Okha and back—a distance of 1,475 miles—in one day.

In mid summer an expedition from the Institute of the Fishing Industry arrived in the Far East to assess the possibilities of seal and whale hunting in the Sea of Okhotsk. This could be done only with the help of aircraft.

Seals and whales, which were plentiful off the coasts of the Tatar Strait and the Sea of Okhotsk, were hunted by the local population, but their methods were very primitive.

I was appointed pilot of the expedition.

The weather was bad, visibility impeded by low clouds. First we went eastwards, seeing no ice for a long time, while the sea raged beneath us. Then one and another floe was spotted until eventually there were many of them. Sighting dark patches on the ice we planed down and found seals which hurriedly dived into the sea, disappearing beneath the floes. We saw more seals on other floes.

Our reconnaissance proved very successful.

A week later we set out again, making a thorough survey of all Shantar Islands. Sometimes we were up for eight hours a day, seeing not only seals but also white whales.

These flights provided some very valuable information, helping to increase the kill.

★ ★ ★

After these flights I worked on the airline where I had an experience which I shall remember all my life.

I had set out from Sakhalin for Khabarovsk where I was due to arrive before dusk. My machine was not adapted for night-flying. At first there was only a gentle breeze, but midway it developed into a strong gale against which the plane made little headway. When only about fifteen minutes' flight remained the sun dipped below the horizon. I ought to have landed and spent the night in some village, but it seemed a pity to do so with Khabarovsk so near at hand. In about ten minutes complete darkness set in and it was impossible to distinguish woods from fields, land from water. Suddenly I saw lights ahead—Khabarovsk.

I came down to about 1,600 feet. To the right of the city was the Amur River, but it was quite dark with no flares anywhere. I turned leftwards, intending to glide down, but the wind carried me away from the city. The lights were left behind and no landmarks were visible.

I continued to bank blindly. The machine trembled. I quickly throttled down and, feeling it getting out of control, hurriedly eased back the stick to gather speed. It plunged down, as if into a chasm, but, luckily, I soon got it under control.

The lights reappeared and, guided by them, I levelled out, opened the throttle and heard the engine hum. Everything was all right now. Flying low I passed over the city, heading for the Amur where two huge bonfires burned on the river-bank. I turned to land, trying to keep the flares in view, and by them determined my altitude.

Feeling the floats touch water I cut off the engine. The frail craft was tossed to and fro in the raging sea, with first one and then another wing dipping into the water. Finally, the machine was washed ashore.

Never since then have I flown at night a machine equipped for day-flights only.

Soon I left the Far East, having flown hundreds of thousands of miles in near to polar conditions.

he pilot who wants to fly in the Arctic, to fight and conquer the grim polar conditions must be expert at flying in fog and snow, and must be able to steer his plane without seeing either the land or sky. Therefore, wherever I happened to be working—on a passenger line, in the special group flying the *Pravda* matrices to the regional centres or on seal reconnaissance in the Caspian Sea—I always tried to accustom myself to the environment of the polar flyer. The flights with the *Pravda* matrices gave me a lot of experience.

When the Civil Aviation Department recruited aviators for the special flying group, they were told:

"The group will be working on an important political assignment. It must be accomplished without fail. No city must be left without the paper, or receive it late through the fault of the pilot. He must be prepared to fly in all seasons of the year and at any time of the day. Let those who have any misgivings, who lack confidence in themselves, say so now."

As I listened I felt half inclined to back out since I had little experience in blind flying. But the closing words deterred me. I was no coward and decided that experience could after all be acquired.

Having several times groped in the clouds or mist I resolved to master the technique of blind flying.

Returning from Leningrad or Kharkov I would deliberately climb 1,900 feet into the clouds and fly blind; then I would swoop down and, on sighting the ground, straighten out and repeat the operation.

After a month's practice I could easily and promptly carry out any assignment in any weather.

My experience in flying over the foggy Caspian was even more valuable.

Early in 1932 the management of the Caspian Seal-Fishery Trust asked Moscow to send a plane for seal reconnoitring in the Caspian

Sea. The Moscow Civil Aviation Department at once ordered me to place myself at the disposal of the trust.

Next day I was at Dzhanbai on the Caspian Sea, where I heard that the first seal-hunting party had come back empty-handed. It appeared that they had gone out on the off chance—without any preliminary survey.

I was eager to know how seals were hunted. One seasoned seal-hunter told me how in the spring, during the thaw, the seals move to the southern section of the sea, and in late autumn they go to the northern pack-ice to cub. That is when the hunting season begins.

The shore ice stretches for about 55 miles and it is there that the seals bring forth their young. Supplied with fodder for their horses the hunters go out in search of game. The strip of sea ice gradually increases in the severe frost, but the cow with her calf remains where she is, on the edge of a lead—she will never abandon her young until she has nursed it to maturity.

In spring the cow and calf make their way to the open sea and that is when the hunters stalk them. Sometimes the track is lost in the jumbled ice and the mammal has to be hunted under the ice with a hook. When struck it will at once reveal its presence by a snort. Then the hunters chop up the ice and find as many as twenty or thirty seals underneath.

Hunting old seal, particularly bulls, is more difficult. The bull remains under water most of the time, emerging only during the mating period. When ice begins to form it makes a hole which it keeps from freezing by blowing.

An old seal is extremely alert. Before showing its head it makes sure there is no one on the ice and then pokes its nose out and sniffs the air. Reassured, it pulls itself out of the water and that is the time to make the kill. During the mating season the seals gather in herds, but at the sight of people they at once flop into the sea. Generally, out of a rookery of a hundred or more animals the hunters manage to kill about fifteen.

The men start out in groups, spreading out to cover more ground. Sometimes a floe breaks away from the pack and the hunters have to sit and wait to see where it will take them. The greatest danger is of being carried out to sea where only a ship can save them.

Horses that have been out on many hunting expeditions give warning of this danger. They begin to snort before a change of wind and refuse to take fodder.

It was a pity I had come so late, the old hunter told me, for if I had been able to indicate the rookeries when the ice was just beginning to form, I should have saved 1,200 horse-sledging parties from fruitless wanderings. "Air reconnaissance will help us a lot," he finished. "If we know there is a plane overhead we'll have no fear of being carried out to sea."

I could see that aircraft would make a tremendous difference in the work of the seal-hunters, with their primitive methods.

The day came for my first flight, and it was not difficult to locate the herds. Wasting no time we wrote a note and on our way back dropped it to the sealers.

Apart from seal reconnaissance we had to establish communication with Kolula and Dolgy islands with which there had been no contact all winter, and also with Astrakhan and Makhachkala.

First I landed on Kolula Island where we were heartily welcomed by the inhabitants, this being the first plane to visit the island. Besides we brought the mail.

Knowing that on Dolgy Island we would have to alight not on ice, but on hard sand, I made a rough sketch of the layout of an airfield and dropped the message. I wrote that I would be back in an hour and would not come down unless a suitable landing field was prepared.

An hour later I circled over Dolgy Island. The airfield was marked off by flags which also showed the direction of the wind. I was able to make a perfect landing.

We returned to Moscow with a message from the Caspian Seal-Fishery Trust, certifying that despite the initial delay sealing was in excess of plan, thanks to aerial survey.

I personally learned a great deal from these flights in conditions which were almost polar and which further prepared me for the work of an arctic pilot.

* * *

Early in 1933 I was ordered out on a long-distance flight from Moscow to Petropavlovsk with a load of urgent freight for Khabarovsk, Okhotsk, Petropavlovsk and other places, from which I was to bring back the mail. In addition I was to test the radius and speed of the P-5 aircraft in severe winter conditions, determine the type of mail and passenger planes most suitable for winter flights, and survey the prospective air route.

I took off at night alone with air-mechanic Seryogin. We had enough petrol to take us to Sverdlovsk, and about two hundred pounds of freight.

In eight hours we safely reached Sverdlovsk where the aerodrome chief, who knew this was a speed flight, had everything ready for us.

"When do you want to get away?" he asked. "We can send you off in half an hour."

The suggestion tempted me to say casually:

"Very well, we'll have lunch and be off."

That was exactly what we did. The machine was fuelled and we decided to fly non-stop to Novosibirsk.

Sverdlovsk informed Omsk that we had started. Omsk was to ask Novosibirsk for the weather forecast and, if this was favourable, to lay out the all-clear signal.

Approaching Omsk I saw two long strips of light, indicating that the route to Novosibirsk was open and the weather good. I was very pleased—we would cover 1,900 miles in a single day!

At that very moment I was hit by a jet of steam, and clouds poured from the engine, blotting out the ground below. The water in the radiator was boiling. I switched off the engine to keep it from overheating and when the steam cleared I started gliding down to earth. Luckily the aerodrome was within sight.

At Omsk I asked the aerodrome staff to replace the faulty pipe and replenish the water supply in the engine.

"Please see that this is done and the engine started without delay," I said to the aerodrome commandant. "Meanwhile I'll have a rest, we've flown 1,560 miles today."

He promised to do everything possible, and so I went to the aviators' quarters and slept.

In about two hours I woke and asked my mechanic:

"Well, is everything ready? Can we set off?"

"Set off! They haven't started the engine yet," retorted Seryogin gloomily.

I hurried to the aerodrome where I saw about 30 men hauling the machine to the hangar. After another hour and a half the engine was quite cold and had to be warmed up. Seeing men carrying buckets of hot water to a nearby plane, I asked:

"Why don't you fetch some for me?"

"We'll fill the other plane first, and then yours."

"But you know I'm on a speed flight and have to be attended to first!"

"We're on this job now, and we'll finish it," came the stubborn reply.

But they did not get their engine started. I was on tenterhooks, turning to everybody for help. Finally, after much confusion everything was ready. Instead of one hour we were held up for twenty-two hours at Omsk.

The journey to Novosibirsk was rough.

While we were at Omsk the weather changed and snow began to fall. At Novosibirsk, Krasnoyarsk and later at Irkutsk we heard the same thing:

"Sorry you didn't set out yesterday—the weather's getting worse."

These words spurred us on. I was particularly interested in weather conditions over Baikal which was the most dangerous lap. However, the meteorologist at Irkutsk reassured me—over the lake the weather was fine.

We hurriedly left Irkutsk, setting the course for Lake Baikal. On our right was the Angara River.

I emerged to the great Siberian lake two or three miles to the left of the river mouth. The altimeter showed a height of 2,500 feet. I set out across Baikal, steering by compass.

Visibility was good. A few minutes after I had passed the rugged bank the machine lurched. I thought we were nearing the opposite bank and turned leftwards. On the right glowed the lights of a railway station—and that was the last I remembered of the flight across Baikal...

This happened on the night of the 13th of February and at daybreak on the 16th I woke up with a bandaged head.

"What happened? Where am I?"

The hospital nurse answered me:

"You had a bad accident over Baikal. You're in the Verkhneudinsk railway hospital."

I asked for Seryogin and was told that he was there too.

Then I dictated a telegram: "Crashed over Baikal. Slightly injured. Please instruct the Irkutsk department to give me a plane to continue the flight to Kamchatka." The nurse took it down but of course did not send it. She knew that after a severe shock people sometimes become immune to pain and do not realize the gravity of their condition.

Presently the nurse told me:

"On the 14th of February, at two o'clock in the morning you were brought here semi-conscious. The doctor ordered us to undress you but you protested, 'What are you doing? I've got to fly.' We said, 'Yes, after you've changed,'" and you believed us.

"You answered all our questions, but confused your name with the mechanic's. You said you were Seryogin but then you corrected yourself and told us you were Vodopyanov. You talked at length about yourself and your work."

I had a series of jagged head wounds, four of which were grave, a fracture of the lower jaw, seven missing teeth and a severe chin injury. There were cuts about the forehead and brows—caused evidently by my goggles which had broken in the crash—and a bad gash on the bridge of my nose.

Some time later when I was taken to Moscow for "complete overhaul" at the Institute of Orthopaedics I learnt more about the crash.

It appeared that the machine had gone into a sharp nosedive over the lake, striking the ice with the skis and airscrew, which means it must have come down at an acute angle. Then the wreckage was dragged along the ragged ice for about 20 yards. I was thrown out on to the ice. The frost stopped the bleeding and brought me to semi-consciousness. It is presumed that I got up, pulled the mechanic free and put him on the ice.

At eight in the morning some workmen from the Mysovaya railway station saw me wandering around the plane, my face splashed with blood and my hands frost-bitten. When they came up I asked them to make a fire and give me a cigarette. They gave me one which I promptly put into my pocket and asked for another. This, too, I put away and then I lost consciousness.

What had caused the accident?

It was probably fatigue. I must have forgotten myself for a bare fraction of a second and lost control of the machine, so that it developed a flat spin which I could not right because of the low altitude.

"You relied too much on your physique," the great pilot, Valery Chkalov, said to me afterwards. "I think you left at midnight, and did you get any sleep before that? Of course not, although you may have tried. You knew you must rest before a flight like that, but nervous strain kept you awake. If a cord is pulled too hard it will inevitably break and that is what happened to you on Baikal— the cord snapped with the strain. One instant of forgetfulness was enough to send you crashing to the ice."

Many people thought that was the end of my flying career, but they were wrong. After five months' treatment by some of the best physicians in the country, I felt sure I would fly again.

My wonderful vocation called me. I wanted to serve my country, the Communist Party and the people.

I recall the long nights in the hospital ward, the white walls and ceiling, the green-shaded table lamp. Many days and nights passed before the hospital physician told me:

"Now you will begin to recover!"

He was right. It was the end of the painful operations and sleepless nights.

My physique had won.

In mid August when I went before a medical committee I was worried—what if they certified me unfit, forbade me to fly? I was even afraid they might ask me to squat and find out that I could not bend my right knee very well.

But I was not asked to squat. The doctors found me fit and said I could make short flights of no more than two hours' duration.

"You're not fit for long flights yet," they told me. "Report for another examination next month."

I was assigned to a special detachment, ferrying planes.

Finally, feeling quite well, I decided to repeat the luckless flight to Kamchatka. I applied for permission, which I received, and began preparing for the flight.

Things were going well when something happened that nearly upset my plans—I was again hauled before a medical committee. The neuropathologist politely asked me how I felt.

"Very well, thank you. Only I'm fed up with committees."

"That's nothing. We want to examine you thoroughly. Tell us about your grandparents. Do you remember them?"

"I remember them all right, but there's nothing to tell. They were sound in mind and body, died of old age..."

"Did they drink?"

"Grandfather didn't drink at all, and neither did my grandmother, of course."

"We'll have to put you in a mental hospital for about a week, for a test."

The idea almost knocked me out.

"I thought I was a bit touched," I said sarcastically.

"No need to worry—it's only a special sanatorium. You'll be back in a week."

There was nothing for it but to agree.

I was placed in an observation ward. Seeing that my companions were quite normal I was somewhat reassured, although I did notice that my movements were being carefully watched and everything I said was noted. The patients asked me to arrange a series of talks, which I did gladly. "Let them write it all down," I thought. I lectured for four evenings, two hours at a time.

Seven days later I left with a sealed envelope addressed to the chief of the Civil Aviation medical department. I got on a tram with my fate in my pocket.

I delivered the message to the senior physician who opened it, and, shielding it with his hand, began to read. I watched, trying to guess what it said from his expression. Then he smiled.

"D'you want me to read it to you?"

"Yes, of course."

"'Comrade Vodopyanov is certified fully fit for flight without any restrictions'."

I sighed with relief.

nly in the Union of Socialist Soviets is it possible for revolutionary organized energy to win such brilliant victories over the elements. Only our country, which has launched and tirelessly continues the fight for the emancipation of toiling humanity, can produce heroes whose amazing energy has evoked the admiration of even our enemies," wrote A. M. Gorky in reference to the Chelyuskin epos which has gone down in history as an unparalleled example of the courage and valour of men faced with imminent disaster. The rescue of the Chelyuskinites was a real triumph for our air force, an indication of the great future of aviation in the Arctic.

Let us briefly recall the stirring events of 1934.

The ice-resisting ship, *Chelyuskin*, sailed from Leningrad, intending to repeat the remarkable feat of the ice-breaker *Sibiryakov* which, in 1932, for the first time in history, covered the route from the White Sea to the Pacific in the course of one brief summer navigation.

For centuries past valiant seafarers had tried to break through the massive ice of the Far North, had dreamed of mastering the great north-eastern sea way—the direct route from Europe to Asia. But the Soviet people alone proved equal to the task. The Soviet Union began an extensive and regular study of the Arctic, set up a network of polar stations and organized many expeditions; all this, taken together, made possible the mastery of the Northern Sea Route and its conversion into a normal sea lane.

The *Chelyuskin* sailed along the Northern Sea Route. The first heavy ice in the Kara Sea damaged the bow but it was soon repaired and the ship continued on her way. She rode through a raging storm in the Laptev and East-Siberian seas, the men on board taking frequent soundings of the sea and studying the weather, the ice and air. The *Chelyuskin* also carried a fresh party of scientific workers who were to be landed on Wrangel Island.

37

The island was sighted late in September but the ship was unable to approach because of the old ice which no ice-breaker could have negotiated. The only thing to do was to steer a course for Vladivostok.

Ahead was the treacherous Chukchi Sea where the *Sibiryakov* had lost a screw. By the time the *Chelyuskin* reached it nine-tenths of its surface was coated with ice. The ship pushed on, sustaining damage which was quickly repaired: no time could be wasted, not a single day, for the short arctic summer was drawing to a close. Soon ice began to form on the channels of open water. The sea was becoming a solid mass.

Progress was slow. An air survey revealed a lane of open water only fifteen miles ahead. From there it would have been easy to reach Bering Strait, but the *Chelyuskin* was already helpless. It was not so much ploughing the ice as slowly drifting westwards with the pack.

Vain attempts to reach the *Chelyuskin* were made by the ice-breaker *Litke* which, despite her own injuries, had rushed to the rescue.

The *Chelyuskin* froze more and more solidly in the ice.

November, December, January and part of February passed without change. The long arctic night was ending and the sun was beginning to appear when heavy ice bore down on the ship. Throughout the brief spells of daylight and long nights reverberated, like distant thunder, the deafening din of pounding and scrunching ice.

The ship's hull shivered from the strain and the men on board listened alertly to the hideous roar. But there was nothing they could do.

A vigilant watch was kept and records were taken of wind and ice. Every member of the crew was briefed, and emergency stores were stacked.

Towards evening on February 12, 1934, the wind increased. The massive ice blocks seemed determined to attack the vessel. The ominous din of assailing ice grew relentlessly. The ruthless assault continued all night. The metal plating was strained to breaking-point.

The *Chelyuskin* camp. Aerial and radio tent

Dawn broke without any relief. At noon a huge iceberg, towering alongside, beset the ship and cut into her bottom. Water flooded the engine-room. The *Chelyuskin* was doomed—the elements had triumphed.

The end of the ship was now a matter of hours. Captain Vladimir

Voronin ordered all hands to stand by to discharge stores and equipment on to the ice. No one hesitated or abandoned the sinking decks.

The ropes fastening the timber and cargo were cut loose so that they could be salvaged when the ship sank.

When the bow began to go down and the upper deck and the stern were under water the order was given to abandon ship.

The captain was the last to leave. A second later the stern was lifted high into the air and the rudder and propeller appeared. There was a terrific roar of rolling cargo and then everything was obscured in a thick blanket of smoke.

When the smoke dispersed the *Chelyuskin* had gone and the ice had come together.

A hundred and four people were marooned on the ice.

The valiant *Chelyuskin* men and their leader Otto Yulyevich Shmidt proved worthy sons of their great country.

Quickly and efficiently they pitched and equipped their camp and at once began making scientific observations.

Often, wakened by the infernal growl of crushing ice, they would have to rush out into the night and move their supplies of food and fuel to a safer place. But, undaunted, they worked as if this were routine duty.

On a small ice-field ten tents with makeshift stoves were pitched. Bottle-glass served as window-panes. Such was the epic Shmidt camp.

These Soviet people, encamped on an ice raft, looked confidently to their country to help and save them. They knew their country, believed in her, and that gave them courage.

And the country spared no effort to rescue them.

A special Government committee was set up under V. Kuibyshev.

The committee was flooded with applications from factory and office workers, students, journalists, sailors and particularly from airmen who wished to take part in the rescue operations.

The decisive role in these operations was assigned to aviation.

Meanwhile, the Chelyuskinites toiled day and night laying out a landing field.

Outside the U.S.S.R. few believed that Soviet pilots could fly successfully over the unexplored route in the very difficult winter conditions to save their countrymen. Foreign newspapers wrote that, even if aircraft did reach the Chukchi Peninsula, they would be unable to land on the ice.

I, at the time, was preparing to repeat the Moscow-Kamchatka flight, cut short by the unhappy incident on Baikal.

The plane was ready: it was winter-proof, equipped for blind flying, the air speed indicator and other gauges were protected against the cold by currents from the accumulator, and auxiliary petrol tanks were installed.

The more I thought about flying conditions on the way to the *Chelyuskin* camp, the more confident I became that my machine was well fitted for the job.

Then I turned to my own qualifications for this crucial flight. I had never been to the Arctic but I had done quite a lot of flying in the Far East—to Sakhalin, over tundra and taiga, in the mists of Okhotsk Sea and the Tatar Strait. Conditions there were almost arctic.

Deciding that I was fit for the job I applied for permission to fly to the rescue of the Chelyuskinites.

The way to the *Chelyuskin* camp lay across tall mountain ranges, across vast stretches of desolate land with hundreds of miles between inhabited localities. No aircraft had ever ventured there before in winter.

I pored over the map, made dozens of different plans and anxiously awaited a reply to my application. I was prepared any moment to get into my machine and set out for the north-east. Scores of sledges, loaded with provisions, ice-breakers and aircraft, were already on their way to the camp. The country waited breathlessly for news.

I had sent in an application to the Moscow Civil Aviation Department asking to be sent to the Chukchi Peninsula.

A few days later the department chief called me in and said:

"I've read your application. You want to help in the relief operations?"

"That's right."

"How old are you?"

"I'm thirty-four."

"Well, wait until you're forty and then go."

I said nothing. The chief walked up and down the room and then, turning abruptly, asked:

"How many are there on the ice?"

"A hundred and four."

"And if you go, there'll be a hundred and six. You'll smash the machine and have to be rescued yourself. That's all."

"It is not," I thought. I wrote to the *Pravda*.

Shortly afterwards I was invited to the Kremlin.

* * *

As I came in Valerian Vladimirovich Kuibyshev rose to meet me. His eyes twinkled with good humour and he was smiling kindly.

I reported in army style.

"Pilot Vodopyanov of the Civil Air Force!"

"I know," said Kuibyshev nodding. Then with a keen look at me he asked:

"Is your machine ready?"

"Quite ready," I replied and added, "I hope to fulfil your assignment."

"Show me the route you've mapped out."

We walked up to a big map.

"From Moscow to Nikolaevsk-on-Amur I shall keep to the existing airline. Then I shall make for Okhotsk, Nogaevo Bay, Gizhiga, Kamenskoye, Anadyr, Vankarem, and from there head straight for the ice camp."

"Has anyone flown along this route in winter—from Nikolaevsk to Chukotka?" asked Kuibyshev.

"No," I said, and told him how a year ago I was to have flown along the Okhotsk coastline to Kamchatka but had met with a serious accident over Baikal.

"I hope this time to carry through the flight successfully and my machine is fully equipped for the job," I said.

Kuibyshev thought for a while and then, glancing at the map, asked suddenly:

"How many accidents have you had?"

"Four."

"Four? Here is what they write about you."

Taking a paper from the table he read:

"'Had seven accidents.' And you say four!"

The blood rushed to my face. In case Kuibyshev should think I was hiding the truth, I began hurriedly to explain.

"I've had only four real crashes, but many more break-downs—about ten altogether. But you can't call a break-down a crash!"

Kuibyshev listened attentively as I went on talking, becoming agitated, for I felt that my fate was in the balance.

"You see what I mean. Supposing I break a wheel ... I replace it and go on my way. We call that a 'break-down'."

Kuibyshev smiled and after a pause asked:

"Are you quite sure you've given this enough thought? It's the Arctic, you know—far more complicated than a flight to Kamchatka."

"I've considered everything."

"Very good!" Kuibyshev said. "Come for an answer tomorrow."

Next day I was back, standing before the map in the same room. But this time Kuibyshev himself mapped out the route.

"You'll start out from Khabarovsk, not Moscow," he said. "The journey to Khabarovsk will be made by train. Dismantle your machine at once and get it loaded on a railway truck."

I was about to protest: why should I, a pilot, go by train when every day was dear. The people on the ice were suffering, waiting to be saved ...

But Kuibyshev was prepared for my objections.

"How can you reach your goal sooner?" he said calmly. "It is still winter—the days are short. Look"—he pointed to the map—"you would be flying eastwards and so you'd have less and less daylight. When it got dark you'd have to land. You couldn't do more than one lap a day. That would mean ten days to Khabarovsk and the express will get you there in nine days. Besides the weather might be unfavourable."

"I was counting on flying day and night."

"No," said Kuibyshev firmly. "I shall permit no night-flying."

"Very well. May I go?"

Kuibyshev held out his hand and in a very warm and friendly way said:

"When you get to Khabarovsk, assemble the machine, try it out in the air, verify everything with the utmost care and don't fly in bad weather. Remember that people are waiting for you on the ice, waiting for you to rescue them. And everything will depend on you yourself."

I remembered these words many times in the course of the journey from Moscow to the *Chelyuskin* ice camp.

★ ★ ★

I arrived at Khabarovsk on March 12 and next day my mechanics, Alexandrov and Ratushkin, began assembling the plane.

Galyshev and Doronin's machines were already lined up, ready to start.

On March 17, at ten in the morning, we took off from Khabarovsk, deciding to fly in formation within sight of one another. Galyshev was appointed senior pilot of the flight.

It was difficult for me to keep on their tail for my P-5 was much faster than their PS-3's. I had to circle, climb, reduce my engine speed, glide and do all sorts of other things to avoid getting in front of them.

At first the weather was fine. We climbed to 2,500 feet but soon encountered a snow-fall. We kept close together to avoid losing sight of the leader. But then the snow grew heavier and we were forced to descend to 170 feet. Visibility was so poor that I lost sight of the leader and a few minutes afterwards I lost Doronin's machine too.

I decided to go alone, as I was familiar with the route. Increasing the speed to 110 miles an hour, I skirted the left bank of the Amur. Suddenly, a PS-3 cut across my path. I jerked back the control stick, climbed into the clouds and lost sight of the ground. I went on climbing until finally I broke through the 8,000-foot cloud bank and emerged into a dazzling sun.

It was dangerous to go on to Nikolaevsk by compass—the weather forecast predicted snow in the area. I could not come down without the risk of hitting one of the many cliffs near Nikolaevsk and it was not safe to fly low because of a possible collision with Galyshev or Doronin, who might have turned back.

I decided to return. Two hours later I was at Khabarovsk, where I was met by my mechanics.

"What's the matter? Why are you back? Engine trouble?"

"The engine's all right—so is the machine," I said.

"Then why did you turn back?"

"The weather's bad, that's why."

Deeply conscious of the importance of the assignment which had been entrusted to me I made sure of every move. Previously, I had been reckless enough, but now I was a changed man.

Next morning I again took the air. It was still snowing and half-way to Nikolaevsk we flew into a blizzard and the machine began to pitch. My mechanic touched me on the shoulder and said:

"Let's go back to Nizhne-Tambovskoye, I saw a smooth stretch of ice on the river."

Just then the machine sank and I was afraid we should strike a hillock. The mechanic was right; the best thing to do was to alight.

Soon after we landed on the ice-bound Amur River a group of youngsters, followed by men, came running up to us and we asked them to take us to the meteorological station. There we learned that the weather at Nikolaevsk was as bad as at Mariinsk—the place where we had landed.

Having conferred with my comrades I decided to wait and as the weather did not improve we had to spend the night there. Next morning I reached Nikolaevsk only to learn that Galyshev and Doronin had already left for Okhotsk.

In the evening I caught up with them there. We were very pleased to be together again.

It was heavy going from Okhotsk to Nogaevo Bay. We were flying in fine weather at an altitude of 6,500 feet but the planes were tossed about mercilessly. The altimeter would show 6,500 feet and then suddenly we would drop to 5,800 feet. It was all right for me because my machine was operational but Galyshev and Doronin had a difficult time with their passenger planes. To add to our troubles there was a strong head wind. It took us six hours to fly 410 miles, a distance my machine could normally cover in three hours twenty minutes.

At Nogaevo we were told that in Japan a whole town had been laid waste and several ships sunk that day. We had been caught in the wing of a typhoon.

We had to stay there for five days. For four days a fierce blizzard obscured the surrounding country. Gizhiga reported several times a day that a snow-storm was raging in the locality and that visibility was 550 yards.

On March 27 we set out for Gizhiga. At first conditions were favourable but then the weather got worse. I flew on ahead to avoid any chance of a collision.

Soon we ran into a blizzard. The visibility was almost nil, but it was dangerous to turn back because of the two machines following.

I sighed with relief when finally we came out of the snow-storm and saw the sea in front of us. Steering clear of the steep coast on our left we reached Gizhiga, but were horrified to find that the airfield was marked off by huge logs; a collision with any of them would have meant a bad smash.

We had asked for a 1,100-yard landing ground and they had prepared one in the form of a narrow strip 1,100 yards long and 150 yards wide. And as luck would have it there was a side wind blowing.

The people at Gizhiga had overdone it. A guide they had picked up said that the letter "T" should be placed against the wind and that is exactly what they had done, stretching the black fabric of the "T" over the whole field. But the wind kept blowing it away and so they secured it with more logs.

I circuited the place once, twice, three times. "This can't go on for ever!" I thought, and planed down, effecting a good landing.

I at once had the aerodrome cleared of the logs and the "T" laid out across the field. The other machines were due to arrive at any moment and, being heavier than mine, would find it more difficult to land.

Galyshev and Doronin did not arrive that day—bad weather had forced them to return to Nogaevo. Next day they were received in accordance with regulations.

The next lap was Kamenskoye, where we found bonfires and the letter "T". Doronin went down first. His machine touched the snow, hit a mound and bounced heavily. The pilot did not panic; throttling on he climbed and then came down for another try. But the chassis collapsed with the impact and the machine, resting on the skis, stopped dead. Doronin jumped out and laid out a sign, forbidding us to land.

We circled, waiting. Galyshev got impatient and alighted on the river a mile from the airfield and began taxiing to some houses. As there were now four knowing people on the ground, I decided not to descend until I got the signal.

Fedotov, Galyshev's air-mechanic, found a level strip of ground and lay down, stretching out his arms to form a "T". I landed beside him.

The chairman of the regional executive committee and other people were very much upset.

"We tried so very hard ... we waited ... measured the airfield with a tape-line to make sure everything would be all right, and then there was this bad luck."

We discovered later that a safe landing could be effected anywhere on the River Penzhina except at the place selected for the airfield. Presently we learnt that the choice had been made by a specialist, a former air-technician. "Here the snow is hard. Heavy aircraft will not sink, and mounds and drifts mean nothing to them," the mysterious "aviator" had declared. He had been asked if it would not be better to receive the machines where we had actually landed but he had said: "The ground is flat, but the snow is soft. The machine may fall through and break its legs."

Next day Doronin's plane was put on its feet and the screw replaced, everyone lending a hand. The damaged undercarriage caused no delay but a snow-storm held us up for five days. For three evenings I lectured on aviation. The Koryaks showed keen interest in aviation, wanting to know whether they would be admitted to a flying school. When I said "yes" they were delighted. It would probably be a good idea to train local pilots for work in this region, since they would not have to get accustomed to the severe climate.

On April 4 we finally reached Anadyr and began to prepare for the last lap.

Some time after we got there two utterly exhausted men in dirty flying suits entered the house where we were.

They were Demirov's mechanics, attached to the Kamanin group.

After warming themselves they told us how they had taken off from Maina-Pylgin the day before, but on reaching Anadyr Bay had been caught in a dense mist and lost their bearings. Seeing some *yarangi* (nomad tents) they had landed to try to find out where they were. But the Chukchi could not enlighten them for they did not know any Russian.

They flew on, alighting six times without seeing any familiar landmarks. Very little petrol remained. They decided to land a seventh time, near a cottage, in the hope of finding a Russian there. But they were again disappointed—this was not a cottage but a fisherman's shed without a living soul inside. In the middle were two drums. Demirov kicked one angrily but it hardly moved. They opened it and discovered ... petrol. Emptying a drum and a half into their tanks they used the remainder to warm water for the engine.

Presently aircraft appeared overhead. They waved, threw up their mittens, fired their pistols and even shouted, but the planes sailed past without noticing them.

Anxious to take advantage of the favourable weather, Demirov ordered the engine to be warmed up, but they could not start it—they had no compressed air, and hands were short. Then Demirov sent the mechanics for help and they came upon us.

The weather improved, but the fuel pump on Galyshev's machine gave way. It would take time to repair and that meant wasting a precious clear day, so Doronin and I decided to start out on our own.

The distance to Vankarem was 800 miles but straight across Anadyr Range it was only 400 miles. I was warned that no one had ever flown that way before.

After a little over an hour I was over Krest Bay and, changing course, steered straight for the range. Here the mountains were not so high and I was able to fly over them quite easily at an altitude of only 5,700 feet.

A strong side wind carried me westwards off my course. I emerged at the lagoon of the Amguyema which I mistook for the Pyngo-pilkhen as they look very much alike on the map. Then I sighted the cape.

Vankarem!

Approaching, I noticed some big buildings and two radio towers. What could it mean? I had been told that Vankarem had only a few nomad tents and a small trading station, but here were houses.

Having circled the place I carefully examined the map and found that that was not Vankarem at all—it was Cape North. We had drifted 125 miles off the course. However, we decided to land and fill our tanks with petrol, for, fully supplied, we could make several flights from Vankarem to the camp without having to refuel. I had heard that Vankarem was short of petrol which had to be hauled there by dog teams from Uelen.

I landed safely. Learning that Doronin, who had left an hour after me, had successfully alighted at Vankarem, I made for the camp that same day.

I climbed to 3,100 feet. On our right we could see clearly the Anadyr Mountains and on our left the Chukchi Sea, studded with ice blocks.

Soon the cape was sighted but it did not look like Vankarem. Had I made another mistake?

I circled round, gradually coming down in an attempt to ascertain my position.

The mechanic touched my shoulder and pointed downward. I thought he was suggesting a landing, but then I saw a dog team. I thought of alighting and asking the men where the elusive Vankarem was but I could not see a suitable landing-place.

Wondering what to do I flew low over the men who waved back enthusiastically. "Thanks," I thought, "but that's not much good to me, I want to know which way to go."

I flew past them once more, trying to make out who they were. They all wore furs and so I decided they were Chukchi, but there was no way of knowing whether they were on their way to or from depot. I decided to drop a message in the hope that one of them would know enough Russian to show us the way.

Five minutes later the message was in their hands. As I circled they read it and pointed eastwards. I expressed my thanks in the way of all airmen—by rocking my wings.

The men in the fur suits proved to be some rescued Chelyuskinites on their way from Vankarem to Uelen.

Landing at Vankarem, I decided to start out at once for the ice camp. While the mechanic cleared the machine of unnecessary loads, Babushkin, acting as aerodrome commandant, told me the course I was to follow.

"After forty minutes' flight," he said, "you'll see black smoke on the horizon. That will be the bonfires at the camp."

In order to be able to take more men on board I decided to leave my mechanic on shore.

I had covered more than 3,150 miles from Khabarovsk to the Chukchi Sea but they were not so reminiscent as the short 100-mile trip to the camp.

I peered ahead, looking for the black smoke. My eyes ached and watered from the strain, and the horizon grew dim. I rubbed my eyes, rested them for a while and then again looked ahead. In exactly forty minutes smoke appeared on my right. I was so happy that I shouted, "Hurrah!"

The camp lay before me, small tents wedged between piled ice blocks. Close by were two life-boats removed from the ship, and from a staff a red flag flapped, very conspicuous against the white background.

A few minutes later I alighted safely on the small ice-field and shouted:

"Who's next for shore? Come along into the plane."

I managed to cram four men into my two-seater. Fifty minutes later I landed them on the mainland and returned to the camp.

On the second trip I took three. But half-way across to Vankarem I noticed a sharp drop in the temperature of the water in the top tank.

At once I began to climb, so that in case of engine failure I could come down nearer the shore. Inwardly I begged the engine not to fail us for at least another ten minutes when we should be out of danger.

However my fears proved groundless. The water did not boil and the engine did not stop. It was the thermometer that had failed.

There were now six men left on the ice. I wanted to go out a third time but was stopped, for Kamanin and Molokov's machines were not in a very good state and my machine could not take all the men. Besides, it would be dangerous to leave only two men overnight.

That night no one slept at Vankarem. For the first time I felt the grim realities of the North and how it strengthened the bonds of friendship. The Chelyuskinites who had been saved worried about their comrades on the ice-floe. They knew that the weather might change any moment and then the last—the fifteenth—airfield would be destroyed. The six men left on the ice would not be able to clear a field for the planes.

Fortunately, the weather did not change.

There was a light haze and I decided to go out without waiting for the weather to clear.

I climbed to 3,100 feet. There was a thin mist over the ice. On my right jutted the mountain peak on Kolyuchin Island.

Then the mist thinned and I could see the hummocks and smoke.

"Good luck," I thought. "The floe has not drifted overnight."

The pilots had to change course every day, sometimes even twice a day for the floe drifted, moving to the right or left.

But as I approached I saw more smoke on my right.

I flew on keeping to the course. Then I found that the clouds of smoke were not flares as I had supposed but masses of vapour coming from cracks in the ice.

For an hour and twenty minutes I forged on. But the camp was hidden by a thin layer of mist. I decided to turn back and wait for it to clear.

By noon visibility had improved. The mechanics had repaired Molokov and Kamanin's machines and the three of us took off together in aircraft of the same type.

Kamanin took Shelyganov, his navigator, with him to make sure we did not stray from the target.

But the vapour had cleared and the mist had lifted. In the distance we could see clearly the smoke from a bonfire.

Krenkel, the radio-operator, sent the last message.

"Three aircraft arrived. Landed safely. Removing radio. Now leaving Shmidt camp."

Kamanin took the navigator and one of the remaining Chelyuskinites. In addition he put eight dogs in parachute cases, slung from the wing. Molokov took two Chelyuskinites, loading the parachute cases with various belongings. I took three, among them Sima Ivanov, a young radio-operator, bound for Wrangel Island.

We were ready to leave when suddenly I noticed something black projecting from the snow. It was two suitcases, both empty. "Their owners will be glad to have them," I thought. Then I saw about a hundred sets of warm underwear and a mattress. I decided to take these too. I was resolved to leave nothing behind.

The machines took off, one after another. Krenkel asked me to make one farewell circuit over the camp. I glanced at my companions and saw them looking down. Krenkel sat frowning.

Forty minutes later we were at Vankarem. The jubilation there is hard to describe. All Vankarem's twenty inhabitants, plus sixty Chelyuskinites, came out to meet us.

The first Heroes of the Soviet Union
Left to right: N. P. Kamanin, M. P. Slepnev, I. V. Doronin,
V. S. Molokov, M. V. Vodopyanov, S. A. Levanevsky,
A. V. Lyapıdevsky

The dogs, let loose, raced around the planes, finding their masters, and dancing about them joyfully. Then came the Chelyuskinites who were fervently embraced by those who had been rescued earlier.

The Chelyuskinites at Vankarem would never forget our last flight to the camp. Those last few hours caused them no little anxiety. On previous occasions either Krenkel or Ivanov would radio the arrival of the planes, and also their safe departure. But this time only the landing was reported for there was no one left to radio the take-off.

The men on shore calculated how long it would take to remove the radio and added an hour for the return trip. According to these calculations the planes were due long before there was any sign of them.

This made them apprehensive. They climbed on to the roof of the trading station looking so intently at the sky that at times they thought they saw squadrons of planes. But the image disappeared as soon as their eyes rested.

Finally a black speck appeared on the horizon, and then a second and a third.

The Chelyuskinites were overjoyed and when we arrived they kept tossing us in the air until I thought they would shake the life out of us. I said to Krenkel:

"This is real solid land. No more drifting south or north... You had tears in your eyes when I made the final circuit over the camp. Were you sorry to leave?"

"Not at all. You brought the tears to my eyes when you planted Ivanov on my legs..."

Krenkel stooped, trying to reach the earth beneath the snow. "Mother earth!"

But someone said:

"It's the sea. The earth is a hundred yards away."

"What! I'm still at sea? I'll rush for land!" he laughed.

We had learned to value the weather and now we decided to lose no time in flying the Chelyuskinites to Uelen. The machines were in good shape and only one thing was lacking—fuel. That was when we fully realized the value of the petrol I had brought from Cape North. I shared it with Molokov and that meant that two machines would reach Uelen with eight Chelyuskinites and return with enough petrol for the remaining planes.

★ ★ ★

On April 13, two months after the death of the ship, a report was made to the Party and the Government that all the Chelyuskinites had been rescued and on the night of April 14 a reply was received from Moscow which read:

"*Lyapidevsky, Levanevsky, Molokov, Kamanin, Slepnev, Vodopyanov, Doronin. Vankarem, Uelen.*

"Applaud your heroic efforts in rescuing the Chelyuskinites. Proud of your triumph over the elements. You have justified the best hopes of the country and proved worthy sons of your great motherland.

"Have made a request to the Central Executive Committee of the U.S.S.R.

54

"1. That there shall be instituted the highest distinction for acts of valour—the title of Hero of the Soviet Union.

"2. That the title of Hero of the Soviet Union shall be bestowed on pilots Lyapidevsky, Levanevsky, Molokov, Kamanin, Slepnev, Vodopyanov and Doronin, who have directly participated in the rescue of the Chelyuskinites.

"3. That these pilots and their air-mechanics be awarded the Order of Lenin and a cash prize of one year's salery.

"*J. Stalin, V. Molotov, K. Voroshilov, V. Kuibyshev, A. Zhdanov.*"

We were overwhelmed and for a long time unable to say anything.

We could not think of words that would express our gratitude to the Party and the Government.

* * *

Next morning just as Molokov and I landed at Uelen a snow-storm began. It was a good thing the *Chelyuskin* camp was no more!

The blizzard kept us grounded for five days. On the sixth day we returned to Vankarem with a supply of petrol and immediately all the machines went into operation.

The people of the Chukchi Peninsula played an important part in the rescue operations by helping to establish an air base at Vankarem, transporting petrol on dog and reindeer sledges and evacuating the shipwrecked *Chelyuskin* men from Vankarem to Uelen.

On the 21st of May we left the shores of the Chukchi Sea by ship. In Vladivostok hundreds of thousands of people rolled out to meet us. Aircraft circled above dropping flowers on deck.

Three days later we were on our way to Moscow in a special train.

There are a hundred and sixty stops between Vladivostok and Moscow. At every station we were hailed with flowers and banners, and everywhere people wanted to know all about the camp and the flights. At one wayside station where the train did not stop but steamed past slowly, an old woman of about seventy with a bundle in her arms ran alongside, shouting:

"Why don't you stop, lads? I've been expecting you. I've got some buns for you!"

The Chelyuskinites had time and again stared death in the face. They had fought the elements for months without weakening, but they could not keep the tears from their eyes in face of their country's warm, kindly welcome.

On June 19, 1934, we reached Moscow, where the whole city turned out to cheer us.

he day following my arrival in Moscow I went to the Civil Aviation Department. I was eager to see my fellow-airmen, to tell them the story of the flights to the ice camp and to thank them for their advice and assistance. To my surprise the personnel officer said:

"Sorry, Mikhail Vasilyevich, but you're no longer with us..."

"What d'you mean?"

"I mean you're no longer in our service—you've been transferred to the polar air service."

At last my ambitions were being realized and I was to fly to the more remote and least-explored regions of the Soviet Arctic. There was plenty of work there for scores of other pilots, besides myself.

"We've been given a great task—to explore and map the Soviet North, approximately one-fourth of the vast territory of the Soviet Union. We shall accomplish it with the enthusiastic and effective help of the whole country, under the direct care and guidance of the Communist Party," said Otto Yulyevich Shmidt, head of Glavsevmorput (the Northern Sea Route Administration) and famous arctic explorer.

Early in 1935 I started out on a flight along the route Moscow-Sverdlovsk-Omsk-Krasnoyarsk-Irkutsk-Chita-Khabarovsk-Nikola-evsk-on-Amur-Okhotsk-Nogaevo Bay-Gizhiga-Anadyr-Uelen-Cape Shmidt—a distance of about 12,500 miles, including the return journey to Khabarovsk.

I had to tackle a number of problems connected with the organization of a mail and passenger service along this route, and also to make recommendations in respect to the type of machine best suited for work in the Far North. V. M. Molotov became interested in the preparations for the flight. On hearing that my machine had no radio, he said I was not to leave until one had been fitted. More than once during the flight I had good reason to thank him for his concern, for things would have gone badly with us if we had had no radio.

I was to start out in company with Matzio Lindel, a seasoned polar aviator. My air-mechanic was Flegont Bassein and the radio-operator was Chelyuskinite Sima Ivanov. Flegont and I were old friends. I had known him during the Civil War when, as a sixteen-year-old lad, he had first joined the Air Force, dreaming of a pilot's certificate. At the age of eighteen he was senior air-mechanic with a military flying squadron, but he still hoped to be a pilot. Poor eyesight prevented this and, eventually, after several unsuccessful solo flights he gave up and devoted all his passion for aviation to planes and engines. He was a first-class air-mechanic.

In 1934, Bassein's pilot crashed on a desolate strip of shore on Wrangel Island, 32 miles off Rodger's Bay, and he set about the formidable task of patching up the machine. His technical brilliance produced some very bold ideas, which he steadily incorporated.

His companions helped him, although they were dubious as to the outcome. But the results surpassed even Bassein's expectations—the machine was saved.

From his looks no one would have thought that Bassein was a veteran polar traveller and a skilled air-mechanic.

He had a boyish face with clear blue eyes and it was hard to believe that he was in his forties. He was of small build, but strong and muscular.

Sima Ivanov was quite different: he was big and heavy and at first glance appeared clumsy—the direct opposite of the slim, well-knit Bassein.

However, Sima, like Flegont, had hands of gold. He was an exceptionally good radio-operator and along with Krenkel he did duty at the Shmidt camp until I took him off in my plane.

Sima Ivanov had not returned to Moscow with the Chelyuskinites, but had gone on to Wrangel Island by air.

The staff of the Wrangel Island polar station still remembered how miraculously he had salvaged the hopelessly damaged radio, which had been idle for close on two years.

Ivanov arrived at the polar station unshaven, unwashed and

almost exhausted after working on the repair of the plane, which had been damaged during a forced landing. But he would not hear of rest, and refused even to wash until he had established communication with Moscow. He returned with fresh wires from the capital.

Radio is immensely important during big arctic flights and so, having a radio-operator like Sima Ivanov on a plane can make all the difference to the success of the enterprise.

We started out on March 1 and five days later reached Khabarovsk. I was happy to land once more at this familiar aerodrome where twelve months before I had taken off for the Chukchi Sea to rescue the *Chelyuskin* men.

The first stage of the flight was over. In the course of thirty-nine flying hours we had covered a distance of 4,700 miles.

But ahead lay the most difficult part of the journey.

Having got the machines ready we took on board the usual mail and also thirty bundles of Osoaviakhim lottery tickets for the Kamenskoye culture centre. It was a cumbersome load, carelessly wrapped in paper and fastened with cord. I did not want to take it but I was persuaded.

There being little room in the luggage compartments built into the wings, the bundles were dumped on the floor of the passenger cabin. This annoyed the air-mechanics and radio-operators as it interfered with their work.

In Khabarovsk, I was handed a radiogram from a teacher on Shantar Islands. The school was running short of copy-books and she asked me to bring a few hundred. I took five hundred with me.

At 10 a. m. on March 11 we took off from Khabarovsk aerodrome and set course for Nikolaevsk-on-Amur. I was again on the old route, viewing the familiar landmarks of Bogorodsk and Malmyzh, and the rugged, hummocky ice on the Amur River.

When another hour had passed things began to happen. On the bank of the Amur River, instead of a tiny hamlet, there now appeared a big town. I glanced at the map, thinking I had deviated from my course. No, it was all right—this was Komsomolsk-on-Amur, a town that had arisen in the past two years. We could see quite clearly the newly built plants, a red-brick mill, a granary and many warehouses. We passed over Sofiisk, once a village but now a town with asphalt streets. How quickly the face of the country was changing!

Near Troitskoye I found I had lost Lindel. What had happened? Only a minute ago he had been close on my right and now he seemed to have vanished into thin air.

"Where's Lindel?" I shouted to Bassein.

He shrugged and pointed to Ivanov who had been vainly trying to get in touch with Lindel for some time.

Alarmed I decided to turn back and see whether Lindel had landed somewhere near. Below, on the white sheet of snow, appeared a dark speck like a plane, but approaching, I discovered it was a haystack. I turned right and left investigating many similar specks, while Lindel, I found out later, was calmly following me, wondering what I was up to. When I circled, I spotted him and we both landed at Nikolaevsk which marked the end of the regular air route. Beyond lay difficult, little-known territory.

Again I was amazed at the scale of construction work.

When I passed the place a year ago I had seen nothing new, but now not far from Nikolaevsk, on the outskirts of Cape Koshka, a new town had been built. People said with pride:

"That's our granary."

"Why granary?"

"Come and we'll show you."

I was eager to see the place and we went by car, which again was a novelty. Hitherto I had either passed in a plane or travelled in a dog or deer sledge. But now a newly built highway led to the new townlet.

Nikolaevsk residents had good reason to be proud of their "granary" which consisted of a large, modern mill with elevators, stores and cottages for the workers.

Next day we decided to head straight for Okhotsk. Taking off at ten thirty, we flew north-west across the mountains.

An aircraft covers many miles in a few minutes and soon we were over Cape Mukhtel. On our left lay Nicholas Bay and Udd (now Chkalov) Island which was our last chance of an emergency landing.

Now we were passing over the Sea of Okhotsk, over rugged ice-fields with rare lanes of open water. We kept listening to the regular drone of the engine, trying both magnetos in turn.

Ahead Big Shantar Island appeared. I throttled down and began to glide. Lindel on my right maintained the same altitude.

We appeared over Yakshino Bay at a height of 1,000 feet. Circuiting the village I recalled how in 1930 I had helped in seal-hunting there. The island, a desolate place then, was now unrecognizable. There was a big sable farm, and on the river-bank were motor launches and boats.

I streamed in from the mountains, flying over the houses at a height of 65 feet. The people ran out, waving their hands in welcome.

I signalled and down went the mail and parcels of copy-books. Then I climbed and, changing course, headed for Ayan across the sea.

We were in constant radio contact with Nikolaevsk, Ayan and Okhotsk. At intervals of 10-15 minutes Nikolaevsk asked for our bearings while Ayan and Okhotsk reported weather conditions.

We had been in flight three hours and had covered less than half the distance. Ahead loomed Ayan. Lindel radioed: "Pump not drawing petrol from auxiliary tanks. Running on main tanks. Wire instructions."

It would take four hours to fly to Okhotsk and the main tanks would not keep him supplied as long as that. It was impossible to land and so I gave the order:

"Alight at once and transfer fuel from auxiliary to main tanks. Then start out for Okhotsk without delay. I shall not land."

The port of Ayan is situated on the western shores of the Sea of Okhotsk. Its bay, surrounded by tall cliffs, is set in a kind of hollow. Here a plane can come down only from the side of the sea. Lindel effected a masterly landing. Reassured, I went on my way.

It was hard going to Okhotsk, I had never known such bumping. Nor was the outlook below very cheering—on the right was the seething sea and on the left the bleak Dzhugdzhur Range. The shore was marked by jagged cliffs with not a hint of flat ground.

Meanwhile our plane lurched more than ever. An invisible force seemed to clutch the machine, lifting it up high and then hurling it downwards for about 700 feet till we thought our safety-belts would snap.

Finally a village came in sight. The steep cliffs ended and stretches of gentle slopes began. We could see natural landing fields—rivers with a smooth coating of snow—and our spirits rose. Besides, it was not so bumpy now.

Six and a half hours after leaving Nikolaevsk we circled over Okhotsk. I carefully surveyed the airfield and turning into the wind, landed safely.

That same evening Lindel arrived.

★ ★ ★

During supper the secretary of the district executive committee spoke of the life of the peoples of the extreme North.

"I've been here three years and I've sledged almost the whole length of the coastline from Ayan to Nogaevo Bay," he said. "I've seen a lot. There are two very backward nomad settlements in the Okhotsk district—Kheidzhan and Ulbeya. These nomads roam from place to place sometimes as far as 300 miles from shore where all the administrative and cultural bodies are concentrated. In winter they hunt and in summer they fish in the mountain streams. Then they are inaccessible except by deer. Not so long ago I went there for the annual rally."

"But the attendance is a hundred per cent," I broke in.

"Exactly! They all turn out to see a newcomer.

"In 1932 I was director of a state deer farm with up to 15,000 animals in my charge. There were two deer purchasing agents on the farm—Zhirokhov, a Yakut, and Lipp, a Kamchadal. Both were affected by a disease common in the taiga. Locally it's known as emiryatchestvo. Doctors say it is caused by people in the taiga having to be always on the alert so that eventually they get so nervous that every sound startles them. For instance, you tell a man affected by this disease: 'I'm going to strike a match—don't let it alarm you.' But in spite of the warning, when you strike the match he begins to shout and beats his hands frantically against everything within reach. Once this happened to Lipp: he was chopping wood when a splinter, that he hadn't noticed, flew into the air and came down on his shoulder. He lost all control of himself, and kept swinging the axe until all his toes were gone. Zhirokhov, the second agent, had different symptoms: when he was frightened by a sudden noise or cry he would shout and repeat everything he heard. One chap, deciding to amuse himself, pushed a cake of soap into his hand and shouted 'eat!' Zhirokhov repeated the command and took a bite at the soap. The joker was strictly warned."

The secretary told us many more interesting stories about life in the Far North. Departing I said:

"Thanks, you're a good speaker. Soon there will be no dark corners in the Soviet Union. The Party and the Government have instructed the Northern Sea Route Administration to begin the development of the remote regions. And letters have been received in Moscow from young people in all parts of the country who want to work in the North.

"We're going to set up a regular air service where few planes have been before. Soon you'll be getting freight and mail not once a year, but every day. Our flight is difficult only because it is the first. We still lack many things—bases, landing fields and a good radio service. Once the equipment is there and a service established flying will be easy. I recall how in 1930 I started a regular air route to Sakhalin. The first few flights were difficult because there was no ground service. But nowadays planes fly there and back every day in forty degrees of frost, in gales and snow-storms and the route isn't considered difficult at all."

Next day we checked the readiness of the planes for the take-off. Workmen were putting firewood round a drum, with a stick jutting out of it and frozen into the ice.

"What's that for?" I asked of Lyuk, a Kamchadal, who was beside me.

"It's very cold and the water has frozen hard—it may burst the drum," he explained.

"Will the stick prevent that?"

"Yes, it forces the ice out and relieves pressure on the sides. See?"

"You're a smart fellow, Lyuk," I said. "Did you invent that yourself?"

"No, the frost did. It's very cold here and containers are scarce. Everybody does the same."

Lyuk put some petrol over the wood and set fire to it. Soon we had warm water which we poured into the radiators.

At eleven a. m. a report was received about weather conditions in Nogaevo Bay and we set out.

The farther we went north the more difficult conditions became for our heavy machines, overloaded with mail.

We found very few suitable landing fields. Now it was all wild country with hundreds of miles between populated areas.

The weather got much worse as we reached Gizhiginskaya Bay. I was forced to fly low but that did not help much because of the mist. Visibility was very poor; there was a grey haze over everything. The situation was not an enviable one.

I was only about 35 miles from Gizhiga but conditions were becoming almost impossible. I had lost sight of Lindel. Should I turn back? Where could I go? There was no intermediate airfield, nowhere to land and wait for better weather; returning was out of the question—there was not enough fuel.

I could not fly low over the sea since everything below was a grey patch. It was best to keep close to the coast, but that was extremely difficult.

The mist did not lift until we reached Gizhiga. To the left of the river mouth four bonfires showed where the airfield had been laid out. Making sure that the airfield was not what it had been the year before, I went in against the wind and landed.

Twenty minutes later Lindel arrived.

Taking advantage of the enforced delay the mechanics decided to get rid of surplus cargo. Expressing the feelings of the crews, Zhukov, Lindel's radio-operator, launched the attack.

"I'm in charge of the mail," he said to me. "Couldn't we leave the Osoaviakhim lottery tickets for Kamenskoye here in Gizhiga? The cargo isn't urgent and although it's not very heavy, it takes up a lot of space. And you know we're very cramped."

"But this is freight, sent by air, and expected by people—it might take a year to reach them by sea," I said dubiously.

"You needn't worry about that," insisted Zhukov. "I've made inquiries and the mail for Kamenskoye is sent off on sledges every other day. It'll be there on the third."

This argument disposed of all my objections.

"If so, go ahead."

In the morning there was fine flying weather. The mist had lifted, the sky was clear and a wind was blowing.

Everything was ready for the take-off—the engines were warmed up and flooded with hot oil. The bundles containing the lottery tickets lay dumped on the snow near the machines; the torn paper flapped in the wind.

We filled the engines with water and were about to run them up. In another minute the propeller blades would whip up snow and scatter the poorly packed lottery tickets, and Zhukov, to prevent this, casually kicked them aside.

The wind raised clouds of soft snow. If it had been a fair wind we could have reached Kamenskoye in a little over an hour, but unfortunately it was a head wind, which would seriously retard our progress and keep us in the air for at least three hours.

Having delivered the mail and taken leave of the hospitable aerodrome staff, we started out.

Gradually the wind abated and the sun glittered on the snow. Flying conditions were ideal.

Beyond the mountains, on the right bank of the River Penzhina, we could see two radio masts and a group of huts. That was Kamen-skoye.

Circuiting I discovered that the landing field was laid out at the foot of the mountain. The signs indicated that we were to land across the river with a side wind. But that did not trouble us now for there was only a light wind.

I alighted first. The machine fell through the snow as if it had been a feather bed. It was just as I thought. Last year the landing ground had been too hard and this time it was too soft.

I at once taxied out of Lindel's way and watched him land. He approached with great care. Descending to about 45 feet, and still some distance from the airfield, he came in at low speed, throttled down, and touched the snow almost on top of the landing "T". "Smart landing," I thought, but I was a bit too soon for at the end of the run the plane suddenly listed and stopped with the right wing deep in the snow.

I ran up and found that everything was all right and the machine was undamaged. There was water under the soft snow and the right ski had sunk into it. With the help of the people who had gathered to meet us the plane was hauled out.

When Lindel's machine had been finally towed into position a post-office official approached me. He had been there for some time and the nomad Koryaks regarded him as one of their own. I had met him the year before.

"Glad to see you, Mikhail Vasilyevich," he said.

Meanwhile two sledges with a guard had driven up and we handed over the mail.

"Why these precautions today?" I asked.

"Special mail, Comrade Vodopyanov."

He himself, assisted by Zhukov, untied and checked the contents of each bag. When, much to the relief of the mechanics, the mail was unloaded, he asked looking worried:

"And where's the main mail?"

"What main mail? That's all we had."

"It isn't all. Here's a radiogram from Khabarovsk reporting that five hundred thousand rubles have been sent by your machines. What have you done with the money?"

"What!" I was indignant. "D'you think we'd play jokes with freight like that? We had no money. I've carried bank-notes to Sakhalin before and they were always packed in leather bags."

"I don't know how the money was packed—all I know is that it was dispatched from Khabarovsk with you."

I was getting worried. Together we went through the mail bags again but found no money. I racked my brains trying to understand what it all meant, when someone said:

"Perhaps it was bank-notes and not lottery tickets you left at Gizhiga?"

"Are you serious?" I asked resentfully. "They couldn't possibly have packed bank-notes in ordinary wrapping paper. Besides we have the bill of lading which clearly specifies the freight. But you never can tell—a check would do no harm."

Instead of guarding the currency which we had not brought, the soldier hurried away to the telegraph station. A wire was sent to Gizhiga, asking them to open some of the packages and see what was in them.

Soon there was a reply—the paper wrappings contained money, a total of half a million rubles. I was very much relieved for it was no joke to have mislaid half a million of state funds!

Why they didn't tell us it was currency and not lottery tickets we were carrying is beyond me, but I'm glad all ended well.

There was no petrol at Kamenskoye and we had to empty all the drums. The fuel was dirty and of unknown quality, but there was no other, and we decided to filter it for in the morning we had to set out for Anadyr.

The mechanics worked all night refuelling the machines. They were assisted by young Koryaks, who displayed great energy, but their ignorance of aviation almost led to disaster.

Standing on the lower wings they cheerfully poured petrol from buckets into a funnel with a suède filter, competing for results. When less than five buckets had been emptied into my machine, one of the tanks of Lindel's machine was full and the Koryaks working with him chaffed our helpers.

"You're a fine bunch of mechanics! Look, we've almost filled the second tank."

Lindel's mechanic became suspicious and climbed on to the wing to inspect the work of his assistants. He found that they had cut a hole in the suède to speed up the flow of petrol. There was nothing for it but to empty the tank and begin again. By morning the petrol was carefully sifted of dirt and the machines refuelled, but we could not set out for there was a howling blizzard; it was impossible to venture out without a wind-blouse—snow got into the fur, which soon became iced up.

We spent the evening in the company of the Koryaks. My description of the *Chelyuskin* rescue operations was followed by a lively chat. One Komsomol member told us about life there in the old days as compared with life under Soviet power.

"We Koryaks are a backward nation," he said. "Our people wander from place to place with their reindeer herds. Communists used to come from the mainland and describe the new life in all parts of the Soviet Union. They urged us to study and build up a new life and showed us how rich kulaks were exploiting us and holding us back.

"We lived in clans, and in each clan were three or four families with fifteen to twenty-five deer and one kulak family with twenty or twenty-five thousand deer. We lived together, looking after the herds in turn, irrespective of how many reindeer the family possessed. Generally, the animals belonging to the rich family were slaughtered for food. This, we thought was very kind of them. We did not understand that they could never have managed without us, that they would have had to hire herdsmen, feed and pay them. And if anyone dared to criticize one of these kulaks he would say, 'We live in communes, as we are taught by the Soviets. Everything we have is owned in common.' And the poor people all their lives had been used to looking on the kulaks as benefactors and attending to their herds along with their own deer, so, for a long time, they could not understand how things could be otherwise. And I'll tell you something really funny—until quite recently we had our own king! This is how it happened: once, probably in the time of Catherine, some merchants came and brought with them a brass crown which they put on the head of the wealthiest reindeer breeder and proclaimed him king. This crown was passed on, as something sacred, from father to son, and a king came into being on Karyak soil. Of course, this 'king' had neither economic nor political power, apart from that he had anyway as a wealthy kulak. But the king was honoured and he always wore his crown. About two years ago we virtually tore the crown off the head of the last king—a wizened old man. There was a great commotion—the old chap didn't want to part with it. 'I'm very old and I won't live long,' he said. 'Let me wear it till I die.'"

It was all very amusing: in 1934, in the seventeenth year of Soviet Government—a king on Soviet territory! The young Komsomol member, carried away by his story, and speaking an even worse mixture of Russian and Koryak, went on:

"Up till a few years ago Koryaks did not understand what the Party and Soviet power mean to us. Communists from the mainland opened our eyes and we realized what a good life was ahead of us. And we, particularly the young people, want to study, want sooner to build up a good, Soviet life in our far-away region. Many of our young people have left for the mainland, but we know they will come back here, to the North, come back learned to help us."

As he finished, we applauded and then the young people danced. The Koryak national dance is very unusual. Generally, it is the feet and legs of dancers which are most active in harmony with other parts of the body. In the Koryak dance it is the opposite—the feet remain motionless, and only the body and hands move. The dancers perform a series of movements of the body, doubling up parallel with the ground without moving a foot.

In conclusion they staged a small play written by local Komsomol members. The play was crude and the acting was bad—none of them had ever seen a real performance—but it was a pleasure to watch them. This little episode, as in a mirror, reflected the new the Koryak people had learnt under Soviet power—to strive for a free life of culture and learning.

On March 26 we proceeded on our journey. We decided to skirt the River Penzhina, by-pass the River Main, emerge at Lake Krasnoye and then follow the River Anadyr to our destination. However, we soon found that it would not be possible to do this. Between the rivers Penzhina and Main rise some small hills which we tried in vain to clear—the visibility had sharply deteriorated and our planes were tossed about in the swift air streams. We had to circuit the mountains. In the passes a fierce head wind almost brought our machines to a standstill—all the engine power was needed to resist the storm. There was no sense in turning back, for we knew that there was not a pint of petrol left in the district we had just left. There was nothing for it but to push on.

Finally, we reached the Anadyr River, but only a few minutes remained before nightfall, and we still had some 125 miles to go.

I directed Ivanov to get in touch with Anadyr and ask about the weather. Anadyr at once replied:

"Conditions favourable. Waiting."

We radioed back:

"We're late. Will arrive after dark. Keep the fires burning."

The sun had already dipped. We were flying at 4,000 feet at a speed of 125 miles an hour. Lindel's machine was hardly visible in the failing light. I wanted to let him know about my talk with Anadyr but his wireless was dead.

All at once Lindel swerved and began swiftly to descend, so that within a minute I completely lost sight of him. It looked as if his engine had failed, but I could not linger, so, plotting the spot on my map, I went on.

Ahead lights flashed and my heart thumped joyfully. But then they disappeared and I wondered if I had begun to see things.

I peered ahead but could see no lights on either side. Then I circled and saw beneath my tilted wing several bonfires. I came down to about 170 feet and noticed that the flames were blown to the right of the line of flares, and so I was forced to land not lengthwise, but across the line.

As soon as I touched people ran to indicate where I was to taxi. I switched off on the river-bank. There were houses on the hill-side and electric lamps on high posts. This could not be Anadyr for there was no electricity there at the time. I clambered out of the machine and found that we had landed at a fishery near Anadyr.

After a brief meeting I asked the director of the fishery:

"Have you got any petrol?"

"There's petrol for you at Anadyr. We laid out this airfield on the off chance that it might be useful—thought we'd persuade you to fly over from Anadyr and show yourself to our workmen. We didn't work in vain—it came in handy."

"I should say so. It saved both us and the machine. But who was it we talked to on the radio? Wasn't it Anadyr?"

"No, you were talking to us. We have our own radio. Anadyr wasn't listening in."

"They sent the morning weather report to you at Kamenskoye and that was all," broke in the fishery's radio-operator, "but I happened to get in touch with your radio-operator and kept track of you."

I warmly shook his hand and thanked the workers of the fishery for the trouble they had taken. Inwardly I very much resented the carelessness of the Anadyr administration.

"So they don't know we've landed?"

"They do not."

Anadyr is at the opposite side of the bay, five miles from the fishery. At my request sledges were sent there at once for petrol—I was determined to start out in search of Lindel next morning. I also asked the radio-operators at Anadyr to send our regular call signals in the hope that he would reply and thus help in the search. Later I learned that Lindel was not the only one in difficulties. Two days before, a machine piloted by Maslennikov, with radio-navigator Padalka on board, had run into a snow-storm and had been forced to land. Sledging parties had been dispatched to look for them.

At daybreak a snow-storm prevented me from going to Lindel's assistance. In the evening he sent a radiogram:

"Landed safely on Anadyr River, 60 miles away. Send bucket to heat water in. Firewood unnecessary, brushwood nearby. Alighted because we feared running short of fuel."

Sledges were sent to look for Lindel, too.

Meantime, we were grounded at the fishery, waiting for better weather. The snow-storm raged on and it was almost unbearable to think of our being forced to pass the time in idle comfort while our comrades were hungry and waiting to be rescued from the snow-swept plains. But it would have been madness to set out in such weather.

In fact it was only about Maslennikov and Padalka that there was any need to worry. They could not give a definite indication of their position and they had very little food. Lindel's plight was not half as bad. He had landed on the river ice and the relief parties, sent out in dog sledges, could not possibly miss him. Besides, he had with him a twenty days' supply of food—including a sack of meat dumplings—a tent and sleeping-bags, as well as cooking facilities.

In planning the rescue of Maslennikov and his companion we first of all reviewed the measures already taken.

Maslennikov had made a forced landing on March 24 and at once radioed Anadyr:

> "Made a good landing. Uninjured and machine undamaged. Think we must be about 25 miles from Anadyr and four to five miles from estuary joining Nicholas Bay, but maybe nearer. Cannot exactly determine our position because of thick clouds blotting out the horizon. Send sledges. Listen in to us tomorrow at 2 p. m."

He was informed that a sledging party had set out in that direction. The day following another radiogram was received:

> "No sledges have reached us. Living in an igloo. Food will last four days. Made several unsuccessful attempts to start engine. Will try again on first clear day. Yesterday Padalka climbed a hillock and concluded we are not where we thought we were. We are far from shore—10 to 12 miles or maybe more. Can see far end of Zolotoi Range which stretches to the Anadyr. We must be deep inland north of Anadyr. Continue search 25-30 miles eastwards, and also a little westward."

The search for Maslennikov was kept up for eight days. Six dog sledges driven by picked kayurs familiar with the surrounding country set out from Anadyr in the direction where it was thought the men were.

Three of the kayurs I had met the year before. The first, Nalivaiko by name, was an old settler from the Ukraine. He was fifty-three but would run behind the sledge like a good athlete. The second was Semyon Savosev, an Ossetian, who had also lived a long time in Anadyr. He was very fond of his dog team but always declared that "mules are better pacers." The third was an ex-shaman—a fifty-year-old Chukchi, Tyrke by name. "Nowadays," he would say, "people are no fools, and so you can't live by deceit—you have to work for a living." I don't know what kind of shaman he was but he certainly made an excellent sledge driver.

It was good to know that local people were taking an active part in the search. On the way five reindeer sledges joined the dog teams sent out from Anadyr. Telepin, a Chukchi from the Polar Star collective farm, came to Anadyr and offered his services.

But the search was not confined to sledging. Air reconnaissance was carried out by Serguchev, our airline pilot held up in Anadyr by the snow-storm. He did not stay out long; a low cloud bank made him turn back without seeing anything.

In a later radiogram Maslennikov and Padalka said:

"Did not see Serguchev. Shall burn oil if we see him or hear his engine. Living on skeleton rations. These will last four days and then can hold out another week on grass and moss. But do all you can to speed up search. We are in good health. Not suffering from hunger but are inconvenienced by the cold and damp clothing. Regards to all. Tell them not to worry."

It was agony to sit idle when these radiograms arrived. But there was nothing we could do for the blizzard had us helpless on the ground.

There had been no news from Lindel for five days. On the sixth a radiogram was received:

"Sledges have arrived. With their help took off and set course for Anadyr. Encountered snow-storm and was forced to land on left bank of gulf, sixteen miles from Anadyr. The machine is safe, and so are we. Send petrol by sledges and cistern for warming water."

There being no more dog sledges in Anadyr a horse sledge with broad runners was sent.

Next day the weather improved and I and my crew set out to look for Maslennikov. But the whole area was wrapped in mist, and we returned without achieving anything.

Chukotka

Before landing I decided to make sure that Lindel had got his petrol. I passed over the Gulf of Anadyr but saw no machine there. That pleased me for it meant that Lindel had got away. Making for the aerodrome across Nerpichy Bay I noticed on the left bank a black speck with a tent pitched near it. Circuiting I saw men clamber out, run aside and flatten themselves out on the snow in the form of the letter "T". "They must be airmen, and this must be a good landing ground if they were signalling us down," I thought.

We landed well.

"What do you mean by giving us the wrong address?" I said. "I sent all you asked for to the Gulf of Anadyr and here you are in Nerpichy."

"Got mixed up. The blinding snow hid everything."

I replenished Lindel's fuel supply from my auxiliary tanks and then flew to Anadyr for hot water. Quickly we installed a large container at the tail end of the cabin, filled it with hot water and returned. Half an hour later the two planes alighted on the fishery's airfield.

The two crews were together again, and the machines in good shape, but we felt we could not leave while Maslennikov was still missing.

The blizzard had not abated and we could not continue relief operations although in his last radiogram Maslennikov had more or less accurately reported his bearings.

"We know of Vodopyanov's flight but did not see him. Landed near a river which we presume to be the mouth of the Volchya. Yesterday Padalka again climbed the hillock. To the south-west and west lies flat slightly elevated country. Get a description of locality and consult some of old residents."

That evening we re-read Maslennikov's radiograms and tried to plot his position on the map. If there was flat land south-west of them, they must be somewhere in the Ushkan Mountains, near the Volchya River. We guessed where they must have landed. The map was ready, but we could not take off, for the weather was still bad. Conditions did not improve until April 3 when we took off for the Volchya River. We followed it as far as the Ushkan Mountains and there, wedged between two tall cliffs, we saw the plane.

Ivanov briefly radioed to Anadyr:

"Machine found, descending."

I circled twice. Not a living soul near the machine. Were they dead?

Gliding down to 300 feet I circuited again seeing first one and then another man come out from under the tail and walk slowly in opposite directions.

"Going to lay out the signs," I thought. But the men made only a few steps and collapsed on the snow. They were apparently too weak to walk.

I did not know which way the wind was blowing or how best to land, but it was no use guessing and so I came down.

The two men walked up, their faces black with soot.

Bassein produced a bag of food which they snatched greedily and disappeared into their "lair."

We began to free the machine and warm up the engine.

Then I looked into the "lair" which was a deep hole high enough to stand in with a smooth floor thickly overgrown with grass. This grass would have lasted them a long while. On the primus stove water was being warmed in a large petrol drum.

"Why are you heating water? Did you know we were coming?"

"No," said Padalka. "We just thought we'd try to get the engine going ourselves."

The two shook our hands warmly.

Maslennikov took off first. Both machines landed safely at Anadyr.

* * *

At last favourable weather set in: reports from Uelen, Vankarem and Cape Shmidt were good.

We had enough time for a thorough discussion of the forthcoming flight. Finally, we decided on the shortest but most difficult route—over the Anadyr Mountains.

Our course lay across a valley with Zolotoi Range on the right and the Ushkan Mountains on the left of us. We struck out across the mountains, intending to reach the Chukchi Sea midway between Vankarem and Cape Shmidt.

We were flying at a height of 5,000 feet. The mountains were enveloped in mist, with the peaks jutting out like sugar-loaves. It was absolutely calm with the horizon clearly visible. The shadow of the plane raced across the clouds.

The mountains were left behind and below us was a valley of clouds. Judging by the hour we should now be coasting the Chukchi Sea. Having learned from bitter experience, Lindel kept close to me.

Striving to avoid the sea, I decided to break through the clouds for one feels safer with the land in sight. I began to plane down and the machine entered the cloud bank. The sun was gone and the ground was invisible. I was flying blind, paying special attention to the height indicator. We had come down to 1,500 feet, but the ground was still invisible. One thousand feet and no land. I was getting worried—if the clouds were at ground level I would crash before I knew where I was. Then for a fraction of a second the land appeared and vanished again. At 750 feet there was still fog and it was only at 600 feet that we could see the shore.

We were on the correct course. On the right was Vankarem with its small trading station and nomad tents.

I was happy to see again the place where we had brought the Chelyuskinites, and where we had heard the news of the Government decoration.

I turned left towards the coast. Cape Shmidt was 112 miles away —only an hour's flight.

Lindel was close on my right.

In fifty minutes we could see houses and other buildings. It was difficult to believe that this was Cape Shmidt in view of the remarkable changes that had been effected in the course of the year.

Many people had gathered at the airfield for they knew we had brought them letters and newspapers. My machine was surrounded even before it had come to a standstill. Instead of welcoming us they called:

"Have you brought the mail?"

Eager hands snatched at the bag, and we had no alternative but to hand our mail there and then.

In those times the arrival of a plane at a polar station was a great event.

Amazing changes had taken place in the Chukchi area. Beginning in 1928, there had been large-scale construction, including the building of boarding-schools, hospitals, veterinary stations, etc.

In 1930 the Chukchi National Region was formed. As time went on the number of schools increased, including even ten-grade, trade and technical schools. Hundreds of Chukchi went to Khabarovsk, Vladivostok, Moscow and Leningrad for higher education, returning as doctors, teachers, aviators or engineers. Every district in the Chukchi region has its culture centre with radio and cinema.

When I was there again in 1950 a new life was flourishing in the region.

At Inchou, once a tiny hamlet near Cape Shmidt, there was a big collective farm. The seal-hunters who founded the collective

77

farm were successfully fulfilling and exceeding production plans, and comfortable cottages as well as a school, bakery and shop were built in the area. The collective farm is well supplied with motor whale-boats, fishing and hunting gear.

There are many similar collective farms—fisheries, seal-hunting and deer farms—in this far-away Chukchi region. Each cottage has a radio and the majority have electric lighting.

The polar station in Cape Shmidt was established in 1933. Previously it was a tiny nomad settlement with no more than four or five tents. The polar party brought building materials, but first they had to live in tents. Soon dwelling houses, a warehouse and a radio station were built.

The settlement gradually developed into a small town as many Chukchi came to settle near the polar station.

After two days we set out on the return journey. Beneath us we saw again the wind-swept tundra, the sea and forest lands.

On April 30 we arrived at Khabarovsk where there was a telegram instructing us to hand over the machines to the Civil Aviation Department and leave for Moscow.

A PILOT'S DREAM

ne day I visited the *Komsomolskaya Pravda* and had a lively conversation with the newspapermen who were all very interested in the flights of Soviet pilots in the northern latitudes of our country.

Suddenly one of them asked, "Where would you like to go now? Which route do you find most interesting?"

I had often asked myself the same question. I had flown over different territory—the Siberian taiga, the Far Eastern mountains, the wild snowy deserts of the North and the hummocky ice of the Chukchi Sea—and was now eager to make use of my experience of arctic conditions by flying to some new unexplored region. I wanted very much to cover the coastline from Arkhangelsk to Uelen but I was even more interested in a flight to the North Pole.

"I would like not just to fly over the Pole but to help in making a careful study of the central polar basin," I said.

The idea of a flight to the Pole appealed to the newspapermen, who fired questions at me:

"What are your views?"

"Is such a thing possible?"

"How could it be done?"

"I have no plans, it's only a dream. But in the Soviet Union the wildest dreams can come true if they serve the interests of the country. With your permission I'm prepared to let my imagination run riot."

And I began to develop my ideas about establishing a drifting station on the North Pole. It was pure fantasy but founded on the accomplishments of Soviet aviation. In my view, aircraft alone could land a scientific expedition well provided with food, scientific instruments and equipment in the heart of the Arctic. I thought several machines should participate for then the pilots could help one another in an emergency.

"You ought to publish your story," suggested someone when I had finished.

"Good idea," said the others. "Call it 'A Pilot's Dream'."

* * *

After this I often caught myself thinking about the North Pole. I tried to forget it but the idea possessed me more and more.

In my rare leisure hours I would take from the shelf a book devoted to some North Pole expedition. Frequently, the dawn would find me still reading about the tragic end of daring explorers on their way to the Pole.

The Pole,—I thought, glancing at the map on the wall—a point in the arctic expanses where all the meridians of the globe met, where the imaginary earth's axis was. The place which held the great secret of weather-making, of wind currents and ice-drifts. For centuries men had striven to disclose its secrets, but nature had guarded them jealously. The ships, balloons and dirigibles in which arctic explorers tried to reach the Pole were either locked in the ice, wrecked by storms or swept to destruction.

Expeditions to the Pole from capitalist countries were not so much in the interests of science as attempts to make records.

"The efforts of Peary, Nansen and other explorers to reach it (i.e., the North Pole—*M.V.*) by dogs and skis, is, in my view, a noble sport, but one which cannot yield any serious practical results," wrote the great Russian scientist Mendeleyev in a well-known paper on arctic exploration (1901).

On reaching the South Pole, Captain Scott, the British polar explorer, saw traces of the Norwegian Amundsen expedition which had forestalled him and made the following entry in his diary:

"The Norwegians have forestalled us and are first at the Pole. All the day-dreams must go; it will be a wearisome return.... We built a cairn, put up our slighted Union Jack.... Well, we have turned our back now on the goal of our ambition.... Good-bye to most of the day-dreams!"

Overwhelmed by misfortune the explorers turned back to die of exhaustion, cold and hunger.

Dying, Scott wrote to his friend:

"... my dear friend, be good to my wife and child. Give the boy a chance in life if the State won't do it."

The last entry of this ghastly diary reads:

"For God's sake, look after our people."

I thought of many brave men who had met their death in the Arctic, but most stirring was the story of Georgi Sedov.

Sedov, son of a poor Azov fisherman, endured hardships from early childhood. In face of many difficulties he eventually obtained his certificate for navigation and hydrography. Working on Kolyma and in Krestovaya Bay he acquired polar experience and realized what an asset the discovery of the North Pole and the study of the central Arctic would be to science. He hoped that his country might have the honour of being the first to reach the Pole.

The tsarist government refused to provide funds for the expedition. Tirelessly and despite all kinds of humiliation he collected paltry donations from the rich to help in his aim.

Sedov's speech showed the expedition's criminal lack of equipment:

"It is not health but something else that worries me most of all. Today is a great day for us and for Russia, but we are setting out without the things we ought to have. We are setting out on a Pole journey with 20 dogs instead of the 80 I had counted on. Our clothes are worn ... provisions on Novaya Zemlya are inadequate and we ourselves are not as strong as we should be."

* * *

On August 27, 1912, Sedov set out from Arkhangelsk on his perilous voyage in a small wooden ship *St. Foka*. He planned to reach one of the islands of Franz Josef Land that same year, winter there and in spring to set out on foot for the North Pole. But these plans miscarried for in the White Sea he was delayed by fierce storms and on the way to Franz Josef Land the frail craft was beset by heavy pack-ice and had to winter there.

The winter was long and dreary and even when the polar night had ended, the ship was still held fast in the ice. As the short summer was drawing to a close the *St. Foka* was released; after great effort Sedov finally reached Franz Josef Land and discovered a convenient haven which he called Tikhaya Bay. He decided to winter there.

The second winter in the ice brought great hardships—half the crew, including Sedov himself, had scurvy. But even then he never for a moment abandoned the idea of reaching the Pole. He waited anxiously for the end of the long, weary night so that he could continue his journey.

Supplies of fuel and food were gradually diminishing. Winter, sickness and malnutrition affected the men's morale and Sedov realized that only the attainment of his aim would raise their spirits.

And so on February 15, 1914, Sedov, with two sailors, Pustoshny and Linnik, set out for the Pole.

They pushed on, encountering numerous obstacles—frozen swells, jagged hummocks and ridges. The dogs could not pull the heavy sledge and so they had to be helped from behind. Each step called for superhuman effort.

On the sixth day Pustoshny and Linnik realized that Sedov could hardly stand. Suddenly he collapsed; they put him on the sledge and continued on their way.

Sometimes Sedov would recover consciousness, raise himself on the sledge and call out to his companions:

"Linnik, Pustoshny, where are you taking me? Not returning, are you? Hand me the compass, the map—yes, that's right, you're on the right track. Thank you, my friends. Onward... onward...."

Then he would lose consciousness again.

For the first days of March the party was confined to the tent by a shrieking blizzard and on the fifth Georgi Sedov died....

The sailors buried him on Cape Auk, Rudolph Island, wrapping the body in tarpaulin and lowering it into a grave dug in the hard frozen ground. Over it they built a cairn and placed beside it the flag which was to have been hoisted on the Pole.

When the news of Sedov's death reached Grigorovich, Minister of the Navy, who had been directly responsible for the poor equipment of the expedition, he said, "I'm sorry the scoundrel didn't come back! I'd have had him prosecuted!"

Progressive people in Russia were concerned about the fate of the Sedov expedition and urged the government to send a search-party. After much haggling the tsarist government finally agreed to organize a relief expedition, the task being given to the Central Department of Hydrography.

As it would have taken a long time for ships to survey the vast ice expanses, Russian explorers recommended the use of aircraft for search operations. As far back as 1913 the northern hydrographic expedition had had an aeroplane at its disposal, but Alexandrov, the pilot, had not had occasion to fly it.

Attempts to explore polar regions by air had been made before that date. The first was by Andrée, a Swedish engineer, who had tried to reach the North Pole from Spitsbergen in a balloon—the *Eagle*.

"We shall fly like eagles and nothing will break our wings," he wrote before setting out for the Far North. But his craft was not adapted to arctic conditions and the daring explorer paid with his life for the flight.

That was in 1897. Nine years later Wellman, an American journalist, made another attempt by balloon, following the same route, but this, too, was a failure.

Wellman repeated the attempt three years later but again unsuccessfully.

The first flyer in the world who, in face of inconceivable difficulties, made successful flights in the Arctic was Ivan Nagursky, a twenty-five-year-old naval pilot with the rank of lieutenant. He suggested that a plane of Russian design (Grigorovich's flying boat) be used in the search for the lost expedition, but this did not meet with the approval of the Admiralty Board, which decided to acquire a seaplane from the Farman firm in France.

Finally, in the spring of 1914 after overcoming numerous obstacles, Nagursky left for France. Almost a month passed before the machine was accepted, for it did not meet with guaranteed requirements. The carrying capacity of the machine was much lower than the stipulated 600 pounds, and its speed too was far below that specified. But there was nothing Nagursky could do.

It took two months to ship the machine to Russia. On July 31 the *Pechora* left Alexandrovsk-on-Murman for Novaya Zemlya. She dropped anchor at Krestovaya Bay and two days later the cases

Over the mountains of Novaya Zemlya

with the aeroplane parts were delivered at the Olgino settlement.

Nagursky and his mechanic Kuznetsov began to assemble the machine, a laborious job which had to be carried out on the open shore in fog, snow, rain and sleet.

On August 8, 1914, Nagursky made two trial flights to adapt himself to the conditions, to test the machine in flight and also to try out the floats for taking off and landing. Then he told his mechanic to get everything ready for a search of the Sedov expedition. Both pilot and mechanic were provided with warm clothing—jackets, sheepskin coats, fur-lined trousers and woollen mittens. They also had sun-glasses. The plane carried a good supply of provisions, a length of steel cable, smoke signal rockets, tools and spare engine parts.

That same day they took off from Krestovaya Bay. It was presumed that the ship of the Sedov expedition was wintering off the western coast of Novaya Zemlya.

Nagursky was to carry out reconnaissance from Krestovaya Bay to Pankratyev Island where he was to land and await the arrival of the ship which had departed in the wake of the plane.

The frail craft with its 70-h. p. engine—the capricious "whirligig" —skirted the desolate shores of Novaya Zemlya. The pilot looked into every bay in the hope of finding the ship. The fine weather which prevailed at Cape Borisov had changed, thick clouds blotted out the sea where brash ice floated.

Nagursky and Kuznetsov kept a careful watch on the sea and coast. At times they had to fly almost blind. Regardless of danger the pilot would cut through a hole in the clouds, examine the shore and climb again.

According to plan Nagursky made straight for Gorboviye Islands which was almost the final point of the flight.

The pilot noticed that in this area "the ice in all the bays was old and solid." There could be no question of landing on the ice for a crash would be unavoidable.

But the pilot did not cut short his reconnaissance and turn back. He reached Pankratyev Island, circled it and seeing the sun appear in the north-west decided to go on as far as Barents Islands. Only then did he return to Cape Borisov where the water was clear of ice.

Nagursky had been up for four hours twenty minutes—an unusually long flight for those years, even over land and in ordinary latitudes.

It was a great exploit.

Landing, they managed with great difficulty to approach the high cliffs and avoid the jagged rocks jutting out from the sea. The pilot and mechanic had to jump into the water to make fast their machine.

Ashore a piercing wind chilled their wet bodies. Nagursky quickly gathered weeds and started a fire. The weary men began to doze but the thought of the ship *Andromeda*, which was due to arrive there, woke the pilot. He jumped to his feet, dragged himself up a slope which could be seen from the sea and fired smoke-rockets, lighting up the cloudy sky with flashes which fell slowly into the stormy sea. Fifteen hours later, guided by Nagursky's signals, the ship reached Cape Borisov.

Sailors brought petrol and oil ashore and the pilot was asked to repeat his reconnaissance of ice conditions near Gorboviye Islands, and to find out if the ship could go on to Zayachy Island and establish a depot there.

Then the second arctic flight began. Reconnaissance showed that the channels between Berch, Lechukhin and Zayachy islands were full of pack-ice which the ship could not negotiate.

Nagursky landed in Arkhangelskaya Bay where for eighteen hours he waited for the *Andromeda*. Next day a storm threatened the safety of the machine which had to be secured without delay. Despite the captain's misgivings Nagursky, with four sailors, safely reached the shore in a life-boat and the plane was saved.

On August 12 Nagursky, continuing his search for the Sedov expedition, went out twice. During the second flight, at a height of only 1,600 feet, the engine failed, but the pilot effected a brilliant landing in the open sea.

Sailors from the ship came in boats and helped to tow the machine ashore.

A few days later the *Gerta* arrived from Franz Josef Land. The captain reported that the *St. Foka* had left Cape Flora in the Barents Sea, making for Novaya Zemlya.

On August 31 Nagursky alighted in Krestovaya Bay from which he made two more flights. That ended the work of the expedition.

Nagursky's flights proved that aircraft could be successfully used in the Arctic. This fearless Russian pilot foresaw the significant role which aviation could play in the study of the Arctic. He said that the North Pole would be conquered by aircraft. And he was right: in 1937, twenty-three years later, Soviet flyers using aircraft built and designed in the U.S.S.R. landed a scientific expedition at the North Pole.

* * *

The triumph of the October Revolution has provided incomparably greater opportunities for the systematic study and development of the North.

In 1918 a Government decree, signed by V. I. Lenin, appropriated a million rubles for the equipment of a hydrographic expedition to the Arctic Ocean.

On April 20, 1920, a special Northern Sea Route Committee was established and in March, 1921, a decree signed by V. I. Lenin provided for the organization of a Floating Naval Scientific Institute. This decree outlined a programme for the study of the Soviet Arctic.

Every year gave Soviet explorers more and more experience, their work became more extensive and their tasks more complicated. And in this titanic effort to conquer the grim arctic expanses the Soviet Air Force played an ever-increasing role. Ten years after Nagursky's flights a plane piloted by Boris Chukhnovsky appeared over Novaya Zemlya.

Boris Grigoryevich Chukhnovsky

Chukhnovsky was the first of the Soviet polar pilots who paved the way for Soviet polar aviation. He was born in 1898 into the family of an afforestation scientist and naturalist. There was a good library in the house and Boris loved books from early childhood. His interest in the Arctic began when he read a book, "On the Ice in the Blackness of Night."

After finishing a secondary school Chukhnovsky joined the Navy. Stationed first in Gatchina and then in Oranienbaum, near St. Petersburg, Chukhnovsky never missed an opportunity of watching the flights of the first Russian aviators. After he went up himself, he firmly decided to become a pilot.

In 1917 Chukhnovsky took a flying course and joined the Red Guards.

In January, 1918, army pilot Chukhnovsky was appointed commander of the Oranienbaum Air Squadron. He was young to occupy such a responsible position, but there were few aviators at that time.

While surveying ice conditions in Finland Bay, he began to realize what great prospects aircraft opened up for the exploration of the Soviet North, for hydrography and ice reconnaissance.

Chukhnovsky frequently met and talked with I. Nagursky. In 1924 a northern hydrographic expedition was organized under N. Matusevich with Chukhnovsky as pilot.

The expedition had at its disposal a two-seater I-20 hydroplane powered with a 185-h.p. engine and supplied with petrol for three and a half hours' flight at a speed of 80 miles per hour.

Chukhnovsky made a trial flight on August 22. Rising to 2,300 feet he flew on beyond Cape Vykhodnoy, some ten miles off the Kara Sea.

Carrying scientific personnel Chukhnovsky reconnoîtred ice conditions in the Kara and Barents seas on twelve separate occasions, proving that regular arctic observation was quite feasible and that only aircraft could give a true picture of ice conditions over the vast sea expanses.

Chukhnovsky's flights made it possible to chart places with shallow water, dangerous to shipping, in regions west and east of the mouth of Matochkin Shar. In clear weather the water in the Barents Sea was transparent, allowing air observation of depths up to 60-100 feet.

The following year the hydrographic expedition received two planes which had to be ferried from Leningrad to Novaya Zemlya. Chukhnovsky headed the aviation group which included Kalvits, a naval pilot.

Otto Kalvits, admired by all pilots for his daring flights, was an old acquaintance of mine. He was born in 1889 in a poor Finnish peasant family, and from early childhood he knew nothing but heavy toil and poverty. By exceptional perseverance he became a mechanic on a merchant ship and during the 1918 naval revolt against the Mannerheim regime he was arrested and sentenced to ten years' imprisonment. But he did not serve his term, escaping to the Soviet Union.

In Samara he finished a flying school and took part in the suppression of the Kronstadt revolt. Then he served in a special Baltic Sea naval reconnaissance detachment. Serious injuries resulting from a crash in 1923 put him out of action for a time, but, thanks to his powerful constitution and will-power, he made a full recovery.

On August 4, 1925, the machines attached to the expedition left Leningrad, reaching their destination at Matochkin Shar on August 29.

By then the ships of the Kara trading expedition were at the mouths of the Siberian rivers. Ice conditions in the southern straits and the Yamal Peninsula, as well as in the Ob and Yenisei area, had been ascertained. But conditions in the sea area east of Novaya Zemlya were unknown. An hour after landing Kalvits went out on reconnaissance returning with the news that for a stretch of eighty to ninety miles from Matochkin Shar the sea in the south-east was completely clear of ice. Another air reconnaissance confirmed that the area north-east of Matochkin Shar was free of ice.

Relying on this data the command of the Kara expedition decided that the ships of the Ob group would return via the channel of Matochkin Shar. Chukhnovsky made another flight in the direction of Bely Island to check on ice conditions and the correctness of the decision. There, too, no ice was sighted. On September 16 the Ob group, accompanied by the ice-breaker *Malygin*, reached Matochkin Shar without coming across any ice.

Air reconnaissance had enabled the ships to choose the best route, and thereby save not only time but also vast quantities of fuel.

The flyers also had to reconnoitre dangerous navigation zones east of Novaya Zemlya and north and south of Matochkin Shar and this too was successfully carried out. A survey on September 19 revealed that Klokov Bay was dangerous to shipping.

It was also established that Brandt and Schubert bays were incorrectly mapped. Stretches of sandbanks and shoals were discovered in Gall Bay which was found to be wrongly plotted on the map.

The data of this air expedition were used for the new navigation regulations in the Kara Sea and for a fuller description of Novaya Zemlya, published in 1930.

Three years later Kalvits made another remarkable flight, covering 3,400 miles along the north-eastern shores of Siberia, from Bering Strait to the mouth of the River Lena, and visiting Wrangel Island, Nizhne-Kolymsk and Blizhny Lyakhovsky Island, and then finishing safely at Bulun.

This flight helped in the study of air navigation conditions in the eastern area of the Northern Sea Route. Soon Soviet pilots were making regular flights from Cape Dezhnev, along the Siberian coastline, to Arkhangelsk.

In 1926 aircraft were used for the first time for seal-hunting in the White Sea. This new use of aviation was very important economically.

Seal-hunting in the White Sea is of ancient origin. In February each year hundreds of thousands of seals would mass on the vast ice sheets, their black skins glistening in the snow. In their wake came the hunters who camped on Morzhovets Island, living in dug-outs or in overturned boats. Storms would often break up the ice and the hunters would be carried out to sea on a floe.

After the October Revolution the seal-hunters were assisted by ice-breakers and eventually by aircraft. The first pilot to win the confidence of the ships' captains and seal-hunters was Mikhail Sergeyevich Babushkin.

Babushkin, son of a factory worker, was born in 1893 in the village of Bordino, near Moscow. In early life he knew many hardships. He served in the army, first as a private at an airfield, then as a mechanic, and eventually as an army pilot.

In 1917 the soldiers elected Babushkin chief of the Gatchina flying school. Defending the young Soviet Republic, he fought the interventionists and Whiteguards in the Far East.

For many years after the Civil War Babushkin was a flight instructor. He demanded much of himself and others, showing by personal example what Soviet pilots should be like. At the same time he was friendly, a good companion and always willing to share his knowledge with others.

In winter work is not easy in the North. In the area of Morzhovets Island 40-45 degrees of frost are common and the snow becomes as hard as sugar. The great difficulty is to start the engine. Mikhail Babushkin and his mechanic, Fyodor Groshev, solved the problem by warming up the engine with hot water and oil.

The skis would slide across the smooth surface of the frozen lake on the island. The four men on the plane—the pilot, mechanic, observer and radio-operator—had to locate a seal-rookery on the ice and radio the ice-breaker how to reach it.

Later Babushkin told me that spotting rookeries was easy enough. The difficulty was to convince the ships' captains that the information was reliable and that the rookeries could be reached. Once a huge one was discovered. The observer immediately radioed the ice-breaker, giving its exact position—square No. 264 on the map. However, the ship did not sail in that direction because of the many shoals in the neighbourhood which made navigation difficult.

When Babushkin had made another reconnaissance and found no seal he went back to the old rookery. It was a clear day and from a height of 2,800 feet he distinctly saw tens of thousands of the animals. The ice sheet, black with seal, extended as far as the eye could see.

"I was annoyed at the hunters' failure to get the catch," said Babushkin. "I decided to talk it over with the captain of the ice-breaker, but I was not sure whether I could land on sea ice, for it had never previously been attempted. I mentioned this to some hunters on shore and they said: 'What are you saying! The ice will hold dozens of machines like yours. An ice-breaker will climb on to the ice and wedge into it without affecting it in the least.'"

Babushkin decided to land and soon found the ice-breaker still in its old position. Alongside the ship was a smooth sheet of ice. He descended and circled over the ice-breaker; the ice seemed reliable and, choosing what he thought was the best direction, he made a safe landing. The hunters gathered round the machine and after a hearty handshake they said this was the first time they had seen a plane. Babushkin explained the construction of the machine, told them how it flies and the great advantages of aviation. The seamen showed the flyers around the ice-breaker and introduced them to the captain. Seated in the cabin, Babushkin turned to business and the captain, flattered by the visit, listened to a detailed description of the unusual seal-rookery. He at once called in his navigators and began to discuss low and high tides, the velocity and direction of the wind, sandbanks, etc. Obviously he had decided to sail for the rookery.

Two hours later the pilots flew back to the island while the ice-breaker steamed towards the place where the seals had been sighted. About a fortnight later Babushkin received a radiogram from the captain:

"Wiring from square No. 264. Hunted seal four days. Spent five days gathering in the kill. Loaded 10,000 heads."

Once a report reached Morzhovets Island from Zimny shore that several hunters had been carried off to sea on an ice-floe which had broken loose. The pilots were instructed to find the hunters and, if it was impossible to land, to report the position of the floe to the ice-breaker.

As soon as conditions permitted Babushkin started out in search of the missing men. But it was eight days before they were found. Utterly exhausted the men tried to wave a welcome to the plane, but collapsed on the ice. They had no food and no fire, and their clothes had long ago become iced-up.

Babushkin dropped a note telling them that the floe was too small to land but that he would immediately report to the ice-breaker and that help was at hand. He also dropped firewood and matches wrapped in waterproof paper, and food packages. A few hours later the ice-breaker *Sedov*, under Captain Voronin, directed by the plane, reached the floe and rescued the hunters.

Within a few years the ships' captains had complete confidence in the assistance given them by aviation.

"Later," said Babushkin, "I had no qualms about landing on the ice-fields in the White Sea for I had learned to size them up from above. During the search operations for the Nobile crew I often had to land on the ice in the Arctic Ocean."

Then he went on to describe what kind of ice was safe and what kind one should beware of.

These accurate observations were invaluable to us polar flyers in the coming years of work in the Arctic.

Afterwards two planes were used for sealing. The second machine was piloted by Ivan Mikheyev, an old friend of mine. The son of a boot-maker and himself a factory worker, he became interested in aviation when he was still a boy. Having no money for tram fares, he would walk to Moscow Aerodrome and watch the flights of the pioneer pilots. Finally his perseverance

Mikhail Sergeyevich Babushkin

was rewarded and he was given employment at the aerodrome workshops where he soon became first a ground-mechanic and then an air-mechanic.

In 1925 Mikheyev participated in the long-distance Moscow-Peking group flight. That same year, rated among the best air-mechanics, he was given permission to learn to fly, which he did in a matter of three months.

Mikheyev soon mastered the technique of flying over the White Sea; he was undeterred by fog, severe frost or the frequent ice movements, when the ice sheet breaks up and a landing is impossible.

One day the radio-operator picked up a call which stirred not only the flyers but all the island's inhabitants.

It was an S.O.S. from Norwegian sealers hunting in Soviet waters. They had sailed to the Soviet shores in seventeen ships hoping to get a share of the booty, but, having no ice-breakers or aircraft at their disposal, the Norwegians had met with disaster. All their ships were locked in ice.

"... Some ships already crushed," read one radiogram. "Surviving members of a wrecked ship crossed the sea ice and reached radio station at village of Iokanga."

The Norwegian Ministry of Trade asked the Soviet Government to find the ice-bound ships and help them.

Next day a telegram was received from Moscow:

"... Send aircraft in search of Norwegian ships in distress somewhere between Kaninskaya Zemlya and Kolguyev Island."

Moved by friendly feelings and a desire to help people in distress, the Soviet pilots thought little of the hazards of such a flight.

It was decided that Mikheyev would fly and Babushkin would direct the operations. Soon Mikheyev, with air-mechanic Groshev and navigator Kryukov on board, waved a farewell to their comrades on shore and set out on their perilous mission.

When Morzhovets Island was left far behind, a wire from the *Malygin* wished the flyers good luck and a safe journey.

The sea below was jammed with brash ice. Soon low clouds were encountered.

Mikheyev decided to get under the cloud bank and push on.

All of a sudden he saw the masts of several motor launches. Some had been locked in the ice and their decks were buried in snow. Then a group of men appeared.

"The very first storm may wreck the ships," thought Mikheyev. As the machine circled, the navigator reported the position of the Norwegian vessels.

The Norwegians were rescued and a few days later the Norwegian Minister of Trade wired his gratitude to the Soviet pilot.

Later Mikheyev once more demonstrated his ability to fly in difficult, near-arctic conditions.

In February 1929 Alexandra Gromtseva, a young teacher, was returning from the small town of Pudozh to the village of Konza-Navolok. It was bitterly cold. Coming down a slope her horse dashed forward, overturning the sledge into a big dip in the ice. There she lay all night frozen into the snow.

The district education department wired Moscow, asking for a plane to carry Gromtseva to Leningrad for an operation. Again it was Mikheyev who made the flight. On February 13 he set out in a blinding snow-storm and, flying very low, eventually reached Leningrad. Next morning he took off for Pudozh. The flight, with visibility at almost nil, was further aggravated by the pilot's fear of crossing the Finnish border. But in spite of everything Mikheyev reached the small town, hidden in the Onega woodlands.

"The patient is developing gangrene and must be operated on at once. Delay would be fatal," the physician at Pudozh told Mikheyev.

On the 15th of February, in severe frost and mist, Mikheyev took off for Leningrad. He flew by compass and late that evening alighted in Leningrad.

The operation was successful and Gromtseva was saved.

Once, returning to Moscow from an arctic flight, I walked out on to the platform at Sverdlovsk and saw passengers crowding round a news-stand. They were talking excitedly with open newspapers in their hands.

Glancing at the paper I was stunned by the announcement:

"The giant 'Maxim Gorky' plane crashed...."

On board were many of my friends, among them the commander of the plane—Ivan Mikheyev.

* * *

The Northern Sea Route Administration was situated in Rasin Street, Moscow. From the ceiling of one of the rooms hung a bronze chandelier of a type usually found on ocean-going vessels. It had a massive cut-glass ball held by two bronze chains. You looked and expected to see it swing.

The room seemed crowded with heavy furniture, including two huge tables in the centre. On one stood a model of a new ice-breaker in a glass case. On the walls were maps of the Arctic. The crowded atmosphere, chandelier, maps and scrupulous tidiness reminded one of a ship's cabin.

This was the study of Otto Yulyevich Shmidt, member of the Academy of Sciences, who was then in charge of the Northern Sea Route Administration.

As I stood in the doorway of the room, so familiar in every detail, the fading light streaking through small windows on my left gave it even more the appearance of a ship's cabin. I knew I must have been called here for something very important for Shmidt was not the man to trouble his staff about trifles. Hesitating I asked:

"May I come in?"

Shmidt welcomed me with a smile and waving me to a chair said suddenly:

"So you've been dreaming about a flight to the North Pole?"

The question did not take me by surprise.

"Yes," I replied firmly but added:

"My ambition is to fly to the Pole but I regard it my duty to go wherever you want to send me."

"You are ambitious, and that is exactly why I asked you to come here," said Shmidt, running his fingers through his beard and smiling.

After a pause he added:

"Your dream may soon come true. The Government has directed us to begin the organization of a scientific station on a drifting ice-floe in the North Pole area. We shall have to fly the men, cargo and scientific equipment to the Pole. I want you to draft a plan for the flight."

Hardly able to restrain my excitement, I rose and thanked Shmidt for his confidence in me.

"You shall have the draft," I said firmly.

"Remember you must provide for every eventuality," added Shmidt, rising too.

* * *

Feeling that I must calm down, I drove out of town.

The summer sun shone brightly. The car raced on at full speed. Houses, shop windows and pedestrians fleeted past, but I was blind and deaf to everything.

One more street, lane and highway, and Moscow was left far behind. I jumped out of the car and flung myself on the grass, resting my head on my hands.

I could not believe that I was to prepare a plan for this remarkable expedition.

The great achievements of our country in recent

Otto Yulyevich Shmidt

years had made it possible to start work on such a gigantic project as the conquest of the Pole.

A polar air force had been established and new air routes organized in the North. The brilliant feats of the *Sibiryakov*, *Chelyuskin* and *Litke* had paved the way for regular shipping along the Northern Sea Route.

Scores of expeditions had gone to the polar basin. Scientists were exploring the hitherto inaccessible islands of Severnaya Zemlya and had discovered new islands in the arctic seas. The scientific outposts in these grim northern areas were increasing in number. Dozens of radio and meteorological stations had appeared on those desolate territories. Gradually the scientists were moving farther and farther north. Thus step by step Soviet explorers had closed in on the North Pole.

Exceedingly valuable information had been obtained about the arctic seas—ice conditions, currents and tides, and wind direction. All these data were useful not only for the promotion of arctic study. The meteorological observations of the polar stations formed the basis for long-term weather forecasts throughout the Soviet Union.

I knew very well what a vast difference observations taken at the Pole would make to the accuracy of these forecasts and to the further study of the Arctic.

"We'll conquer the North Pole," I said to myself.

Many years' work in the Arctic had prepared the way for the conquest of the Pole. The splendid achievements of the Soviet aircraft industry were well known. Soviet designers had built machines capable of flying to the Pole and landing there. In this way a group of scientists, supplied with all the necessary scientific gear, equipment and provisions could be landed on the ice. In a year or so flyers could return for the wintering party, regardless of drift.

Such an expedition would naturally require painstaking preparation. The flight would have to be made by several aircraft and a landing at the Pole would depend on conditions prevailing there.

I do not know how long I lay thus stretched out on the grass.

Overhead, in a blue cloudless sky, planes flew past. I watched them, recalling my first glimpse of an aeroplane.

My father and I were thatching a shed. I was standing on the roof receiving the straw as my father handed it to me.

Suddenly I heard a strange sound in the distance.

My father said:

"Misha, look at the aeroplane in the sky."

The sound grew and in another minute a huge bird passed over our hut.

Turning sharply, I lost my balance and fell from the roof on to the straw.

"I see men—there they are, on the wings!" I cried at the top of my voice.

Afterwards I learnt that they were not men I had seen but engines mounted on the wings and that the machine which had impressed me so much was the giant aircraft called *Ilya Muromets*. I was anxious to see the strange monster, so, as soon as we finished thatching the shed, I hurried off to the railway station: I saw the machine land somewhere near, but I was not allowed to approach it. Disappointed, I went home, thinking:

"Whatever happens, I'm going to see that aeroplane...."

* * *

I lay watching the sky. Above me aircraft continued to circle and perform various stunts.

"One turn, two, three...."—I watched the plane going into a spin—"five, six, seven.... Splendid!" Almost as it reached the ground the plane levelled out and soared up again.

Then I noticed a machine which was behaving strangely in the air and I realized that this was a training flight. "Must be excited," I thought, recollecting my first experience at the controls.

That was in 1926. I had asked Tomashevsky, the pilot, to let me go to Serpukhov with him instead of his air-mechanic. Tomashevsky looked at me and smiled:

"D'you want to fly very much?"

"Very!"

"Then, come along."

I was a ground-mechanic in those days. Tomashevsky had often flown on engines which I had repaired and he was always pleased with them. That was why he had agreed to take me.

It was a passenger plane with the pilot's seat on the left and the mechanic's on the right.

Taxiing up to the runway the pilot opened the throttle, pushed the control lever forward and the machine began to gather speed. He got his tail well up, keeping it horizontal without swerving to right or left. A few seconds later the plane was in the air.

At an altitude of 1,000 feet we circled the aerodrome and then steered for Krasnaya Presnya, and from there to Serpukhov.

I listened to the regular drone of the engine. I had never flown in a plane with dual control, and here right in front of me was the second control lever. I watched the confident movements of the pilot and was overcome by a desire to take hold of the second lever, put my feet on the rudder bar and pilot the machine.

On the left railway tracks appeared. I looked down and saw clearly the fields, woods and highway. The weather was fine and visibility was good.

Tomashevsky guessed what I was after. He smiled and, nodding at the controls, shouted:

"Go ahead!"

This was the first time my hands had touched the stick and my feet the rudder bar. Tomashevsky indicated the direction I was to follow, told me to keep the railway under the left wing and, letting go of the control lever, took his feet off the rudder bar.

Now the plane was obeying my will alone.

At first it behaved well but then its nose went up and it began to climb. Afraid of changing its position too sharply, I eased back gently. The pilot smiled.

"You don't have to be so timid," he cried. "Pull harder or you'll have it standing on its tail."

I pulled the control lever forward and the machine began to lose height. Then I pulled back and it again climbed. It seemed to be sailing through huge waves, now dipping its nose, now rising on its tail or reeling from right to left.

Tomashevsky was still smiling.

"Keep calm! Don't exert yourself so much! We've passed Podolsk already," he shouted.

But Podolsk didn't interest me. I didn't even notice it. The plane behaved as if it were drunk. I tried pushing the control lever backwards and forwards. Sweat poured down my face, but I could not get the plane on an even keel. Finally the pilot put his feet on the rudder, took over the controls and with virtually one movement corrected my mistakes.

"Now, hold her like that!" he cried and again turned the controls over to me. The machine was now flying more or less straight.

"That's right," came the pilot's voice. "Splendid!"

Encouraged I steered more confidently and brought the plane to Serpukhov.

I was tremendously grateful to Tomashevsky, who had sat patiently for forty minutes, suffering all the discomforts of my clumsy piloting.

Over Serpukhov Tomashevsky took over and in his firm hands the machine behaved well.

Over the aerodrome we turned sharply and landed.

"Very good, Vodopyanov," said Tomashevsky. "You'll make a good pilot."

"It's nice of you to say so, Apollinari Ivanovich," I answered, very much embarrassed. "But I daren't dream of such a thing. I just want to learn to fly a bit."

An hour later we set out on the return journey. As soon as we were well in the air the pilot, much to my satisfaction, again turned over the controls to me.

The hour's wait in Serpukhov had set my nerves at rest and I was now able to fly more or less straight. I was in charge all the way to Moscow. When we got out of the cabin, Tomashevsky gripped my hand and said:

"You must learn."

From then on I was obsessed with the idea of learning to fly, of qualifying for a pilot's certificate.

An opportunity presented itself two years later, in 1928, when our detachment received several AVRO training machines. I decided to try my luck and asked my chief if I might learn to fly.

Permission was soon received and I began to assemble the machine. Once I was approached by air-mechanics Osipov and Kamishev, who had taken part in the big Moscow-Peking flight and who were also eager to become pilots. I suggested they should ask the chief to let them learn to fly with me for together we should have the machine ready sooner.

Permission was granted and when pilot Zhirkovich had tested our machine in the air we started training.

Being experienced air-mechanics, it was easier for us to train than for the beginners.

Three months later we took examinations and received our flying certificates. On my way home that day I kept taking the certificate out of my pocket and reading:

"Comrade Vodopyanov ... third-class pilot...."

I was so happy that I could scarcely believe my eyes—only three months had passed and I was a pilot.

The sun had set long ago. No planes were doing stunts in the sky, but I was still lying on the grass absorbed in my recollections. It was quite dark by the time I got home.

★ ★ ★

This was not the first time I had prepared for a big flight, but I had never worked with such enthusiasm and excitement as I did for the flight to the North Pole.

My thoughts turned to Nansen, Peary and Amundsen, the old and tried arctic explorers. Their books alone could answer the question that worried me most: would it be possible to find a floe suitable for the landing of aircraft at the Pole?

Amundsen set me thinking. In his "Flight Across the Arctic Ocean" he wrote:

"We did not see a single landing-place for a plane on the entire journey from Svalbard to Alaska. Not even one! ... Despite Bird's brilliant flight, our advice is: 'Don't penetrate deep into the ice-fields until aeroplanes are perfected to such an extent that there will be no fear of a forced landing!'"

Not very cheerful! According to Amundsen, it was impossible to build a runway or land in the high latitudes.

I also read Amundsen's description of his expedition in 1925 when he tried to reach the North Pole with two aircraft.

In latitude 88° N. shortage of fuel had forced him to land. Only on the twenty-fourth day, abandoning one plane, was the expedition able to escape.

Amundsen's machines had been equipped for landing on ice and water, which was a great advantage, and yet the expedition had failed. But I just could not force myself to believe that there was not a single floe at or near the Pole where a plane on skis could make a safe landing.

There was not an islet for thousands of miles around—so why should the ice break up?

Then I took up a book by Fridtjof Nansen which cheered me considerably.

In 1893 Nansen set out for the Pole in a ship called *Fram* which far from the Pole froze into the ice and drifted as far as latitude 84° N. Realizing that they were being carried away from the Pole Nansen along with Lieutenant Johansen abandoned ship and sledged towards the Pole. On the very first day the fearless explorers covered seven miles without a halt.

This was a considerable distance which it would hardly be possible to cover in such a short time over uneven ice, for they had to help the dogs to pull their heavily loaded sledges.

Nansen's books raised my spirits.

"Before us stretched a smooth ice sheet," he wrote in his diary. These words made me exclaim:

"So there are landing fields there! The thing is quite possible!"

Peary's book, too, added to my confidence. Amid descriptions of the difficulties of sledging on rough ice and deep snow I came across heartening lines such as:

"It was a fine marching morning, clear and sunlit, with a temperature of minus 25°, and the wind of the past few days had subsided to a gentle breeze. The going was the best we had had since leaving the land. The floes were large and old, hard and level, with patches of sapphire blue ice (the pools of the preceding summer)."

Further on Peary wrote:

"As soon as we struck the level old floes we tried to make up for lost time."

I was now quite sure that ice conditions in the central polar basin favoured even the most daring flight, and I seemed to see endless ice-fields and an aircraft on them.

As I read these books and analyzed the explorers' efforts to conquer the North Pole, I realized why all these expeditions were doomed to failure. These men had courage and will-power, but they were alone. Often they were regarded as lunatics. There was no one they could turn to for help—they could depend only on themselves and their close friends. But we had the backing of our mighty and beloved country.

When I had familiarized myself with the writings of the polar explorers, I began to think: how was I to cram into a short paper the plan for such a grand flight?

Obsessed with the idea of flying to the Pole I began to jot down ideas that kept me awake many a night.

I vividly imagined the conditions we should encounter, the kind of ice we should meet on the Pole, and described in detail how to equip the expedition, what machines were preferable, and the best men for the job.

I imagined two detachments starting out for the Pole on the same type of aircraft, with the same equipment and differing only in the character of the pilots in charge. One, whom I called Besfamilny, was well disciplined, steadfast and self-possessed; the other, Blinov, was self-assured and had an eye for records.

I thought of myself as half-Besfamilny, half-Blinov.

Wanting to be first to reach the Pole, Blinov was over-hasty, did not test the machine, and crashed.

Besfamilny planned the flight very carefully, waited patiently for clear weather and was first to hoist the Soviet flag at the top of the world.

When I had written the last chapter of "A Pilot's Dream," I had firmly decided to be Besfamilny and not Blinov.

Work on the book and draft was in the main finished.

I went to Shmidt and, placing the manuscript on the table, said:

"Otto Yulyevich, here's a draft plan for the air group of the expedition."

Shmidt looked surprised.

"But that's a whole story."

I was rather embarrassed. "I don't know how to write official papers, but you'll find everything there and I think that is what matters most."

"Yes," agreed Shmidt, "that's the main thing. I think I have ample data for a draft plan to present to the Government."

A month passed and in response to a telephone call I went to see Shmidt. When I arrived he was talking to Mark Ivanovich Shevelev, chief of the Polar Aviation Department. Both looked excited.

Standing up from behind the table, Shmidt said:

"The Government has approved the plan for landing a scientific expedition on a drifting ice-floe in the North Pole area. I have read your manuscript, Mikhail Vasilyevich, and I like it. Go ahead with your plans. First of all fly to Franz Josef Land and choose a depot nearer the Pole. The flight will no doubt give you a lot of experience."

I left as if I were walking on air.

The "pilot's dream" was coming true.

It was the end of March and the weather was bad. Moscow was in the grip of a damp cyclone. It was three degrees below and the coating of ice on the wind-screen made it difficult to see passing people and cars. The snow-scraper was choked and out of action.

The chauffeur muttered gloomily:

"What beastly weather!"

I agreed, adding:

"I wouldn't like to be in the air in this weather—the wings would be ice-heavy in no time. And tomorrow or the day after we'll have to set out for the Arctic."

We didn't notice the time pass when we drew up at the entrance to the Polar Aviation Department.

Mark Ivanovich Shevelev rose from the table and, shaking my hand cordially, asked:

"Are the machines ready?"

"Everything is shipshape."

"You'll examine all possible landing-places on the way to Franz Josef Land," said Shevelev, "and if they're unsuitable for the main expedition you'll have to find new ones. But your most important job will be thoroughly to survey the archipelago and try to find a site for the expedition on one of the most northerly islands as close to the Pole as possible."

We parted until the time of the start.

At home, as I had expected, I found my crew gathered.

The crew was formed long before from men with common experience and who knew each other well. The air-mechanic was Flegont Ivanovich Bassein, my companion on many flights, and the radio-operator was Serafim Alexandrovich Ivanov.

"We start tomorrow," I said. "Off you go and have some rest. You'll get final instructions before the start."

On March 29, 1936, at ten in the morning, two planes took off from an aerodrome near Moscow and flew north.

Back to the Arctic! Hungrily I inhaled the pure, clear air. How easy it is to breathe in the northern expanses! From my pilot's cabin I could see great snow-drifts in the hazy horizon and below the silent ice desert.

The plane was conquering space...

On March 30 we reached Naryan Mar, capital of the Nenets National Area. It was a new town which had sprung into being during the past few years. That was quite natural. Before the Great Socialist Revolution all the nomad tribes of the Bolshezemelskaya and Malozemelskaya tundra were regarded as savages by tsarist officials, who called them "samoedy" (barbarians). The tsarist government had neither the will nor the means to develop this rich territory which was at the mercy of greedy merchants who plundered the native population and introduced tsarist "civilization" in the form of vodka and syphilis. The Soviet State concerned itself with the wellfare of the nomad tribes, helping them to develop their economy and culture. For the first time in their history these people had acquired the right to their own nationality, their own alphabet and territory.

The Nenets National Area is larger than a good many West European countries, extending for 560 miles from west to east and roughly 200 miles from south to north, but until recently this vast region had no roads. Communication was possible only in winter by deer or dog sledges. Anyone wanting to go from Naryan Mar to Pesha, the district centre, for example, could do so only during the four winter months, when it would take him four or five days. From April to November Pesha was cut off from the regional centre. Conditions were no better in the other areas. Such a state of affairs was, of course, intolerable; if one calculated the time officials spent going from place to place it would be found that they spent their lives travelling.

Poor communication held up the development of this national area until the aeroplane came to the rescue.

In the autumn of 1935 the Nenets regional executive committee purchased two light, one-engine SP aircraft and early in 1936 they acquired an ambulance plane. Polar flyers Sushchinsky and Klıbanov established a network of air routes across the tundra.

A trip from Naryan Mar to Pesha was now possible at any time of the year and travelling time was cut from four or five days to two hours forty minutes. Sushchinsky and Klıbanov worked tirelessly to overcome difficulties. They studied the area, made their own maps and mastered the technique of flying over the tundra.

Standard flying suits were entirely unsuitable for winter flights in this area and crews had to use fur blouses and trousers and fur boots worn by local people; these provided warmth and comfort and were indispensable in case of a forced landing.

The appearance of aircraft in the tundra promoted cultural development, for whenever a plane landed in a populated locality everyone living up to 25—30 miles around would gather to see the machine and the "air driver." Seeing their interest in aviation, the members of the crew arranged talks for adults and children, and took them for "joy rides."

The ambulance plane was first used to bring medical aid to a man on a deer farm. It also carried a doctor to the Nesino fishery where a fisherman's wife lay dangerously ill after the birth of a child. In both instances timely help saved the patient's life, and the news spread like wildfire to every nomad settlement. Aircraft became very popular with the Nenets people and pilots—welcome and honoured guests.

In the evening Sushchinsky and Klibanov visited us and, following the local custom, we offered them tea. After the usual talk about friends and acquaintances the conversation naturally drifted to a topic which interested us all—to flights beyond the Arctic Circle.We asked the two pilots to give us the benefit of their experience, which they gladly did.

"I was the first to establish an airline from Naryan Mar to Kolokolkovskaya, situated on the shore of the Barents Sea," said Sushchinsky. "I had some adventures which I believe would be useful to every pilot who has no experience of flying here..."

In January 1936 Sushchinsky set out with two co-operative

officials for one of the settlements. He had enough petrol for four hours' flying and three days' food supply.

At first the weather was favourable, visibility good and he flew low so that he could familiarize himself with the landmarks. Below was the monotonous, snow-swept tundra with not a bush or tree in sight. At times, about twelve miles to the left, he would get a glimpse of a narrow black strip of river, its banks overgrown with brushwood. This was the only landmark which confirmed that he was on the right course.

Soon the black strip disappeared completely, signifying apparently that they were nearing Kolokolkovskaya Bay. Sushchinsky came down to 650 feet, distinguishing with difficulty the low, ice-jammed bay, obscured by drifts. A thick fog moving in from the sea blocked the way to the settlement about nineteen miles away. He did not feel like turning back, but trying to spy the settlement in the fog was not inviting either. So he began to circle before the curtain of fog, turning on the tap to let the petrol flow from the top tank into the lower tank, which he had been using so far. But apparently the pipe was choked for no petrol came through. As the fuel in the bottom tank was almost exhausted and would not be enough for the return journey, the only possible course was to land. But to alight twelve miles from his destination seemed simply indecent for a pilot, and he decided to go on in spite of the fog and try to find the place.

Flying in the fog soon convinced him that the search was hopeless, but it was just as risky to land for everything below was a milky white and it was impossible to tell fog from snow. Fortunately, Sushchinsky happened to see some black specks which he used as guides in landing.

Leaving the machine with the engine running, the men went to see what had helped them to land. They found three barrels, two empty and one sealed. Sushchinsky's passengers, the co-operative officials, said they were sure the sealed barrel contained salt fish which the fishermen had, for some reason, abandoned. This cheered them for a barrel of salt fish would be a welcome addition to their modest three-day food supply. Wishing further to reassure his passengers Sushchinsky said gaily:

"With supplies like that we can go on 'partridging' for a week!" The word "partridge," meaning to live in the tundra like the partridge, kept warm by the snow, was used in place of the unpleasant "forced landing."

The engine was still running, consuming precious fuel, but Sushchinsky did not want to switch off, still hoping that the weather would improve. Instead, it grew worse. There was more wind and a snow-storm began, forcing them to "partridge" whether they liked it or not. Reluctantly Sushchinsky taxied nearer to the barrels and cut off the engine.

Night in the North is long and dreary, lasting more than twenty hours. They had no need to hurry and during the night, taking turns with their only shovel, they anchored the plane and built a kind of snow hut, which gave protection from wind but not from cold. It was quite impossible to sit there with the temperature 27 below zero. Sushchinsky suffered most of all for he had nothing but his fur coat and the air mercilessly absorbed the heat generated by his body. The passengers in native dress were far more comfortable and even managed a few hours' sleep whereas the pilot had to scramble out every half hour to exercise his cramped limbs.

At daybreak the weather improved. They were all beginning to feel hungry and leaving one passenger to make tea on a torch the others headed for the precious barrel. They were looking forward to a hearty meal, and arguing what kind of fish the barrel contained. Then they cut a hole in the bottom of the barrel with a spade and out came ... ordinary salt!

There was nothing for it but to look for a way out. Scanning the surrounding country with glasses they discovered not far away what seemed to be a tundra deer road. This meant that sooner or later someone would come that way and they set up a permanent watch. When the visibility had improved, the look-out shouted: "I see a deer sledge!"

They began to whistle, shout and run round the plane, but the sledge, passing about a mile away, turned aside without seeing them or perhaps without wishing to see them.

But their disappointment was brief. The sledge soon reappeared and came towards them. It appeared that the Nenets had gone into the tundra to check his traps and, seeing them, had decided to invite them to his tent. He didn't think the "air drivers" needed help rather than hospitality.

After a day in the nomad tent the weather improved and they flew on to their destination.

"Since then," said Sushchinsky, "I have never flown without a native suit."

Klibanov, his young co-pilot, told us about his first "partridging" experience when he had suffered for his ignorance of tundra life. His emergency rations consisted of two bars of chocolate and some biscuits. He had not thought of taking skis or a gun and, although there were partridges everywhere, the men had to go hungry, for they could not take even a few steps in the deep snow. To add to his troubles Klibanov was wearing a leather flying suit and was virtually frozen. Katushenok, the air-mechanic, had had more sense and was quite comfortable in his Nenets dress and fur boots.

There were 25 degrees of frost. For three nights they tried everything—sitting in the machine, under it and in a hole in the snow—but it was just as cold everywhere. On the fourth day, as no help seemed to be forthcoming they decided to make skis for themselves from the runners. However, Sushchinsky's plane arrived in time to prevent this happening.

This "partridging business" had taught him a good lesson. At the time his only thought had been to get out of the place and never to set foot there again. But no sooner was he back at Naryan Mar than he forgot his troubles and was pleading for fuel to be sent for the machine which had been left in the tundra.

His worst "partridging" experience was during a regular flight from Pesha to Indiga, on the Timansky Kamen, when the plane was caught in a fierce gale. The speed indicator failed, visibility was nil and flying was impossible; they had to land as best they could and wait. And wait they did.

A blinding snow-storm obscured everything around them and their position was aggravated by the severe cold which ranged from forty to forty-eight degrees of frost. Their only chance to keep warm was to tighten the belts over their fur coats, take their arms out of the sleeves, pull their heads in and convert the native dress into a sleeping-bag.

Thus they sat for four days without once leaving the cabin. On the fifth day the gale died down and they decided to brave the cold and make for Indiga on foot since it was utterly impossible to warm up the engine. They had not very far to go, and, having learned from bitter "partridging" experience, they now carried skis with them, so all went well.

These two landings made Klibanov all the more eager to conquer the tundra but they taught him also that the tundra must not be trifled with. Eventually they learned to decipher weather reports and to analyze them before taking off on a flight.

In bad weather it is almost impossible to fly in the tundra. Low flying is very difficult because the bleak arctic wastes are very deceiving. Frequently, the pilot thinks he is high up in the sky when actually his skis are skimming the snow. He is flying almost blind, straining to catch sight of something below.

In fine weather it is pleasant to fly over the tundra. Looking down, you think you are above the clouds. Nomad tents are occasionally seen and at the sound of the engine the deer breeders rush out to get a glimpse of the plane. Once, one of them insisted that a machine passing over his tent had stopped in mid air, looked to see how the Nenets people were living and then proceeded on its journey. Whenever a pilot lands near a nomad tent he is at once surrounded by hospitable people who place before him the compulsory bowl of tea which precedes the general "aiburdaniye" (eating). This includes a chunk of raw frozen deer meat, and as a special honour the host will treat his guest to a marrowbone, which really does taste good. Then he will offer him his best "bed" (deer skins).

Not so very long ago the Nenets tent was a smoke-filled, filthy hole, swarming with vermin. Now all that has changed. Small iron stoves have replaced fires and culture centres have taught the people to wash and keep clean. Once, Klibanov and two Indiga state-farm workers spent a night in the tent of Alexei Dvoinikov, a Nenets nomad. In the morning the workers sat down to breakfast without washing themselves. Seeing this, their host said half-jokingly that they would get nothing until they had washed. They dutifully did so.

The Nenets are intelligent people. They wanted to know how the heavy aircraft could fly and often Klibanov, sitting with a bone in his hand, had to go into details about flying and other things connected with aviation. Many of the young people were eager to train as pilots or air-mechanics and they were confident that this was possible. Indeed, in the Soviet country, there is no reason why they shouldn't become pilots.

With this, Klibanov, the young, persevering Naryan Mar aviator, finished his story. The first streaks of dawn found us still listening to our comrades and we were very sorry when they rose to go.

At six in the morning the planes were ready for the next leg, which would take us to Amderma.

The going was good. When we crossed Dolgy Island in the Barents Sea, Ivanov radioed to Amderma to expect us in about thirty or forty minutes. Meanwhile, at Amderma a strong wind began to sweep the snow and the horizontal visibility was down to about 33 feet. The local aerodrome staff decided that we would turn back. They were unaware that the snow did not rise to any great height and did not hinder flight. When we suddenly appeared over the roof-tops they were quite unprepared and we had to circle for some time before they laid out the landing signs.

In a few days the weather improved and we decided to fly non-stop to Cape Zhelaniya—the northernmost point of Novaya Zemlya. But the take-off was delayed for an hour owing to some trouble with the second machine. This proved very costly. The sun vanished and we ran into a thick cloud bank and then into snow. The pilot of the second machine was getting nervy, constantly changing course and paying no heed to my signals. Afraid of losing him I kept on his tail. The weather grew worse and, after circuiting the Kara Sea, we were forced down at Vaygach Island, not very far from where we had taken off. Again we were held up by the treacherous weather. Finally, on April 9 both machines reached Cape Zhelaniya.

We were now only 310 miles from our destination, but this flight across the Barents Sea was the most difficult part of the journey.

After a good rest we took off again. Below us floated small ice sheets divided by lanes of open water. The monotonous scene continued without change for about three hours. We were expecting any moment to see the islands of the Franz Josef Archipelago, when the weather again became bad. We flew into clouds and I lost sight of the second machine in which Akkuratov, the navigator, was plotting the course. It was warm in the machine although the thermometer on the wing registered 31 degrees below zero.

Finally we sighted land on our left.

"The archipelago!" shouted Bassein.

I agreed but did not know which of the many islands this was.

While Ivanov was trying to get in touch with Tikhaya Bay we again found ourselves over sea ice. There was no answer from Tikhaya.

I decided not to waste petrol and land on the island we had just passed. But as I turned I nearly hit the steep shore, rising before me.

Soon another islet loomed in sight and then a larger one with a flat stretch of ice between them.

From my enclosed cockpit I observed the surface drift which helped me to determine the direction of the wind and land.

"Look here," grunted Sima Ivanov, "you took me off one floe and now you're dumping me on another."

The wind made it impossible to turn the machine without outside help. The engine had to be slowed down; Sima jumped out, taking hold of the right wing tip. I opened the engine and the plane turned obediently and ran forward towards the island.

Ivanov, falling behind, was at once out of sight. The visibility on the ground, already poor, was reduced to a yard or two by the whirlwind of snow which was raised by the screw. Afraid of losing Ivanov I stopped and soon, guided by the noise of the engine, he caught up with me.

As a result of this brief excursion in 30 degrees of frost with a strong wind blowing, white patches appeared on Ivanov's face.

Bassein took off his woollen scarf and made him rub his frost-bitten cheeks with it.

I taxied up to the island, stopped the engine and opened the tap under the radiator. A stream of hot water, rippling merrily, thawed a hole in the snow.

The heart of the machine was gradually getting cold and with its warmth went all hope of speedy deliverance from our unwelcome captivity. Without water it is impossible to start an engine even if it is equipped with a starter for use in low temperatures.

Even here, in the shelter of a cape on this unknown islet, the wind raged ceaselessly. It was the beginning of another blizzard.

I knew the people at the polar stations and on the mainland would be terribly worried and that we ought to send a radiogram, but I realized also that it would be useless to attempt to start the emergency dynamotor in this wind.

I shared my gloomy thoughts with my companions. The radio-operator, agreeing with me, nodded towards the mechanic, who was silent, holding a bandaged hand to his face.

It was only then that I learnt about Bassein's accident. When taking off from Cape Zhelaniya he had discovered that the tail skid was broken.

While he was picking it up, the big skis froze in the snow.

The machine could not be moved without additional help and that could not be obtained swiftly. We had taxied up to the runway and were about a mile from the party that had come to see us off. In their cumbersome fur clothing they would have been slow in reaching us.

Bassein decided to try to get the plane in the air without outside help and, passing the broken skid on to Ivanov, he began rocking the machine by the left wing.

When the plane broke clear, Bassein climbed on to the left wing, forgetting in his haste about the dynamo that was installed there. The air resistance grew and the dynamo propeller revolved at a speed which made it invisible. His hand was caught, the propeller cutting through his fur mittens and leather glove, and injuring two fingers.

Bassein jumped in when the machine was in motion, took his seat and I, unaware of the accident, got away.

The heating system in the plane functioned only when the engine was running. No sooner had we shut it off than it began to be almost as cold inside as outside—thirty-one degrees of frost. The thin plywood walls of the fuselage were, of course, ill-adapted to hold warmth for any length of time.

We thought we had landed between three and four in the afternoon but actually it was after midnight.

We decided to rest, and Ivanov produced sleeping-bags, fur-lined overalls, and other polar equipment.

"Enough of your Moscow swank," he joked, handing out the kit. "When in the Arctic be kind enough to dress as befits the occasion!"

Putting on our overalls and fur hats we began to allocate the floor space.

"I want accommodation in the tail, near the skid—my favourite place," said Bassein. "At least I can stretch my legs there."

We willingly agreed. Then Ivanov generously offered the passenger cabin to me and without waiting for a reply occupied the pilot's cockpit.

The most difficult thing for me is to struggle into a sleeping-bag. That night I made my first attempt. Ivanov had had two months' training at the *Chelyuskin* ice camp and thought nothing of jumping into a sleeping-bag. Bassein also had had some experience, and he had the advantage of being small.

But I with my build was helpless and Ivanov had great difficulty in pushing me into my bag.

Then I just could not get warm. I tossed and turned, my teeth chattering, until finally I could stand it no longer and asked Ivanov to light the primus stove. After that it was a little warmer.

I turned in for the night, hoping that in a few hours the weather would improve, and we would get the radio going and contact the polar stations. My hopes were vain although the wind did abate a little.

Realizing that we would get no sleep anyway, Ivanov and

I climbed out of the machine and began to pitch a tent.

Choosing a spot which was near the plane and sheltered from the wind, Ivanov traced a square with a shovel and, with the frenzy of men dreaming of warmth, we began to dig a place for the tent.

Warmed, we recovered our spirits. Without realizing it we talked loudly, laughing and joking, our voices resounding in the distance, and breaking the silence of this deserted, ice-bound island. Hearing us, and guessing that we had managed to get warm, Bassein crept out of his den.

"Here's a relief party," cried Ivanov.

"Relief party! I'm a number one invalid," retorted Bassein gravely.

While we were busy pitching the tent and spreading the floor-cloth and sleeping-bags Bassein jumped about exercising his cramped limbs. He had left his bag in the machine.

"I'm going to sleep in the passenger cabin and you can freeze in your tent," he growled.

"Mind you don't freeze yourself."

"We'll see..."

Soon the primus stove was sending out a pleasant warmth and stretched out in front of it we began to feel hungry.

"Wouldn't be a bad idea to lunch," remarked Bassein dreamily.

He volunteered to be chief cook of our "partridge haunt" as he had nicknamed our abode, and there and then began to issue orders. Acting on his instructions Ivanov and I brought the bulk of our emergency rations into the tent.

Bassein was busy cooking for a long time, but what he was making is difficult to describe as I do not think the recipe could be found in any cookery-book. It was as follows: when the snow in the pot melted and the water boiled he added a few spoonfuls of milk-powder, two bars of chocolate and two spoonfuls of butter. But that was not all: the contents of our pot gradually assumed a greenish and then a blackish colouring. This puzzled and worried us as we hungrily watched our cook. We thought the butter was bad, but there was nothing wrong with it. A careful investigation revealed that the colouring of the broth came from the deer fur of our overalls and sleeping-bags! There was little room in our small tent and a lot of the hair had got into the pot, giving it its strange colour. But the potful of "polar" broth braced us up and we started to repair our radio.

The frost persisted. We had to work without mittens, our fingers freezing to the metal parts. Ordinarily the job could be done in about ten or fifteen minutes but we tinkered with the thing for nearly two hours.

With great difficulty we succeeded in fixing the wireless. Ivanov took the key and began tapping out our call signs. He had done so only once when the driving belt of the motor snapped.

Finally we were able to send out a message and hear what was taking place in the world.

Suddenly we heard Moscow calling. A message to Tikhaya Bay said that the Polar Aviation Department was sending two planes in search of our crew. The knowledge that the country was following our every movement and that help would be forthcoming as soon as it was needed gave us courage and strength.

Then we intercepted a message from Akkuratov to Moscow, reporting that bad weather had forced him to return to Cape Zhelaniya but that as soon as conditions permitted he would go out in search of Vodopyanov.

Towards the end of the second day the visibility improved. I took my glasses, climbed to the top of the cape which sheltered us from the wind and looked about me.

All at once I saw on the smooth snowy surface a black shape with a coating of snow like that of a hat pulled over the eyes.

I peered ahead, thinking it must be either a hut or a depot.

Near every lonely building in the Arctic there is generally a cairn concealing a bottle with a note inside which will tell the finder the co-ordinates of the island.

"It is undoubtedly a hut," said Ivanov confidently, "and not far off either—only about a couple of miles."

"More work and less talk," I said joyfully and, grabbing a gun in the event of an encounter with the white-furred king of these places, I set out in that direction.

The thing that had puzzled us, and had given rise to such hope proved to be much nearer than we had supposed. I counted five hundred steps, but instead of finding a hut or a depot I stopped before a most ordinary stone, so small that, if it had not been frozen fast in the ground, I could easily have carried it to the plane.

This was our first experience of the common optical illusion or mirage, found in the Arctic. Previously we had known of it only from books.

Annoyed by our adventure, we recollected that it was midnight and time to turn in. Bassein said he would sleep in the machine; Ivanov and I decided to stay in the tent and had a good night's rest.

The weather continued to improve. On the third day visibility was quite good. To the south-west was a chain of islands, clearly visible to the naked eye. On the one nearest us towered a lofty mountain.

"D'you think that mountain's very far?" I asked Bassein.

"Not a bit," he replied confidently, "four or five miles at most."

"Mightn't it be another optical illusion?"

Bassein stared at me in astonishment.

"Rubbish! The visibility is excellent today. Look!" Pointing to the stone which we had mistaken for a hut, he said cheerfully:

"Now you can see quite easily that it is neither a hut nor a depot."

As I, too, had the impression that the mountainous island was not very far off, I decided to climb it and take my bearings.

Thinking I would soon be back, I took only a gun and a bar of chocolate with me, just in case something happened. Bassein almost forced on me a few lumps of sugar, which I detested.

I started out without any fear of losing myself. On my left were the waves of the Barents Sea, an excellent guide.

It was months since I had gone for a long walk, and now I was happy to be striding along on a clear, crisp frosty day.

I walked for an hour but the island seemed no nearer and the going became more difficult: hummocky ice and icebergs instead of smooth surface. More and more often I looked back, sometimes losing sight of the plane behind the jumbled ice. The distance grew, the machine was becoming a faint dark speck, but the island was still far away.

Gradually it dawned on me that I was again the victim of a mirage. Should I go on or turn back? In outline it looked like Hooker Island on whose north-western shore lay Tıkhaya Bay.

There seemed to be no doubt about it, but knowing the archipelago only from the map I could not be quite sure, and it was impossible to guess even the approximate distance to my goal.

"Suppose you're wrong?" I argued with myself. "Maybe it isn't Hooker Island at all. What then? You'll get there all right, but your strength will give out on the way back. You're feeling the strain already."

The strange thing was that I had been on the march for close on three hours without seeming to get any nearer to the island which seemed farther away than ever. Therefore, taking a last look at the much-desired, but inaccessible island, I turned and marched back along my trail.

Then came the first signs of weariness. I ate my bar of chocolate and felt very thirsty. After a few more steps I was dying to sit down and rest. But there being no place for rest, I trudged on.

The snow was dazzling. My sun-glasses were fogged with my breathing and I could see nothing. Lowering them I went on.

At first I kept looking back in case I might meet a polar bear, but now I was using the gun as a stick to lean on, and caring little about bears. Exhausted and out of breath, I at last reached the plane and tumbled into the tent. At that moment our "partridge haunt" seemed paradise to me.

It was some time before I was sufficiently recovered to tell my story.

Bassein was staggered. "What a country! You can't believe your own eyes here."

As the time passed and we were still unable to take our bearings it became more and more evident that we were unlikely to be found soon and that the best thing would be to try to get away. I suggested taking stock of our fuel, and all the available petrol went into the two upper tanks. That was enough for two hours' flight, but in addition to petrol we needed hot water for the take-off—six pailfuls of it.

Removing the auxiliary tank we filled it with snow and began to heat it on a primus stove and a torch; then we covered it with all the canvas cases and leather coats we could muster. It took us nearly twenty-four hours to heat the water.

Finally came the solemn moment: the water was ready. Trying not to spill a single drop we poured it into the engine.

The weather was ideal. The sun shone brightly on the virgin snow, which sparkled in all the colours of the rainbow.

As we busied ourselves with the water we discovered that the mirage had played another trick on us. What we had taken for sea-waves was nothing more than an ice ridge sloping down a neighbouring island. That really was a revelation, for we had reported our position as being a few miles from the sea.

We carried a cylinder of compressed air with which we managed to start the engine. We were overjoyed. Bumping into one another we hurriedly gathered up our things and threw them into the luggage compartment and passenger cabin. The food was followed by canvas cases, tent, sleeping-bags, primus, torch, etc.

Every minute of idle engine running reduced the petrol supply and our chance of reaching Tikhaya Bay.

As soon as the others were seated I opened the throttle and the machine rose into the air. At about eight thousand feet I was able to take my bearings.

The mountainous island which I had tried to reach on foot proved to be Vilchek Land. We approached it after fifteen minutes' flight—a distance of at least twenty-five miles.

Tikhaya Bay was about 115 miles away, but we were hampered by a strong head wind. We had not a pint of petrol to spare.

Having worked out my compass course I steered for Tikhaya Bay. Ivanov tried in vain to get in touch with Tikhaya to find out what the weather was like there.

Near Gall Island we went into a cloud bank. Afraid of missing the Bay in the mist I had to go under the clouds and skirt the island from the Barents Sea.

Soon the mist was almost at sea level and flying was very difficult. Below us hummocky pack-ice alternated with channels of open water. We had been in the air for about an hour and a half and according to the time should now be approaching Hooker Island.

Bassein suggested that we should look for a smooth stretch of ice, land and wait for the mist to clear.

"If we go on like this we'll run out of petrol and have none to light the primus," he argued.

Meanwhile Ivanov passed a note:

"Clouds over Tikhaya. Visibility 3.5 miles."

I didn't know what to do. As we flew over smooth ice my hand would move towards the engine switch. But while I hesitated the level strip would end and hummocks would appear again.

The machine, regardless of my indecision, moved on at the same speed. On my right were the steep sloping shores of the islands.

I tried to keep them in view. From Gall we proceeded westwards, but then the compass needle began to swing to the north.

"Can this be Hooker Island?"

Manoeuvring over the rugged coastline I told Ivanov to ask Tikhaya Bay for another weather report.

"I'm not in touch with Tikhaya," he replied impatiently.

"It's only a few minutes since you got the weather forecast from them!"

"I didn't get it from them. I intercepted the daily bulletin that Tikhaya Bay sends out to Cape Zhelaniya. And now they're talking to Moscow again!"

I swore under my breath.

There were only a few pints of fuel left in the tanks. Bassein again suggested landing.

"When the petrol runs out it'll be too late to land," he insisted. "Even if we come down safely, it'll not be much good—we can't last long without fuel."

As we argued a dark cliff appeared on our left. Before I had realized where we were two masts and several small houses grew out of the mist.

Tikhaya Bay!

Polar station. Tikhaya Bay

For an instant my heart stopped. Bassein gave me a hug and Ivanov clapped his hands gleefully.

"Make haste!" they shouted in unison.

Barely reaching the aerodrome and determining the wind direction by the flags I made straight for the ground without the usual circling.

There was of course no one to meet us. But as we taxied down the runway the station staff and the crew of the second plane ran out to meet us.

Flushed and excited, they gathered around us.

"We were going to give you a grand welcome," the chief of the station said ruefully, breathless with running, "but your sudden arrival has spoiled everything."

Having at last escaped from the ice, we felt like kissing every one of our dear, embarrassed companions. But I doubt if they would have liked it, for glancing at Ivanov and Bassein I realized that our faces were thick with grime, whereas the others were, of course, clean and tidy.

After a while we were taken to the baths. I wanted to shave and only then, in front of the mirror, discovered frost-bite on my cheeks and chin.

"It might have been worse," I mumbled to myself. "It's not the first time I've had a change of skin."

* * *

This was the first time in the history of aviation that aircraft had crossed the Barents Sea and reached Franz Josef Land.

This archipelago bears the name of a former Austrian emperor but by right it ought to have been named after the Russian scientist and revolutionary, P. A. Kropotkin.

P. A. Kropotkin, then secretary of the Russian Geographical Society, suspected the existence of this archipelago as early as 1870. When studying the ice-drift in the Arctic he concluded that unknown land existed somewhere in the North, between Spitsbergen and Novaya Zemlya. This was evident from the centuries-old ice north-west of Novaya Zemlya, from the rock and earth found on floating ice sheets, and from other less significant factors. Kropotkin planned a polar expedition to discover this "unknown land," but the plan was never carried out because the Ministry of Finance refused to provide funds.

The truth of this contention by the Russian scientist and revolutionary was soon proved, for in 1873 chance brought two Austrian explorers, Weyprecht and Payer, to the land whose existence Kropotkin had foreseen. There is not the slightest doubt that the discovery was accidental, for they had been drifting for over a year on a ship frozen into an ice-field many feet thick, and to use Payer's own words "had turned from free explorers into passengers on an ice-floe."

That was how the vast archipelago of some twelve thousand square miles, which Payer named Franz Josef Land, was discovered.

Kropotkin wrote bitterly at the time: "The land we had seen through the polar gloom was discovered by Payer and Weyprecht."

In the course of half a century—from 1873 to 1929—about a

hundred and thirty expeditions visited Franz Josef Land. Almost every country in the world sent its representatives: Russia, Norway, Britain, America, Austria, Germany, France and Italy. However, the majority went there not for scientific but for mercenary aims.

The Soviet Union was the first country to undertake a planned scientific survey of the archipelago. In 1928 the Soviet flag was hoisted there and twelve months later the Shmidt expedition began a systematic exploration of the islands. That same year the first house was built on one of the islands (Hooker Island) and a wintering party arrived.

The station staff there gave us a warm, friendly welcome. Tikhaya Bay lies in the north-west of Hooker Island, which occupies a central position in the archipelago, and cuts into the island for almost two miles. In the north, east and west it is sheltered by cliffs up to six hundred feet high, heaped with glaciers.

It was the most beautiful spot we had seen beyond the Arctic Circle during our month's flight. The island and the bay are particularly good to look at when the bright orange sun shines through the twenty-four hours of the polar day. The sea, ice, basaltic cliffs, and the six hundred feet high Ruby Rock, which juts out of the sea right in front of the station, sparkle in a myriad of colours.

It seems a pity there are so few sunny summer days at Tikhaya Bay. The sun rises there in mid February and disappears at the end of October. Then comes the impenetrable polar murk, broken occasionally by the wonderful aurora.

Since the temperature on Franz Josef Land averages 14.3 degrees of frost all the year round the ordinary division into "winter" and "summer" does not apply to these places any more than the conception of "day" and "night." Actually the high northern latitudes of the Arctic are a land of eternal winter. When people speak of the arctic winter they mean the polar night, for then the temperature is lowest and hurricanes rage, accompanied by the dreaded arctic blizzards, but in Tikhaya Bay winds and especially thick fog are frequent in "summer" too.

Ninety per cent of the archipelago's area is covered by huge

125

glaciers, their monster tongues lolling down the steep shores into the sea and there forming masses of floating icebergs. Only one-tenth of the land surface is ice-free and there the polar station was built.

Meteorological observation is carried on throughout the twenty-four hours of the day.

Icebergs. Left—Ruby Rock

Every hour of the day, in all kinds of weather—sunshine, raging blizzards or storms—readings have to be taken and weather forecasts submitted to the radio-operator. Two men keep watch all the year round and not once has a weather report been late in reaching the mainland.

Meteorology is only part of the varied and complex scientific work done by the station staff. Their observations concerning terrestrial magnetism are of especial importance as Tikhaya Bay is closer to the magnetic pole than any other polar station.

A study of the characteristics of the earth's magnetic field, apart from its scientific interest, is of great practical assistance to air and sea navigation, particularly as the staff of the Tikhaya station collate their observations with a view to determining the degree of regularity of magnetic storms. Their findings show that magnetic storms in the Franz Josef Land area can make the compass needle deviate as much as six degrees one way or another. A pilot would prefer running into a storm or blizzard if he could avoid one of these magnetic storms, imperceptible to the eye or ear.

Our machine hade covred 2,800 miles in adverse meteorological conditions, and so before setting out on the last and most important lap—the flight over the archipelago—the plane had to be carefully overhauled.

Working and resting we watched the doings of the wintering party. Nothing was missing which the country could possibly provide for these people's comfort. In latitude 80° N. everything imaginable had been done to make life tolerable in the grim Arctic. The houses where the people lived were solid and comfortable. These polar explorers had long passed the stage of makeshift shanties heated with blubber or primus stoves, of the cold and damp.

Each man had a separate, well-heated room with electric light and telephone. There were baths and a spacious dining-room. The cook had no need to exert himself to vary the menu: the station had pigs and cows, the stores were stacked with ham, all kinds of smoked sausage, beef-rolls, tinned foods, flour, sugar, cheese, chocolate, cocoa, coffee and wine. There was food enough for several years.

When off duty they got together in their commodious "mess-room" to listen in to Moscow, play a game of billiards, hear the piano or a string band, or see a film. This room also contained a well-selected library.

Indoors nothing reminded you of a polar winter. But outside, in the "street," the North is at once telling. You see bear skins hanging about. The wind knocks you off your feet and you are bewildered by the grandeur of Ruby Rock, which, as a rule, lies behind a curtain of snow or mist.

* * *

The planes were ready for a reconnaissance flight but thick clouds and snow-storms held us up. It was not until April 26 that favourable weather set in. I immediately ordered a start, arranging that the machine with Akkuratov, the navigator, would go first.

Near the shore was an ice-hummock which the pilot tried to avoid. But in taxiing round it, his right ski floundered into a pocket of soft snow. The plane was hauled out and towed to safety but its wing was damaged.

It seemed a pity not to make use of such fine weather and so I decided to go alone. The heavily loaded machine made a run of at least 700 yards and then almost reluctantly began to climb. I set the course for Rudolph Island.

At first the radio functioned perfectly, maintaining regular communication with Tikhaya and bringing us their weather reports. But when Rudolph Island was in sight Ivanov passed me a note:

"Radio dead. No contact. I can't make out what's the matter. We'll have to land to repair it."

On my right, beneath the wing, lay Rudolph Island. I easily recognized Teplitz Bay which I had known only from the map. On the shore were three small huts one of which I knew had been built by the American Ziegler-Fial expedition in 1903. This expedition, organized at huge cost, was to have surveyed Franz Josef Archipelago and then to have set out for the North Pole. But failing to achieve either object, the expedition returned to the United States.

The two other huts had been built by Soviet explorers in 1932, during the Second International Polar Year.

South of the station lay a long strip of smooth surface where I thought a landing could be effected. But the machine was overloaded and there was the danger of breaking a ski.

Weather conditions were exceptionally good, with visibility at least sixty-five miles and the engine in perfect trim. In view of all this, I decided to fly farther north, survey ice conditions from Rudolph Island to latitude 83-84^0 N. and, having used up some of the petrol and reduced the dead weight of the machine, land in Teplitz Bay to repair the radio.

Climbing to four thousand feet I steered north by compass. We were 600 miles from the North Pole.

Below us, stretching for miles, was a wonderful panorama of polar ice. In places the uneven pack-ice formed the most intricate design, and the ice looked as if it had been put through a giant mincer. Here and there towered great icebergs of fantastic shape. Farther north the surface grew smoother and the icebergs less frequent.

I gazed spellbound at this scenic magnificence of might and calm, trying to take in every minute detail, when I was interrupted by a sudden push on the shoulder and a shout above the noise of the engine:

"The land's disappearing!"

I swung round, heading for Rudolph Island.

We calculated that we had reached latitude 83° N. but we could not be sure for we had made our deductions from the duration and speed of the flight. If I had had a navigator with me I would have gone on to 85 degrees.

East of Rudolph Island stretched a strip of open water about 20 miles wide with more ice beyond it.

I circuited the island several times finding a number of places suitable for taking off and landing with heavy aircraft.

Then I skirted the island from the south, making for the familiar huts. The machine was now lighter and a landing was safer, but coming down, I felt troubled.

Leaving Ivanov in charge of the plane with the engine on, Bassein and I went to explore the huts.

The first thing we saw was a big barn, which must have been roofed with canvas: through time this had rotted and had been carried away by the wind, but bits of it still dangled from the skeleton roof. From under the snow broken cases and empty barrels jutted out. Evidently this had been the depot of the Ziegler-Fial expedition.

Near it was a wooden hut with bear trails round it. We peered through the window: the room was snowed up almost to the ceiling.

Nearer to the shore was the well-preserved hut and depot of

9

Ice hummocks off the shores of Rudolph Island

the Soviet expedition. We opened the door wondering why the bears had not been able to get in. They had been there time and again, leaving traces of their teeth and claws on the solid door. Then why hadn't they got at the contents?

The riddle was solved by our observant Bassein: the door could not be pushed open, but had to be pulled, and this the gourmands had not enough sense to do.

The things we found in that depot! From the ceiling hung bacon and smoked sausage. The shelves were stacked with cartridge-cases and gunpowder, candy and cranberry juice, all arranged in orderly fashion as in a model food store. This supply would have lasted the three of us for many years, and, judging by the bear trails, fresh meat would also be plentiful.

Our investigations completed we set out on the return journey.

Meanwhile Ivanov had repaired the radio and communicated with Tikhaya Bay. The operator there reported:

"Weather worse, visibility two miles, mist 200 yards."

Below broken clouds floated, now and then blotting out the coastline. Over one island the machine suddenly swooped, the speed dropping from 110 to 65 miles.

Instinctively I pushed the control lever forward and the plane went into a steep dive. The speed at once increased to 140 miles an hour and a few seconds later I levelled out.

The situation was restored but the machine had lost height by 1,000 feet. This apparently had been caused by a strong down current.

Through a hole in the clouds I saw Hooker Island and a patch of clear water near Tikhaya Bay and so I reduced the engine speed and began to glide to earth.

On the runway the "T" was laid out, and we alighted safely.

We could now start on the return flight to Moscow but for the impenetrable fog of the polar spring. The temperature rose sharply and was now never below two degrees. There was a southerly wind and the ice in Tikhaya Bay, including our runway, was being steadily crushed and carried out to sea. The water came near an old iceberg which had been grounded for two years and then one night the waves floated the berg out to sea.

The runway grew smaller every day, increasing the anxiety of the crew.

May Day came and we celebrated together with the station staff. The heavy cloud banks, the cold glitter of the icebergs and even the shrieking wind which crumbled the remains of our runway could not damp our spirits.

A broadcast from the Red Square made us think of Moscow and the marching columns of demonstrators. We felt quite happy.

The wind had completely wrecked our runway. With great difficulty we found another on a narrow strip of shore ice from which we had first to remove some ice-hummocks with ammonal.

When the station staff learned that we intended to get away on the first suitable day they began to write letters to their friends and relatives with whom they had had no communication for almost a year: the last mail had left on an ice-breaker in August of the previous year.

At last conditions were favourable. Weather reports from all points along our route were good. We could set out.

Conditions had changed since our arrival. Now, beneath us lay the open sea. There was no ice as far as the eye could reach.

The engine began to tremble as if it were about to fly out of its frame and there was a smell of burning. Something serious had happened and below us was water. I decided to go on, steering straight for Tikhaya Bay. We were losing height but we managed to reach Tikhaya and land safely. The second machine crashed, landing on its nose.

The crew scrambled out of the damaged cockpit, their hands and faces cut by broken glass, but otherwise unhurt.

An inspection revealed a broken airscrew, several dents and holes in the wing, and shattered struts and runners. Alongside lay the cause of the crash—an ice splinter. The left ski had caught on the piece of ice and the machine had turned turtle.

The engine of my plane was quite dead and so the only thing to do was to make one machine out of two.

After three days of strenuous effort, we four, including navigator Akkuratov, set out for Cape Zhelaniya.

We left the bay in clear, sunny weather but soon, near Salm Island, at the southern end of Franz Josef Land, low clouds advanced towards us, almost touching the sea.

"We'll try the old method," I said to myself.

It was a thick layer but I broke through and was glad I had done so. At intervals of ten to fifteen minutes holes appeared, so that I could judge fairly accurately the character of the ice below us.

After three hours' flight, I knew that we must be nearing Novaya Zemlya, so I dived through a hole in the clouds and flew on beneath them.

At ten to twelve we landed safely at Cape Zhelaniya where we were greeted warmly by the station staff.

We were hungry and only too pleased to accept an invitation to lunch.

During the meal the chief told us a story which seemed funny but might easily have ended in tragedy.

"At eleven thirty when we got your last radio message," he said, "the men on duty went to the airfield to light the bonfires and lay out the landing sign.

"It has always been a rule with us never to venture out without a gun, in case we meet a bear. But this time, the men, with their hands full of signal cloth, firewood and blubber, forgot about guns.

"They laid out the landing signs, lit the bonfires and kept feeding the fires with blubber, which burns well and makes a black smoke, easily seen. But burning blubber has a characteristic smell, which all bears love. The men recalled this when it was too late, and a huge polar bear came ambling towards them.

"So they had a guest, but nothing to welcome him with—no guns. He advanced boldly as if he knew they were helpless. But when he was only about a hundred feet away he came upon an empty barrel, and began to nose about it. This was the saving of the men for we heard them shouting.

"When we ran out and saw a white speck beside a black barrel we realized what was the matter. We grabbed our guns, called the dogs and ran to the rescue.

"Scenting the dogs the bear turned tail, but he could not shake them off. One dog snapped him from behind and he launched out angrily with his paw but missed, just as another dog clutched his hind foot. There was a lively tussle but the fight did not last long for a bullet sent the bear sprawling on the ice.

"And so the polar Mikhail did not meet his Moscow namesake," concluded our narrator.

In the evening a broadcast was arranged with all the polar stations taking part. It relieved the monotony of arctic life for a dozen polar stations and gave further proof of the significance of radio in the Far North, of the excellent quality of our polar radio stations and the good work done by radio-operators.

For me it was an opportunity to describe my flight to the staff of the polar stations and, on behalf of the crews, to thank them for their devoted, selfless work, which had been largely responsible for the success of the undertaking.

When I finished, questions poured in from all parts of the Arctic.

Suddenly the familiar voice of Ernst Krenkel, who was wintering on one of the islands, came from the loud speaker.

"What's the ice like north of Rudolph Island? Is it suitable for the landing of heavy aircraft? Where have you decided to establish the depot?"

I answered all these questions as best I could, knowing that Krenkel was to participate in the expedition.

"So we're going to winter at the Pole!" he cried confidently.

Next day we took the mail and set out for Matochkin Shar. On May 17 we left the station there and were soon at Yugorsky Shar.

The runway was quite good, but we spent only a few hours there, for the weather urged us on. Naryan Mar reported that there was little snow there and that a landing on skis could be effected only on the ice of the Pechora River, but this "aerodrome" would not last long either.

Loading the machine with mail and fur we left Yugorsky Shar and landed at Naryan Mar the same day.

The ice of the Pechora where our plane had landed was now a thaw pool. It was just as difficult to take off on skis as on wheels. But we knew that a landing on skis farther south was out of the question so we changed them for wheels and asked Arkhangelsk, Kotlas and Vologda about conditions there. The replies were not very reassuring. Only at Vologda was a landing possible, but this, too, was risky.

When we took off I sat at the controls thinking: "I can't go back and land my heavy machine on wheels. Therefore we must go on to Vologda at all costs."

Below us was a stretch of woodland, the trees half submerged in water. We were passing over limitless bogs where no landing was possible; even if we did miraculously survive we would never get out of the bogs alive.

After seven hours' flight we emerged to a railway, sighting small clearings at rare intervals. The plane rolled and pitched and Ivanov, who was very sensitive to air sickness, had great difficulty in maintaining contact with the ground stations. Seeing this, Bassein tried to induce me to land.

134

"Mikhail Vasilyevich," he said, "let's come down. It's quite dry here; I'm sure we'll land safely."

Paying no heed I went on, because I felt that the farther south we got the more fields there would be and the easier it would be to land.

Eight hours had passed since the take-off. Our petrol would last another half hour.

Things were becoming really bad. Ivanov was knocked out and we had absolutely no contact with the ground. When we left Naryan Mar the temperature was two degrees below zero and now it was eighteen above. The engine was overheating and I expected the water to boil any minute. Making use of the turbulent air flow, I fought my way up without increasing the revolutions of the engine. With great difficulty I managed to climb to 3,800 feet, where it was cooler. The danger of overheating the engine had passed and I sighed with relief.

Vologda was 43 miles away and we had already been flying non-stop for eight and a half hours. I managed to save a little fuel by varying the mixture ratio. But would it suffice?

The town was now in sight. Only a few more minutes to go and the petrol might give out any moment.

But the engine did not fail us, and here was Vologda. I circled the aerodrome as if nothing had happened and made a perfect landing. Immediately afterwards the engine stopped—the tanks were quite dry.

At six thirty on the evening of May 21 we touched down at Moscow aerodrome. The long flight from Moscow to Franz Josef Land and back was at an end.

he day after my arrival in Moscow from Franz Josef Land I sat in Shmidt's study reporting on my flight to an audience which included the management of the Northern Sea Route Administration and the men who were to spend the winter at the Pole. I suggested that the main depot be established on Rudolph Island—the extreme northerly point of the archipelago.

The island is coated with ice, but its dome slopes gently so that aircraft can take off with any load.

"What would you consider the best time for a flight to the North Pole?" asked Mark Ivanovich Shevelev.

"I think April and May are the best months," I said. "The sun is high at that time, but it is still cold and the aircraft skis will slide well."

"But are there any ice sheets fit for the landing of heavy machines north of Rudolph Island?" inquired Otto Yulyevich.

"I'm sure we'll find a suitable ice-floe for landing the expedition in the vicinity of the North Pole."

Otto Yulyevich nodded approvingly and after a pause said enthusiastically:

"We are Bolsheviks and shall overcome the difficulties. The depot will be established on Rudolph Island and preparations must begin at once."

Turning to Papanin, he said:

"We are placing the ice-breaker *Rusanov* at your disposal. Build houses on the island, take the winter party there and also the major equipment for the North Pole expedition."

"Very good," replied Ivan Dmitriyevich Papanin briefly.

"You, Mark Ivanovich and Mikhail Vasilyevich, will have to see to the planes," Shmidt said to us. "Get in touch with the aircraft plants and arrange all the details."

It was considered essential that the machines for the forthcoming expedition should have the maximum carrying capacity and range and it was decided that the G-2 machines were best suited for the purpose. We also needed a lighter plane for reconnaissance and Shevelev suggested the twin-engined G-1 which we agreed was a good choice.

"Bear in mind, comrades, that you have little time before the take-off," Shmidt said in parting.

These were wonderful days. The impossible was becoming possible under pressure of eager enthusiasts.

The ice-breaker *Rusanov* was steadily grinding her way through heavy ice to Franz Josef Land, carrying equipment for the new, most northerly air base in the world. The ship's cargo included many cases with the thrilling label, "Pole."

Just over six months remained before the flight. I often thought of how Robert Peary had devoted twenty-three years of his life to the realization of his dream.

We were fortunate to be living at a different time and in a different country, where everything is done to further socialist construction.

The whole country—factories, laboratories and institutes—were hard at work to fit us out for our long journey.

One plant was reconditioning the heavy machines, another designing powerful engines for operation in low temperatures. Radio factories were constructing special equipment.

The Institute of Public Feeding provided an excellent variety of tasty and nourishing food concentrates.

Every hour the whole country was interested in the success of the enterprise which the Party and the Government had entrusted to us. The workers were proud to help in equipping the expedition, and our own work was easier for we knew we had millions of friends about us.

The crews chosen for the flight were all seasoned arctic flyers. My co-pilot on the flagship, U.S.S.R. N-170, was the well-known polar aviator, Mikhail Sergeyevich Babushkin, and the navigator was Ivan Timofeyevich Spirin. In 1921 Spirin and I served in the *Ilya Muromets* air squadron. In 1934 he and Gromov flew 75 hours non-stop over a circuit course, covering 7,760 miles.

The commander of the second plane, U.S.S.R. N-171, was Vasily Sergeyevich Molokov—hero of the *Chelyuskin* relief expedition. I made Vasıly Sergeyevich's acquaintance during the *Chelyuskin* rescue operations in 1934, but I had heard about him long before.

Ice cliff on Rudolph Island

I remember the young man with streaks of grey hair whom I first met on the grim snow-swept Cape Vankarem.

"That's Uupenaskhen—a fine hunter," said the Chukchi, distinguishing Molokov from the rest of us. The Chukchi are shrewd; they at once picked out our most valued and seasoned flyer.

Reserved, cool and disciplined, Molokov is responsive and friendly, but he always tries to keep in the background so as not to overshadow somebody else.

Vasily Sergeyevich's early life was quite ordinary. He was born in the Moscow suburbs, now known as Molokovo, and participated in the Civil War. In 1921, he finished a flying school. Then he was squadron instruction leader training some very distinguished flyers, among them Levanevsky, Doronin and Lyapidevsky.

In 1929 Molokov worked for the civil aviation and was the first civilian pilot to operate a regular night route. These flights steeled the pilot and improved his skill. When he joined the polar air service he was already experienced. Soon he won distinction for his remarkable achievements, including a one-day winter flight from Krasnoyarsk to Igarka—a distance of 1,125 miles—which was quite a feat in those days.

Molokov again distinguished himself during the *Chelyuskin* rescue operations when he managed to squeeze four men into the rear seat, designed to hold one passenger, and to carry two more in parachute cases slung to the wings.

Thanks to his resourcefulness Molokov evacuated thirty-nine of the *Chelyuskin* men—more than any other pilot.

On his return he was given a high award for his services.

In 1935 he made another remarkable flight to the Arctic, covering a distance of 12,500 miles, and the year following, in exceptionally adverse meteorological conditions, he surveyed the extreme North and the Northern Sea Route from Bering Strait to Arkhangelsk.

He was given a grand reception in Moscow where Vyacheslav Mikhailovich Molotov was ta the aerodrome to meet him.

From Moscow the U.S.S.R. N-2 went to Krasnoyarsk where it safely landed finishing the last lap of a brilliant flight.

Molokov's fine record made him a worthy member of the air crew of the North Pole expedition.

Anatoly Dmitriyevich Alexeyev—the commander of the U.S.S.R. N-172—knows how to overcome the worst flying weather. Once, piloting a flying boat in the spring thaw and mist, he evacuated a sick man from one of the most northerly polar stations—something which had been considered well-nigh impossible.

Alexeyev does not look a bit a pilot and certainly not a polar flyer. The first impression is that he is rather timid, but in the course of his polar service he has come out unscathed from many a tight corner.

Alexeyev's father was a railway clerk at a Moscow station.

Alexeyev recalls his childhood when his parents had to save every penny; but they were eager to give their children a good start in life.

At the age of eight his father wanted him to learn a trade but his mother insisted that he should go to school. He did not study well in the primary grades, but afterwards steadily improved.

Soon after the October Revolution his mother died, the family was broken up and Anatoly had to shift for himself.

In 1921 he finished an officers' electrical engineering school and was appointed first to an electrical engineering unit and then to the Sevastopol Naval Flying School, where he was an instructor in electrical engineering. A few years afterwards he joined the first torpedo squadron, where he met Boris Grigoryevich Chukhnovsky. Under his influence Alexeyev became interested in the North and began to study navigation. Some time later he obtained an observer-pilot's certificate.

In 1928 an Italian expedition under Umberto Nobile made an attempt to reach the Pole in the dirigible *Italia*. On May 24 the ship reached the Pole but could not land a party on the ice.

On the way back it crashed off Spitsbergen. There was a sudden escape of gas and the dirigible rapidly lost height, struck the ice, then rose clear and drifted off with some of the crew. The details of their death are unknown.

The others, including Umberto Nobile, were flung on to the ice. Some food and a wireless set were also thrown out.

When the first attempts to establish radio communication with the outside world failed, three members of the expedition set out on foot, hoping to sight a trading vessel and report the accident.

The first to hear Nobile's distress signals was a Soviet amateur wireless operator, Shmidt, in the village of Voznesenye-Vokhma, Viatka Region.

The catastrophe set the world astir. Relief operations by different countries included the services of eighteen ships and twenty-one aircraft, but the efforts of the Soviet Union were the most effective. Only Nobile was saved by the Swedish aviator Lundborg.

The search undertaken by the U.S.S.R. was based on the combined operations of aircraft and ice-breakers.

With great difficulty the ice-breaker *Krasin* ground its way to the Seven Islands where a plane was lowered and assembled on the ice. Losing no time, Chukhnovsky and Alexeyev went out in search of the lost expedition. On July 10 they spotted two men on a small ice-floe. A landing was impossible and there was no chance of reaching the ice-breaker, for they had run out of petrol. There was nothing for it but to land on the first suitable ice sheet.

A radio message from the plane gave the location of the men and urged the commander not to bother about the plane, but go to the help of the castaways.

Two half-dead, frost-bitten Italians were taken on board the Soviet ship. Their companion, Dr. Malmgren of Sweden, a young geophysicist, had been abandoned, utterly exhausted, fourteen days after leaving camp. Then the ship took the flyers and the plane on board and later in the day rescued the remaining members of the Nobile expedition.

In 1932 Alexeyev gave up the work of navigator to become a pilot. It is interesting to note that Golovin, the youngest participant in the North Pole expedition, had been his flight instructor.

In 1934 Alexeyev made a brilliant flight to Severnaya Zemlya. The story runs thus.

Not a single ship had been able to reach Domashny Island, land the new party, and replenish supplies of food and fuel. One of the polar party of four, headed by N. P. Demme, had scurvy—the dread disease of the North.

V. V. Kuibyshev ordered that they should be evacuated by air and the station closed.

The task was entrusted to Lindel and Lavrov, but as they approached the island their engine failed and Lindel, who was at the wheel, crash-landed, wrecking the machine beyond repair. The aviators made their way to the station on foot where six people were now marooned in place of four.

Another machine, piloted by Anatoly Dmitriyevich Alexeyev, was sent to their assistance.

Twice Alexeyev tried to get through to Novaya Zemlya, but was each time compelled to return owing to bad weather. The third attempt was successful; he reached the island and landed on a narrow lane of open water, which threatened to close at any moment and crush the plane.

He rushed to the station and told them to pack and board the machine. But Demme was a woman of strong character. "We three are in good health," she said. "We can hold out till next year."

"Should we close up?" she asked the others.

Two healthy men and one very ill with scurvy said:

"We leave it to you to decide."

Alexeyev had to do quite a lot of arguing before he could prevail upon her to go. Finally, she agreed but only when Alexeyev had given her the wireless message from V. V. Kuibyshev.

The return trip was just as difficult. A fog was descending over the sea, making even low flight impossible. Alexeyev broke through the clouds, steering southward.

Zhukov, the navigator, succeeded in making contact with the ice-breaker *Sibiryakov* whose captain advised them to head in his direction. "The weather is good," he wired, "and there is a channel of open water near the ship."

In about an hour the clouds were left behind and the aviators sighted the ice-breaker. They landed alongside and turned over the party and sixteen dogs.

Alexeyev is a splendid polar flyer. I always admired his skill, which combined the experience of navigator and pilot.

Ilya Pavlovich Mazuruk, the pilot of the fourth ship, the U.S.S.R. N-169, comes from my own district.

Until quite recently Ilya Mazuruk was working at the Lipetsk power station. The Komsomol (Young Communist League) helped him to achieve his great ambition—to enter a flying school. There he displayed his energy, resourcefulness and discipline. It so happened that Mazuruk replaced me on the Khabarovsk-Sakhalin line. He told me of many interesting experiences, one of which impressed me particularly.

One bleak winter day, when tiny particles of snow were whirling in the air, Mazuruk had to take twelve passengers and 400 pounds of mail to Sakhalin in a three-engined plane.

At first all went well, but over the Tatar Strait, at a place where it rarely freezes, and only 25 miles from Sakhalin, the central engine suddenly gave out. The plane began to lose height and their only chance of escape was to lighten it.

Mazuruk at once ordered the mail and equipment to be thrown overboard. Everything possible went over the side but the machine was still heavy. Realizing the danger the passengers began to pass on their personal belongings, but that too was not enough. The plane was only 300 feet from the sea when suddenly Barukin, the air-mechanic, began to strip, and said he was going to let the petrol out of the auxiliary tanks at the far end of the wings. This would relieve the machine of 400 pounds of dead weight.

But would he complete the operation before the machine touched the water? The black waves were very near: one more minute, one false move and the skis would catch on the crest of a wave, and that would be the end.

But then, clumsily, as though unwillingly, the machine began to climb. At the same moment the frost-bitten mechanic emerged from the wing. He had had to bore a hole in the tank with a screwdriver; the petrol had gushed out of the tank on to his face and hands, and the cold had done the rest.

Mazuruk shouted to the mechanic to smash the compass glass and use the alcohol to rub the frost-bitten parts, but, horrified, he waved away the suggestion.

"What! How will you steer without a compass?"

The reply made the pilot forget his predicament. With men of this kind, he thought, he had nothing to fear.

Through the snow the contours of a rocky shore came in sight. A few minutes later the taiga appeared and then a small clearing, but at that moment the second engine failed and the machine began rapidly to lose height. Realizing that he would not reach the glade, the pilot ordered the passengers to fasten themselves to their seats, and turning into the wind, effected a successful landing on bushes. Except for a few scratches on its paint the machine was undamaged.

Waist-deep in snow, the men struggled through the thickets, and finally reached a settlement.

When the Evenks heard of the misfortune they at once offered to help. Before long Mazuruk and Barukin, accompanied by ten

Evenks, left in deer sledges for the taiga. It took four days of hard work to cut a way through the bushes and tow the machine to a clearing where a take-off was possible. And when they had all but succeeded a badly secured rope almost shattered their hopes. The deer pulled, wrenching loose a landing gear strut. The machine was left with only one leg.

The pilot and mechanic, tired and dirty, flung themselves down despairingly on some twigs beside the fire: it was impossible to get away and nowhere to do the repairs. Just then an aged Evenk came up and began to comfort them.

"I like you, air drivers," he said. "I'll work all night and make a leg for your machine from black birch. It's like iron! We make runners for our sledges from it."

Mazuruk thanked the old man, but said that it would be no use for the machine's legs were made at a factory and from special material.

But the old man insisted. All night long he worked with his knife, carving a wooden stump and fitting it to the plane. In the morning the leg was ready.

Having fitted the strut in place the men began to rock the plane up and down. The strut withstood the strain.

The deer easily towed the machine to the clearing. The mechanic trimmed the engines, but suddenly it was discovered that oil was short. Acting on the advice of the same old man, the crew replenished their supplies with cod-liver oil and took off.

With a wooden leg fitted to their machine and cod-liver oil in the engines they flew a distance of 80 miles, landing without any damage to the strut.

Mazuruk flew a total of 44,000 miles in the Far East, carrying mail and about a thousand passengers.

Pavel Georgiyevich Golovin, a well-known polar flyer, was put in charge of the two-engined U.S.S.R. N-166 reconnaissance plane.

Aviation had attracted Golovin at an early age. Residing in Naro-Fominsk, he attended a flying model class where he acquired his first knowledge of aerodynamics and himself built several models. Later he joined a glider class and devoted himself to glider construction.

Ships' commanders I. P. Mazuruk, A. D. Alexeyev, V. S. Molokov
and M. V. Vodopyanov

In 1924 the local ODVF Society (Society for the Promotion of
Aviation) sent him to a glider meet in the Crimea. There he first
saw gliders in flight and became an enthusiast.

In 1927 the Komsomol helped him to enter an engineering school
in Moscow. There he also set up a glider class and worked on a new
design. When finished the glider was taken to the Osoaviakhim
gliding centre.

There Golovin spent most of his free time, making some very
successful flights.

Eventually the persevering glider-pilot was sent to a flying school.
He completed the course and became a flight instructor, but did
not abandon gliding.

In 1932 Golovin took part in a glider contest in the Crimea where
he made a series of flights, one of which brought him world fame.
He flew over the Kara-dag mountain peak, the sea, Feodosiya and
returned to Klementyev Mountain, establishing a world endurance
record with a passenger.

Here is the story as told by Golovin himself:

145

"On the twenty-ninth of October a shock-cord dispatched my glider into the air. I made a steep turn, breasting the air currents along the slopes of Uzun-Syrt Mountain.

"It was ten in the morning. I flew back and forth along the slopes, while my passenger played a mouth-organ.

"It was past noon, but we were still on our route, covering each time three or four miles. The sun blazed. The stream-line flow was very strong.

"Soon thermal currents began to rise from the heated ground. At first cautiously, and then more and more boldly, I began to steer clear of the mountain, when suddenly I noticed a shadow on the wing. It was an eagle flying overhead—we could see its claws and strong, sharp beak.

"With outstretched wings, the eagle sailed before us. Following it I noticed that the glider was steadily climbing. I could feel it being pushed up by the currents of heated air. It appears that the eagles are familiar with these up-currents and fly with little effort. Whenever our line of flight exactly coincided with that of the eagle the glider gained height.

"At about six in the evening it began to get dark. The eagle had long since disappeared. I switched the lights on and off, including the red lights on the wings. Then, peering into the darkness, I noticed three flares at the take-off.

"A moist, warm wind was blowing from the sea and the thermal lift steadily increased. We were being jerked up more and more. The bonfires down below seemed tiny specks.

"I decided to make an experiment which I had planned long ago: to steer round Uzun-Syrt Mountain. Soon I approached the summit of Kara-dag, enveloped in white and grey clouds. In the west, on the sea-shore, lights twinkled. Below we could just make out the steep cliffs and the sea. I went back to Uzun-Syrt and turned on the lights and signal flares so that the people on ground duty would see us. Seeing them wave torchlights I realized that we had been spotted and switching off the lights headed for the sea. It was delightful to cruise in mid air in the quiet of night!

"While my passenger dozed I skirted Koktebel and made two

P. G. Golovin and A. D. Alexeyev

big circuits over the sea. The further I got from shore the more height I lost. It was none too pleasant to lose height over the sea. Then I decided to head straight for Feodosiya. The altimeter showed that we were 4,500 feet above the starting point—the maximum achieved during the flight.

"Soon lights appeared on the horizon. My glider sped towards them with a fair wind. It was the town of Feodosiya, which I circled several times.

"Enough for today,' I said to myself, although I could have stayed up much longer.

"I made for Uzun-Syrt to the tune of 'The Indian Guest' played on a mouth-organ by my now wide-awake companion. Those were nerve-racking moments. There was hardly any wind. Taking advantage of occasional thermal up-currents I climbed and, doing my best to use them sparingly, glided on to the next lift force..."

At the Moscow flying school Golovin, instructor, met a very gifted student—A. D. Alexeyev—whose arctic stories aroused his interest. Golovin became a polar flyer whose remarkable exploits brought him great fame.

* * *

The crews prepared carefully for the forthcoming flight. Notwithstanding their extensive experience, the ship's commanders and their assistants practised blind flying and the piloting of heavy aircraft. We all, including myself, again became apprentices. My trainer was Major Babkin. I tried to be very diligent and was very pleased when he happened to praise me.

The navigators also were hard at work, plotting the plane's course by the sun compass and studying the new radio equipment. The mechanics were given a special course on engine maintenance.

At the height of this activity I was told to report to the Polar Aviation Department.

"Something's happened," I thought, alarmed.

The chief greeted me and at once gave me a radiogram. I read it once ... twice ... but could make nothing of it.

"Aviaarctic, Shevelev, Moscow.

"Took off for Rudolph on the eighth. Returned to Tikhaya on the tenth. The entire string of islands from Tikhaya to Rudolph unfit for depot. Rudolph no good at all. On the way back landed on Ketlitz Island. Its northern section is a plane, an inner glacier, with no lead to the sea. The shores are rocky and up to 65 feet high. I am familiar with the glacier. In about ten years the ice may grow so much that it will bridge the shore and slope down to the sea. Then a crack will form and the depot will be put out of commission."

This was from the pilot I had left in Tikhaya Bay during my flight to Franz Josef Land. He was to help the scientific personnel to survey the newly discovered islands of Franz Josef Land in a U-2 plane and this surprise radiogram was the outcome of his flights.

Amid the ice-fields

The chief looked at me and laughed but his eyes were serious. I lifted my hands in dismay: could I have blundered so badly? Besides the message produced a very strange impression.

The chief tried to calm me:

"He seems to be over-cautious, suggests building a depot that will last ten years. Do you understand him to mean that in ten years Ketlitz Island also will be of no use?"

"I don't understand him at all," I replied with a hopeless gesture. "Why is Rudolph Island absolutely no good. Of course there's a suitable airfield on Ketlitz Island and a winter station could be built close to it. On Rudolph Island the runway would have to be built on the dome, one or two miles from the station. But we'll have lorries and tractors on Rudolph Island—all we'll need is a hut for the mechanics and workshops."

"Ketlitz Island is no use at all. It's too far from the Pole, we wouldn't have enough petrol."

At this time Papanin was trying to break through to Rudolph Island. The ice-breaker *Rusanov* was beset by ice. At times she was thrown back through the British Channel to Tikhaya Bay, but the crew persisted stubbornly.

I called Papanin on the wireless and had the following conversation with him:

Vodopyanov. Greetings to all. Why are you silent? Where have you established the main depot? Have you surveyed Rudolph Island?

Papanin. Greetings from Rudolph Island. Surveyed the runway and found it quite good. Its length in various directions is roughly a mile and more. Pilot Iyeske and navigator Rubinstein are leaving for Rudolph Island tomorrow with instructions to make a precision chart of various compass points. I shall take this chart to Moscow. Establishing the main depot on Rudolph Island and on Rudolph only .... Don't worry about the depot. Everything will be carried out in full. Doing all we can. The work is well under way; the assignment will be fulfilled.

I sighed with relief. All was going well. We had a depot on Rudolph Island, in latitude 82° N. Several days later a lively discussion on the forthcoming North Pole expedition was started by some of the leading newspapers.

n 1937, a story entitled "A Landing on the Pole" by M. T. Slepnev, Hero of the Soviet Union, appeared in one of the January issues of the newspaper *Izvestia*.

The story opened thus:

"Lavrenty Grebnev was in favour of a para landing at the Pole. Yegor Provatorov dreamed of landing at the Pole in a plane. They were returning from a conference at the Kremlin. Both were given a hearing.

"Each tried to prove his case. The country's leaders questioned them carefully, listened to their arguments, calmed them with a witty remark or a businesslike observation, and suggested that a combined expedition be organized, to try out both the Grebnev and the Provatorov methods.

"The machine piloted by Provatorov reached the Pole. The field below was a jumble of rough ice. There was nothing for it but to land on a small cake seamed with fractures and wedged between towering glaciers. The heavy machine touched the ice, ran into a crack and was smashed. The crew just managed to jump clear when the ice gave way and the wreckage slipped over the side into the sea.

"The luckless men discovered they had provisions for no more than seven or eight days. The radio had gone to the bottom with the plane. But soon Lavrenty Grebnev came, or rather jumped, to their rescue from the sky. He descended first, and then, at his signal, men and dogs were parachuted in specially designed cases.

"A stretch of ice was levelled out on which a four-engined machine landed safely and picked up the daring party."

This briefly was the climax of the story which aroused keen interest and started an animated discussion.

Replying to Slepnev, Hero of the Soviet Union Molokov wrote:

"If I were asked to choose between the two ways of reaching

the Pole I would uphold Provatorov's idea of flying to the Pole in a heavy machine and landing there.

"We have no experience of parachute jumping in the polar region. I don't think it would be possible to parachute some of the delicate gear required for scientific work at the Pole. I also doubt that a wireless can be safely dropped by parachute.

"Provatorov's method is more reliable. The crash described in the story is not so terrible. An air expedition to the Pole, if one is organized, should be undertaken by several planes, piloted by seasoned Soviet polar flyers, and a landing ought to be successful."

A. D. Alexeyev, who later won the title of Hero of the Soviet Union for the North Pole flight, at first opposed the idea. He believed that there was not the slightest chance of finding a natural runway at the Pole.

"It might be possible," he said, "to find a flat field with a thin coating of ice between piled blocks but it would not hold a heavy machine. Old ice-fields, 15 or 20 feet thick, are always covered with ice blocks three to twenty feet high.

"I think it is quite possible that a more or less flat stretch of ice could be found which four or five men could transform into a runway in the course of three or four days.

"Therefore the problem boils down to landing an advance party which would find and level out a field for the landing of aircraft."

I was very interested in what Molokov and Alexeyev had to say on the matter. Their views convinced me that our best aviators were seriously considering the feasibility of an expedition to the North Pole.

I did not doubt the correctness of my theory that a heavy machine could be landed in the vicinity of the Pole, but I was eager to convince others and wrote an article on the subject.

After stating my views on the organization of a drifting station on an ice-floe, I turned to the question of the flight and landing.

"Is a landing at the Pole possible?" I wrote. "Of course, it is. I have done a lot of flying in the Arctic, in both east and west. Once I flew north of Franz Josef Land as far as latitude 83° N. Unlike the Chukchi Sea where the ice is a mass of tiny fragments as if it had been put through a giant mincer, the ice on the Barents Sea, in the western part of the Arctic Ocean, is fairly smooth. Several expeditions have confirmed that flat ice-fields are frequently to be found there.

"The achievements of our Soviet parachutists have given rise to the idea of landing a parachute party at the Pole. I doubt if this is possible.

"We know that conditions at the Pole are rather different from those at Tushino Aerodrome, for example. When the parachutist leaves his aircraft over the Pole he will have to come down not with a bouquet of flowers as in an air display, but with a two years' supply of food, a tent, various equipment, arms, ammunition and a large variety of scientific gear. All this cannot be landed by parachute. Besides, not all scientists are parachutists.

"The conquest of the Pole is quite possible. It is not a dream of amateur explorers.

"If need be, Soviet aviators and Soviet scientists will fly to the North Pole and harness it as they are now harnessing the arctic coastline and the Northern Sea Route...."

I had the support also of Mikhail Sergeyevich Babushkin, an old polar flyer and an expert on ice-landings.

"Of late the interest in arctic flights to the Pole and over the Pole has grown very considerably. Are such flights really possible? Undoubtedly they are!

"Our ordinary transport planes can do it. A flight over the Arctic Sea will be no more hazardous than along the northern air routes on the mainland. As far as temperatures are concerned those on the air routes are more difficult to negotiate.

"All we need is to increase the range of the planes by adding auxiliary fuel tanks and to equip them with superior instruments for blind flying and for flights in low clouds.

"The magnetic compass is useless for such a flight. We must be freed from dependence on magnetic attraction which has not yet been studied in the North Pole area.

"We must use the sun compass and the radio compass, install a direction-finder and improve the radio equipment...."

"I repeat that the flight is quite possible. When the need arises to land a scientific expedition at the North Pole and the Party and the Government call on us polar aviators to do the job, we shall be ready and I feel certain that we shall successfully accomplish the assignment."

I. V. Doronin, Hero of the Soviet Union, did not quite share this opinion.

"In my view," he wrote, "the advance plane should be a flying boat and not a land-plane on skis, for it will be very difficult to land a plane safely in the vicinity of the Pole. From above some ice sheets look flat, but the snow hides treacherous little blocks which spell disaster. Sometimes cracks bridged with thin ice run across a field. This ice will break on landing, which is more dangerous for a land-plane. And it is quite impossible to determine beforehand the thickness of the ice, particularly if we bear in mind the specific sunlight in the region.

"A flying boat has far more chance of landing safely on an un-adapted stretch of ice than has a land-plane. It will not go under if the thin ice collapses. Besides, the pilot will, we presume, find wide channels of open water on which to land his boat and then, when it is unloaded, tow it on to the pack."

Not only aviators, scientists also took part in the discussion. One professor wrote in an article "Aircraft or Parachute Landing at the Pole?":

"I see no special difficulties in a parachute landing at the Pole, for parachutists can always calculate the descent and to a certain degree choose their place of landing. We must have the views of the parachutists.

"Air contact with the mainland will be necessary at least once every six days in order to replenish supplies. . . .

"The use of airships is also worth considering. The Soviet Union is building ships large enough for the purpose. The *Zeppelin* flight in 1931 proves that airships are a doubtless advantage for polar exploration. They do not require a landing field and can land a party on the ice and take it back on board without any prelimin-aries.

"The airship does not have to fear the hazards of engine failure, for sooner or later it will reach the mainland by free flight.

"Furthermore, the airship can serve both the geographical Pole and the pole of relative inaccessibility* by maintaining a regular freight service with the two points...."

I confess that the article made me smile. The professor knew very little about polar aviation for he had everything wrong.

Among my most ardent opponents was Captain Yakov Moshkovsky—the famous parachute jumper, who afterwards took part in the North Pole expedition.

"M. V. Vodopyanov, Hero of the Soviet Union, bewilders me," he wrote. "Soviet parachutists have proved time and again that they can jump not only with flowers during air displays. I have but to mention the mass parachute jumps during manoeuvres and the brilliance with which they are carried out.

"The quality of our men and parachutes leaves no doubt as to the success of the operation.

"A Pole landing is not a Jules Verne adventure. We may rely on our gallant parachutists to accomplish the feat."

I had to answer Moshkovsky and his supporters and prove to them that they were wrong. And so amid the frenzy of preparations for the expedition I gave all my spare time to writing an article.

"No one, myself included, questions the courage of our parachutists. I am sure that if need be they would jump not only on ice but into a raging sea. If need be! But is this necessary in the situation described in many articles? I, for one, do not think so....

"If Soviet aviators and scientists ever go to the Pole it will not be to display their valour or in pursuit of world records. They will go there for scientific purposes, to unravel the many arctic mysteries. That alone would merit the outlay of state funds.

"The conquest of the North Pole is a serious task, and one that will take time. Such problems are not solved in a day or a month,

---

* The pole of relative inaccessibility is the area in the polar basin which is farthest from land, and in the past inaccessible. Avation has now refuted the idea. — — *Author's note.*

but take years. The first expedition will require at least a year. This means that throughout that time the scientific and other personnel of the North Pole station will have to be provided with all the necessities so that they do not suffer undue privations. Consider the weight of the supplies even if the party is restricted to four or five men.

"Such a landing would require dozens if not hundreds of large parachutes. Suppose only one comes down on rough ice and breaks or even damages a radio valve, or a thermometer belonging to the meteorological station and the party is unable to conduct any observations. Such a thing is quite possible.

"We have no precise data on ice conditions in the vicinity of the geographical Pole. Some say that the ice there is young and hummocky with large channels of open water and thaw pools. Others, on the contrary, assert that the Pole is covered with thick pack-ice and many flat fields. From my own observations I am inclined to support the latter version.

"But supposing those who say that the Pole is covered with young hummocky ice are right. Seeing this, the leader orders the party to jump and the parachutists land on the jagged ice at the risk of their lives. By a happy coincidence no one is killed or injured, and no one is drowned in the pools.

"The men alight and find that the ice is unsuitable for the landing of a plane and that it will take several days to prepare a landing field. The pilots drop food and tools for their valiant companions and return to their base.

"Let us further assume that the parachuted radio equipment is intact and that the party is able to communicate with the base. They report: 'All our efforts to prepare a landing field have proved futile.'

"Now, how is the plane to pick up the parachutists? This reminds me of an article which recently appeared in the *Rabochaya Moskva*. The author—a professor—admits that a situation like the one we had just described is quite possible but he sees nothing tragic in the plight of the fearless parachutists. He thinks that all that is required is to establish regular air communication between the mainland

and the party at the Pole by planes or airships making a trip 'at least once every six days.'

"It is not as easy to fly in the changeable and treacherous Arctic as some people imagine!

"I think the only way to establish a drifting station at the North Pole with the least possible risk and the best possible results is to land a heavy aircraft or flying boat (if you like) at a place chosen from the air. The flight must be undertaken not by one but by three or four planes. One lands at the risk of damaging its under-carriage. It is a risk that cannot be avoided. It goes without saying that the machine will neither fall through nor sink—all that is rot. This machine must carry, in addition to the crew, all the members of the party, all the major scientific gear and a six months' food supply.

"This party can level out a runway for the other machines, which will bring the minor equipment, the year's basic provisions and, having taken on board the crew of the shattered machine, return to their base. Twelve months later they will return to take off the party. . . ."

The discussion was over, but all were aware that that was not the final word. Only the flight to the Pole would prove who was right.

t the Central Moscow Aerodrome two rooms were placed at our disposal. One was littered with boxes, wrappings, rubber mattresses and packages. But more things kept arriving every day.

I looked gloomily at all this valuable material scattered on the floor. It was already the seventeenth of March and our start had been fixed for the fifteenth. Bad weather, fog and clouds had made it impossible to try out the machines or the wireless. The factory tests had been quite successful.

We planned to fly four ships in the direction of Arkhangelsk, find a suitable lake 350-450 miles from Moscow, land on this natural aerodrome and spend about a week there. The idea was to see whether we could start the engines and return without outside assistance. But now we realized that there would be no time for such a dress rehearsal.

Spring set in unexpectedly. The winter runway was living its last.

On the eighteenth of March there was a spell of cold weather. I arrived at the aerodrome very early, but my companions had forestalled me. The mechanics were fussing round getting the machines ready for a try-out.

Chief navigator Ivan Timofeyevich Spirin, stocky and soldierly, coughed as he studied a diagram.

Spirin had joined us from the Soviet Army. He is not only a splendid navigator but also a good pilot. Reserved and rather dry, he put his heart and soul into the forthcoming expedition.

"The weather today is reliable," I said, firmly clasping his hand. But inwardly I thought, "What if it gets bad again?"

"We'll get the trials over all right," Spirin replied, smiling encouragingly as if he had read my thoughts.

Then he turned to the navigators, Ritsland, Zhukov and Akkuratov, and gave them final instructions:

"We'll try out the transmitters and receivers without the engineers today. Don't forget there'll be a wireless-operator on the flagship only. You navigators are also the radio-operators. Our job is to see how the direction-finders and radio compasses work."

When all was ready for the take-off, Shevelev arrived.

"Are you going with us, Mark Ivanovich?" I asked.

"Of course, that's why I'm here."

Late in the day the tests were successfully completed. I was particularly pleased with the working of the air-brake: it weighed very little but functioned extremely well.

The idea of an air-brake had occurred to me when we discussed the problem of how to land a plane on a small runway. After some hard thinking I finally decided that a parachute would solve the problem and turned to the parachutists for advice; they advised me to talk to a parachute designer. The latter agreed to help and soon suggested fitting a brake to the tail unit.

"During a landing," he said, "when your speed is considerably reduced, you'll pull the rip-cord and the parachute will open."

"What if it opens in the air—then we're finished?" I asked with a laugh.

"The parachute would immediately break loose, for it is designed for a speed of roughly 50 miles an hour and in flight it is double that."

Such a brake suited me perfectly so I asked him to get it ready as soon as possible.

The pilots and navigators got plenty of training during these trial flights on the heavy machines, and our mechanics had a chance to prove that they were perfectly familiar with the AM-34 engines.

The machines, fitted with skis, stood ready for the start, but we were delayed by bad weather along the route.

On the evening of March 20 Shevelev and the commanders of the planes gathered in Shmidt's study. The conference opened with a weather report. Vera Alexandrovna Samoilova, our brilliant weather expert, had not had a proper night's sleep for a long time. Day and night she and her assistants collected information about the weather, plotted it on the chart, and briefly reported the forecasts to us.

From the moment Vera Alexandrovna walked in smiling apologetically, I guessed that she brought bad news.

"The weather between Moscow and Arkhangelsk will be worse tomorrow: visibility is expected to be from 200 to 1,000 yards and there is a danger of icing," she said without lifting her eyes.

Notwithstanding my worries about the start I could not help being amused by her expression. One would have thought that she herself was responsible for the bad weather.

Otto Yulyevich took the chart, examined it carefully and, turning to us, said:

"Comrades, it will again be impossible to get away tomorrow. A violent cyclone is advancing from the south-west."

Then I said: "If we can't start tomorrow and warm weather is anticipated, I suggest that we immediately change the skis for wheels, for otherwise we shan't be able to take off."

I proposed that the skis be sent by train to Arkhangelsk and from there to the aerodrome at Kholmogory.

"I suggest we wait another day," said Shevelev. "We may be able to get away on skis after all, and that would save a lot of trouble."

It was decided to wait another day.

With this Otto Yulyevich closed the conference, saying that we would meet at six the following afternoon.

A grey dawn gloomed through the window. The snow thawed and drops of water streamed down the panes. Feeling very moody I left for the aerodrome.

There I got into an aero-sleigh and with the aerodrome commandant searched for a runway suitable for taking off on skis. Everywhere were black thawed patches. These could, of course, be covered with snow, but that did not eliminate the risk of seriously damaging or even wrecking the skis in taxiing.

Having inspected the aerodrome I went to the planes and found the mechanics hard at work. What a restless lot—the planes had been ready long ago, but they were still looking for a faulty screw.

I was showered with questions. Everyone wanted to know how soon we should start.

"When the weather clears up," I said irritably, although I knew quite well that the mechanics felt the delay as keenly as I did.

The eyes of every member of the expedition seemed to say, "I hope I was there already!"

"Comrade Commander," said Ilya Mazuruk, "I damaged the left ski of my machine in taxiing. May I replace it?"

"Wait till I speak to the people at the meteorological station and then we'll decide what to do."

I was told that the weather was expected to improve, which meant that we could start next day.

"Change the skis for wheels," I said.

The order was passed on to all the flight commanders.

Having personally instructed the engineers to supervise the work I hurried off to the Northern Sea Route Administration.

At six sharp Vera Alexandrovna spread out her weather charts and began reporting to Shmidt:

"The cyclone, as I had anticipated, passed between Vologda and Arkhangelsk. Had you set out today, you would have run right into it."

Otto Yulyevich nodded approvingly.

"Good work. And what about tomorrow?"

"There'll be a cyclone tomorrow too, but less violent. It is advancing very slowly, so that it will not cut across your path before noon. I would advise you to start out as early as possible. You'll meet thick clouds with occasional rifts along the whole route. The visibility is expected to be from three to six miles. That's all I can say."

"Very good. Thank you," said Otto Yulyevich and without taking his eyes off the chart asked the ships' commanders whether they thought a take-off was possible next day.

I said "yes" and suggested fixing the start for six so that we could reach Kholmogory before noon.

The others supported me. Otto Yulyevich listened attentively to each of us.

"You know best," he said. "I'm no aviation expert. If you say we can start tomorrow, well and good. We'll meet at the aerodrome at five in the morning. Meanwhile go and rest."

"Where to?" asked the chauffeur.

"Home."

We crossed the Red Square. The hands of the clock on Spasskaya Tower pointed to twenty-five past seven.

Moscow was aglow with lights. I glanced at the sky. It was dark and cloudy, and no stars.

"What if we don't get away tomorrow?" I thought and then I said to the chauffeur, "Turn for the aerodrome."

The car turned and raced off towards Central Aerodrome.

The times I had started out from this aerodrome on big flights! I had flown five times to Khabarovsk, twice to the Chukchi Sea, to Franz Josef Land and tomorrow I was going ... to the Pole!

Approaching the machine I found Bassein busying himself with the engine.

"What are you doing here, Flegont? Shevelev told me he'd sent you home."

"I can't stay at home, Mikhail Vasilyevich. Besides, I have to look after the workers."

From the cabin came two mechanics, Morozov and Petenin. To be frank, I was not surprised to see them there.

"Can't stay at home," I said to myself, thinking of what my air-mechanic had said.

"We start at six tomorrow. Don't let us down, comrades..."

"We shan't, Mikhail Vasilyevich."

It was the same on all the other machines. The mechanics did not leave until the workmen had finished everything.

When I got home it was nearly eleven. The news that we were leaving next morning had spread among our relatives and friends.

The dining-room was full. I sat down beside Fyodor Ivanovich Groshev who looked at me and smiled. We had long ago learned to understand each other without words.

I had first met Groshev at the *Ilya Muromets* air squadron where he was a senior mechanic and I a petrol carter. I became particularly drawn to this sturdy young man of tireless energy, with his black moustache and eyes that seemed to see right through you.

With dirty hands, he went from engine to engine helping the

men to get the machines ready for battle. And yet he always found time for me, a rank-and-file soldier. He taught me the mysteries of the engine, and rejoiced at my successes. I had him to thank for the fact that I had become a decent mechanic.

We never lost sight of one another—"old friendship never rusts." Groshev frequently accompanied Babushkin on seal reconnaissance flights and he was with Babushkin in 1928 when they set out in search of Nobile. In 1930, on my first major flight from Moscow to Khabarovsk, Groshev was my air-mechanic as far as Irkutsk. He had now given up flying and was the manager of a test station at a repair works.

I was very pleased to spend this last evening with one of my best friends.

"Marusya, where are the kids?" I asked my wife.

"They're in bed. It's late."

"We're not asleep," came excited voices from the nursery. "We're waiting for you, Dad. Come on, Daddy, hurry up!"

I opened the door of the nursery.

"It's dark here."

"We put the light out because we wanted Mamma to think we were asleep," explained five-year-old Misha.

He jumped out of his cot. I took him into my arms, kissed, and then put him back to bed and tucked the blanket under him.

"Daddy, you going away tomorrow?"

"Not going—flying," corrected Vova and Vera in chorus.

"Yes, I'm going to fly, very far, to the Arctic. If you're good, d'you know what I'll bring you?"

"What?"

What could I bring back from the Pole, I wondered.

Vera came to my rescue. "Dad, bring him a little bear."

"That's right. I'll bring a little white bear."

"A live one, Daddy, a live one?"

"Of course, a live one. And now sleep!"

I kissed the children and returned to the dining-room.

★　★　★

At five sharp I was at the aerodrome. The planes were some distance apart. Mazuruk's and mine were near the aerodrome buildings and Molokov and Alexeyev's farther away with about half a mile between them. Golovin's machine was still farther away.

The puddles of thawed snow made walking difficult and the car useless. Using the aero-sleigh, I quickly inspected the planes. The mechanics were at their posts and hot water was being brought to warm up the engines.

I arranged with the ships' commanders that I would taxi up to the runway first, followed by Molokov, Alexeyev, Mazuruk and Golovin.

Now it was only a question of weather. There were slight gusts of wind along the Moscow route, but they would be no obstacle.

As soon as Otto Yulyevich arrived he and I ascended the first floor of the aerodrome building.

Vera Alexandrovna was at the telephone, taking down the weather report.

"What's the weather like on the route?"

"Just a minute," she said, her ear pressed to the receiver.

We stood by the window in silence. Finally, Vera Alexandrovna hung up.

"Flying is possible. There's a slight snow-fall in places, and visibility ranges from one to three miles. But the weather is deteriorating."

"May I give the order to start the engines?" I asked the chief of the expedition.

"Yes, do."

Acting on my instructions the mechanics hurried off to their planes. I listened carefully and heard the whir of one, two, three of Molokov's engines. Then Alexeyev's engines began to hum. But my fourth engine went on strike—the water had cooled and the heater, worse luck, was still working on Mazuruk's machine.

We had to wait, but time was precious and it was already nine o'clock. It was decided to send out Golovin first; he could act as scout and radio weather conditions.

At eleven thirty, after Golovin had passed Vologda, I went to Otto Yulyevich to report that the other machines were ready to go.

Shmidt hurried off to Vera Alexandrovna, who had received six weather reports and now hesitated.

"I can't promise that the weather will be quite as good for you as it is for Golovin."

I thought of the hours of terrific strain which we and the aerodrome staff had gone through. Of course, it was a useful rehearsal. If we went next day the engines could be started without delay. But what would the weather be like tomorrow?

"D'you think we ought to start, Mikhail Vasilyevich?" asked Shmidt, interrupting my thoughts.

"Even if the weather is twice as bad on the route, we can still make it," I replied firmly.

"I agree with Mikhail Vasilyevich. The weather is tolerable," said Shevelev.

Otto Yulyevich gave the order for an immediate start.

Then the leave-taking began. There were forty-three of us going to the Arctic, so you may well imagine what a crowd of relatives had come to see us off.

When the members of the expedition had embraced their dear ones and taken their seats I taxied up for the take-off. In my wake followed the machines of Molokov, Alexeyev and Mazuruk. Ahead, driving an aero-sleigh, was the aerodrome commandant, pointing out the way.

The weather was becoming decidedly worse with a strong wind blowing. But the machines were all ready for the start.

In the distance, near the main building, a crowd had gathered to see us off. So far they alone knew about the flight to the Pole. If the news had got round the towns and villages, millions of people would now be gazing at the sky and joining with our friends and relatives in wishing us good luck.

The commandant held a red flag. Then he raised a white one. "Ready!"

The white flag waved. I opened the throttle and four engines soared into the air.

It was the twenty-second of March, 1937, and the hour 12.30 p.m. The flight to the North Pole had begun.

At the edge of the aerodrome the plane bumped. Below we caught a glimpse of Byelorussian Railway Station and Mayakovsky Square. And there was the Kremlin!

I swung round.

Pointing towards Khodynka Aerodrome, Babushkin made signs to show that two machines were now in the air. Bassein was giving all his attention to the engines, but he did not forget to take a parting look at Moscow. There it was, our beautiful capital which I had seen so often from above, and which gave me each time a new thrill. I silently bade Moscow farewell.

The door of the navigator's cabin swung open and Spirin walked in. He tried to appear calm but his lively grin gave him away.

"North," he said, coming over to me and setting the needles of our compasses.

"Right," I answered and waving cheerfully he went back to his place.

It was 12.40 and all four aircraft were on the course, flying in formation.

The altitude was a thousand feet, visibility good, but it was unpleasantly bumpy.

Fifteen minutes later Dzerdzeyevsky, the expedition's weather expert, told me the weather was getting worse. "Snow-fall in some places."

"That's nothing. We'll get through, so long as there's no icing."

"We've covered a hundred and fifty miles. Ground speed over one hundred and thirty miles an hour," reported Spirin.

I had merely to turn my head to see our orange-blue birds. Facing me was the instrument panel which would help me to find my way in fog and darkness.

Sitting at the controls I thought of a man passing through an unlit street at night. He walks warily, stumbles and is about to fall when he remembers he has an electric torch in his pocket. In a second the torch is on, lighting the way of the pedestrian who goes on light-heartedly.

In the same way a pilot flying blind runs the risk of collision, but the moment he switches on his instruments he can see better than the man with a torch in the dark. And when he turns on his automatic pilot he can take things easy, knowing that the plane will keep to the course.

The wind was favourable but we ran into a cloud bank and I glided down to 700 feet. Ahead of us was a black wall which looked as if it would soon envelop the planes and conceal the ground. But we knew it wasn't a mist at all, but snow or rain.

Visibility became much worse. The snow forced us down another 300 feet, so that we were skimming the trees and country-houses.

I imagine the noise we made flying over the countryside; the windows must have trembled when our four giant planes passed over the roof-tops, cutting the air with their powerful wings.

The snow-fall had become heavier and we were flying by compass, but I was able to maintain contact with all the machines for the radio communication was excellent.

After five hours' flight Kholmogory was sighted, the birthplace of Mikhail Vasilyevich Lomonosov. More than two hundred years ago a country lad from the village of Denisovka, near Kholmogory, decided to walk to Moscow in quest of learning.

Lomonosov wanted to become a scientist, but this was not easy for a poor peasant. He knew want and vagrancy, and had to pose as a nobleman's son to win a way to education, until finally his outstanding talent and perseverance broke through all barriers. Lomonosov became a great scientist, who left a rich heritage in many branches of science and art. A man of the people, he heard the pulse of life even through the thick walls of the Academy and always sought not only to explain but to change the world.

He dreamed of Russians harnessing the Northern Sea Route, and conquering the North Pole. Soviet people carried out the first of these projects, for Soviet ships now sail from Arkhangelsk to Vladivostok in the course of one navigation season.

It fell to us to fulfil the second ambition of the great Russian scientist.

And here was the aerodrome. The vast field was covered with

snow and there was not a sign of thaw. We had at last escaped the grip of spring and now we could get away on skis.

Circling, I examined the ground below. The landing field was lined with red flags and in the forefront flags marked the danger zone.

The white sheet came nearer and nearer. I landed first. The snow was deep, but safe enough for our wheels.

When the machine grounded I hurriedly taxied aside to make room for Molokov, Mazuruk and Alexeyev.

We slept like logs that night but in the morning we had an unpleasant surprise: it had begun to thaw, and water was dripping from the roofs.

"Where's the Arctic?" inquired Spirin of everyone. "I had heard so much about the arctic cold that I dressed for sixty degrees of frost, and now it's raining. What am I to do?"

"Wait, we're only at the gates of the Arctic. You'll get plenty of cold yet," Babushkin said soothingly.

On the third day we got our skis and all hands turned to, working until late at night.

The machines were on skis, the engines thoroughly overhauled and the fuel tanks filled.

"Boris Lvovich," I said to Dzerdzeyevsky, "when can we expect to get away?"

"The weather will be bad for at least another three days," replied the expert calmly.

"I don't believe your reports. It's all rot. We start tomorrow."

"What do you mean?" Dzerdzeyevsky was very much annoyed. "How can the weather be fine tomorrow when clouds are coming from the south?"

"That's nothing. It'll change by tomorrow. The wind's fair. We'll get away early in the morning and be at Naryan Mar in no time."

"There really is a strong, fair wind blowing, but a take-off will be impossible just the same."

"Come along to the rest-house, comrades. We'll trust our weather expert this once," I muttered with a wave of the hand.

Exchanging wheels for skis

We read and played billiards, chess and dominoes to kill time. Otto Yulyevich combined with Babushkin against Sima Ivanov and myself. We played a total of 500 games of dominoes during the flight.

We wanted to get off as soon as possible and our enforced idleness was very irksome. Every morning Otto Yulyevich asked Dzerdzeyevsky:

"How's the weather on the route?"

"None too good."

We surrounded the weather man and argued:

"We've had enough of it, Boris Lvovich. Mind, the weather is good tomorrow!"

★   ★   ★

It was decided that Golovin would start out first. So far his crew consisted of two mechanics and Volkov, the navigator, who acted also as radio-operator. During the flight from Moscow to Kholmogory Golovin's radio had been frequently out of order because Volkov, busy plotting the course, had not had time to mend it.

Therefore, Otto Yulyevich added radio-operator Stromilov to the crew and ordered Golovin to return at once if his radio showed any signs of failure.

On the twenty-seventh of March the weather slightly improved. Golovin was ordered to fly to Naryan Mar and to report on the weather along the way.

Dawn found the mechanics still fussing with the engines. Stromilov was busy with the radio. Golovin and Volkov got into their seats.

The reconnaissance crew wore warmer clothing than we did for their cockpit was open. In addition to double fur-lined coats and fur hats they had fur masks. The two looked like grizzly bears groping their way to the navigation instruments and control column. Golovin and Volkov were so cramped in their tiny cabins that it was quite an effort to turn right or left, and utterly impossible to see what was happening behind them.

When everything was ready the mechanics clambered into the machine. Golovin opened the throttle, the engines roared, but the skis seemed to stick to the soft snow, and the plane to have been nailed to the spot.

Some men rocked the tail to help the pilot break loose. For five minutes Golovin had the engines running at full speed, but to no purpose.

There was nothing for it but to cut off the engines. The mechanics let them cool and then started them again. More hands helped. Golovin opened the throttle, and the machine rolled forward— the joint effort had succeeded.

Ahead lay a flat field. The machine was facing the wind. Without reducing the throttle Golovin rose into the air. The men who had helped to rock the machine ran behind, shouting and waving. Golovin wagged his wings in greeting, set the course for the north and a few minutes later the plane disappeared from view.

They were well on their way when the radio-operator reported that the radio was dead.

"It can only be repaired on the ground," he said.

This was hard luck but, mindful of what Otto Yulyevich had said, Golovin reluctantly turned back.

Soon Kholmogory Aerodrome loomed in sight and Golovin alighted. Taxiing to his station, he suddenly saw a man amazingly like his mechanic.

"What an extraordinary resemblance," he thought. "I'd have sworn it was Terentyev."

Just then the living image of the second mechanic approached.

"What the devil," wondered Golovin. "Are they my mechanics or an arctic mirage?"

The "arctic mirage" proved to be the real thing. When Golovin taxied up and was met by his mechanics, he did not know what to think. "How ever did I manage to lose them?" he wondered.

The explanation was simple. When the plane was being rocked the mechanics had climbed down to help. Golovin and Volkov, sitting in front, did not see this and Stromilov, absorbed in his wireless, paid no attention. When, finally, the plane was moved from its position Golovin ascended. He heard people shouting and saw them waving from the ground, but he thought they were rejoicing at the successful take-off and wishing him good luck. And if Golovin had not had to return he would have landed at Naryan Mar and wondered how his mechanics had contrived to disappear in mid air.

We, in our big planes, were unable to leave that day.

* * *

The sky was overcast and a mist was descending. Although the weather at Naryan Mar was fine, I thought it was too soon to fly.

"The visibility is so poor that we can easily lose each other with all sorts of unpleasant consequences," I said. "We'd better wait for the weather to improve."

"Who's that advocating caution? Oh, it's Vodopyanov," drawled Spirin derisively. "Since when have you become so cautious? As far as I know you used to fly in all kinds of weather."

"I do now, if necessary. When I was taking *Pravda* matrices from Moscow to Leningrad, I, of course, didn't bother about the weather. I had to deliver them at Leningrad Aerodrome by five in the morning or else the paper wouldn't appear in time. At present things are different. It's true that we are working on an extremely important assignment, but we are not pressed for time. So what right have we to risk our lives, risk smashing the machines, and jeopardize the success of the expedition?"

A few days before the take-off I had been received by V. M. Molotov, who questioned me minutely on every detail of the forthcoming flight and finally, taking my hand, said several times, "Don't hurry."

I did not forget this wise counsel, nor what V. V. Kuibyshev had told me during the *Chelyuskin* relief operations. Besides, my own experience had taught me that one must learn not only to fly but also to wait.

The snow was loose and wet. Wondering how the machines would behave in such weather I asked a pilot to go up in a U-2 light plane. He warmed up the engine, and opened the throttle, but the skis would not glide. Before the pilot knew where he was, the tail had risen and the machine was nose down in the snow.

Finally, Dzerdzeyevsky came and told us that the weather was expected to improve and that we were to be ready to start out the following day.

There was a light frost in the morning and the machines went up one by one. Spirin determined the direction of the wind, the drift and the ground speed. We set the course.

We spent a long time at Kholmogory. The "gates to the Arctic" only opened on the eleventh day. What lay in store for us at Naryan Mar?

Flying north-east, it was interesting to note how gradually the landscape was changing.

Ahead stretched the River Mezen, fringed with green pines, lakes and bogs. In front was the dark sea.

A favourable side wind was blowing. Our ground speed was 132 miles and we were drifting off our course in the direction of the sea; the river was our only guide, so we had to fly by compass.

We passed the Mezen. Forests were becoming few and far between, and small patches of green shrubbery stood out like islets against the white snowy background. Soon they too disappeared and the tundra began. Vast, endless expanses lay hidden beneath the snow. Thick, gray clouds obscured the sky.

We were passing over Cheshskaya Bay. Last year, during my flight to Franz Josef Land, it was covered with ice and could hardly be distinguished from the surrounding tundra. But now the winds had carried the ice into the sea.

Spirin changed course and we turned towards Naryan Mar. Soon the River Pechora would appear and on it the centre of the polar region.

In three hours fifteen minutes we landed safely on a spacious airfield laid out on the river ice.

It was eight degrees below zero; the machines glided easily along the smooth hard snow.

Bassein winked cheerfully:

"The spring will never catch up with us now," he said.

We were given an enthusiastic welcome. There was a stand ready for every plane and even lashings frozen into the ice to hold them.

"Comrades," cried Shevelev, "let's toss up Spirin—it's his first day in the Arctic."

"He's not the only one. We have many novices among us," I added.

"Congratulations, comrades!" said Alexeyev, butting in. "We've given the spring the slip at last. From this airfield we'll get away with any load."

"Yes, we don't have to worry about the take-off any more," agreed a number of voices.

The mechanics put the canvas covers on the engines and fastened the machines. Then we all left for town in the best of spirits.

During the evening meal, arranged specially for us, we sang and joked. Everyone was sure that the spring would play no more tricks on us and that we had left all our misfortunes on the other side of the polar circle.

At a brief conference we decided to refuel and start out for Rudolph Island next day.

★ ★ ★

We slept well and wakened next morning to another thaw. We were very angry, levelling all our fury against the innocent Dzerdzeyevsky.

"The winter has again eluded us," muttered Sima through set teeth.

The news that day was bad: at Novaya Zemlya a hurricane raged, Rudolph Island was swept by a blizzard and Naryan Mar was still in the grip of spring.

Towards evening the weather got worse. First there was sleet and then it began to rain.

We were stuck fast. On the third day the snow was a wet mass. The ice had given way under the weight of the heavy machines and pools began to form. The planes had to be hauled to another place.

"Where's your Arctic?" snorted Spirin. "Is this what you call the North?"

"You wait," I growled. "The Arctic'll show you yet."

"Will it, though? You've been promising us severe cold long ago," persisted Spirin. "We'll never get away with our cargo. Why, the place is a real bog."

"There's going to be a lecture on meteorology by Dzerdzeyevsky today," I announced.

"What's that for?" asked Bassein.

"So that we could learn to read a weather chart and not just blame our meteorologist," retorted Golovin.

That evening Dzerdzeyevsky gave an interesting account of the origin of cyclones and anticyclones. He spoke about air currents so fascinatingly that his audience listened to every word he said. It was nice and cosy in the room. The "weather man," upright, with a neat little black beard, was very popular. We respected him and trusted the accuracy of his reports. But why not have a little fun?

"If it hadn't been for Dzerdzeyevsky, we'd have been at the Pole long ago," Spirin said calmly after the lecture.

"What d'you mean?" objected the meteorologist. "Look what

a cyclone is passing through the Barents Sea. And what if ice began to form? I see you have no faith in meteorology."

"Give us good weather and we'll believe you," returned the audience in chorus.

"When flying is possible I'll tell you."

"All right. We'll wait...."

From that day we began to think in terms of weather and talked about nothing else. During the midday meal an unpopular dish would be referred to as an occlusion and a good one as an anticyclone.

Day after day, at nine in the evening, the commanders gathered in Shmidt's room and studied the morning, afternoon and evening weather reports.

The days of waiting seemed endless. Our hosts did their best to make our stay pleasant. The Nenets entertained us, arranged amateur performances, sang their national songs. We had daily invitations to the local club for either a performance or a cinema show. But each day of enforced idleness seemed eternal. We didn't like to question Dzerdzeyevsky, for his reports looked so hopeless.

Then one day he announced:

"The weather is expected to be fine tomorrow. We must get ready for the start."

Everyone beamed. Shmidt ordered all members of the expedition to bed at once.

"Don't forget that at five in the morning you must all be at the airfield," he said before departing.

The start was fixed for seven. Golovin as the reconnaissance pilot was to start out an hour earlier.

At daybreak the weather did improve slightly. But the longed-for frost did not come. I worried about the take-off: we had decided to fly non-stop to Rudolph and had overloaded the machines with petrol.

At six sharp Pavel Golovin taxied up to the start.

The comparatively light machine raced along the field for fifty-two seconds before becoming airborne. The runway was barely long enough.

When twenty minutes had passed Golovin reported:

"Flying at an altitude of 1,900 feet. Above us impenetrable clouds. Visibility good."

Having given the order to start the engines, I managed with the help of jacks to break loose and taxi up to the start. I opened the throttle but the plane could not develop speed, and the skis sank in the soft snow. Only after one minute and twenty seconds was I able to break away from the Pechora ice.

The crew was jubilant.

I circled, waiting for my comrades to get away. My place on the runway was taken by Molokov. I saw his machine run the whole length of the airfield and, failing to get away, taxi back to the starting point.

Suddenly came a radio message:

"Golovin returning because of bad weather. Thick fog overhanging the sea, machine threatened with icing."

I replied asking Golovin to break through the cloud bank and ascertain its height. But before Ivanov could convey the message Golovin had come down.

Then Spirin approached and said:

"Things are bad, Mikhail Vasilyevich. Landing with such a load is a risky business."

I was fully aware of the fact, but answered:

"It's all right, the snow is soft—we'll make it. What do you think, Mikhail Sergeyevich?"

Babushkin shrugged his shoulders:

"I hope it'll be all right."

I decided to climb and use up more petrol before landing.

Increasing the engine speed, I climbed into the clouds. The glass of the flash-light and the navigator's cockpit became immediately iced up. The visibility was very bad and so I had to steer by instruments.

The machine climbed steadily. At a height of 5,000 feet we got a glimpse of the sun which appeared very bright. The ice on the

176

glass gradually thawed and I was able to look ahead. It was fine flying weather!

"D'you think the clouds will be at the same height all along the route to Franz Josef Land?" I asked Dzerdzeyevsky.

"I think conditions ahead will be better," replied the weather expert.

Spirin suggested that we should fly on the course for about fifteen minutes and I agreed. Standing beside me, the navigator looked admiringly at the cloud bank which somewhere, far, far away, merged with the blue sky.

When a quarter of an hour had passed I turned back. I did so reluctantly, for Ivanov had just received a weather report: it was fine at Novaya Zemlya and Franz Josef Land; part of the way would have to be covered over the clouds, but that was nothing. Over the sea there would be no landmarks anyway and I would have to rely on the magnetic and sun compasses. Our instruments were first class. Spirin could take his bearings by the sun without seeing the land, sea or floating ice. He could also determine the ground speed and plot the course by the sun.

After a word with Spirin I got in touch with the ground station and reported to Shmidt:

"Weather fine. Suggest going to Rudolph Island without reconnaissance."

The reply said:

"Molokov cannot get away."

I began to come down. We had lightened the plane by only half a ton during the hour's flight. That, of course, was not much and the machine was still overloaded. The men on the ground watched us apprehensively and I, too, was worried, but I had no option, for I couldn't leave my companions in the lurch.

I decided to come down very low and touch lightly so that the tail would drop of its own accord; that would soften the impact.

Contrary to expectations all went well. The plane glided softly along the soggy snow, splashes flying from under the skis.

We were surrounded by our excited comrades who greeted us as if we had been away for at least six months.

One worker said jokingly:

"You didn't go away after all. I shan't be able to see you off tomorrow, for I'm on duty."

"Don't worry," remarked another. "We'll be seeing them off many times yet. The runway will be even worse tomorrow."

"We'll start out in the morning," I said firmly.

Next day we got ready to fly above the clouds. Mazuruk had already told us how he intended to spend the day on Rudolph Island.

Golovin took the air first.

This time we decided to follow two hours later. The reconnaissance plane would by then have covered about 250 miles and would report weather conditions.

Golovin again went under the clouds, but got caught in a fog over the sea and returned. However, this time he did not land but broke through the mist near the airfield.

A few minutes later he radioed:

"Flying above the clouds at an altitude of 4,700 feet. Visibility excellent."

Every twenty or thirty minutes he radioed:

"Weather good, flight possible."

Exactly two hours after the reconnaissance plane had left, I got into my plane and tried to rise. But the skis sank in the slush leaving a trail of muddy water. I could not get clear; the plane seemed stuck to the snow. Several times I taxied back to the starting point, trying again and again to break away, but in vain.

After a brief conference Otto Yulyevich decided we should empty two tons of petrol and fly to Matochkin Shar instead of Rudolph Island.

Golovin was instructed to change course for Matochkin Shar and wait for us there.

An hour later the machines rose, broke through the clouds and steered northward. Beneath us were clouds and above a bright sun.

Soon holes in the clouds appeared and we caught glimpses of the sea brimming with brash ice; here and there were dark lanes of open water. The farther we went the more holes we saw, and the thinner became the clouds.

Everyone was preoccupied with his work. The navigators were busy plotting the course; the pilots were steering; the mechanics climbed into the wings every ten or fifteen minutes to see how the engines were running; the radio-operators were maintaining communication with the ground and the other planes; the correspondents were jotting down their impressions. The winter party alone sat idle, their eyes glued to the windows.

Novaya Zemlya lay in front of us. In the distance loomed the familiar contours of Matochkin Shar. We were approaching our goal. Only two more stages remained—Rudolph Island and the Pole.

It was pleasant to rest in a comfortable room with smiling, friendly faces around us. Our thoughts turned to homes and families. Our people at home must be worrying about us, and probably our wires were little comfort to them.

We were making little headway, very little.

* * *

The Matochkin Shar Strait intersects Novaya Zemlya, dividing it into the southern and northern parts, and joins the Barents and the Kara seas.

The Arctic holds many surprises for the traveller. The weather is nearly always bad, but Matochkin Shar is especially famous for its local winds. Often, when the wind is mild in the surrounding area, there is a raging storm in the strait.

That was why we had wanted to head straight for Franz Josef Land. Our worst fears were confirmed, for the day following our arrival a fierce blizzard began. Denuding the mountains and raising whirlwinds of snow 45—60 feet high, the hurricane carried it from the shores of the Barents Sea into the Kara Sea. The visibility was almost nil. Outside a milky haze obscured everything.

We set up a regular watch near the machines. A rope led from the depot to the planes to guide us, for otherwise we could easily have got lost.

Seated in a warm room, we were recalling our arctic experiences when suddenly the door swung open and in walked Spirin, smothered in snow.

"Is that you?" we laughed.

"It's blowing a full gale," sighed Spirin, removing his mask and fur suit.

"Where's the Arctic?" said Shevelev mimicking Spirin. "You wanted so much to make its acquaintance."

The fierce gale made the windows rattle.

"We're acquainted now," replied Spirin. "It's impossible to face the wind—it chokes you and knocks you off your feet. I crawled uphill on my hands and knees. Our machines are in a bad way too. I'd never have thought the wind could turn the propeller with the engine off. It's astonishing, I say."

Looking through my list I turned to Babushkin.

"Your watch, Mikhail Sergeyevich."

Babushkin dressed hurriedly and walked out. The wind howled and shrieked as the door shut behind him. "Nothing can keep the snow out," muttered Spirin sighing again. "And you should see the insides of the planes! You'd think the doors were shut tight, but the cabins and wings are full of snow."

"And what if you meet weather like that on the route?" interrupted the doctor of the winter party.

"At high altitudes it's not so bad," said I intervening, "but if we had to land, nothing would be left of the machine."

Suddenly Shevelev rose and said:

"I don't like recalling the incident," he began with a catch in his voice, "but I'll tell you the story of our unfortunate landing in this strait in September, 1932.

"The Northern Sea Route Administration had only five machines which were used for ice reconnaissance and for piloting ships. In one of them, a twin-engined flying boat, I once went out on a long reconnaissance flight. We intended to skirt Novaya Zemlya as far as Cape Zhelaniya, cross the Barents Sea, and make for Franz Josef Land. There, in the strait was the so-called Belushya Bay, where we had a fuel depot.

"It was getting dark. Our petrol was nearly all gone. We decided to spend the night at the depot and start out again early next morning.

"There were six of us in the machine. Over the sea it was calm, with practically no wind.

"We entered the strait from the Kara Sea and passed over the polar station, where we are now. I saw Portsel, the pilot, ease the engine and gradually lose height. The co-pilot was watching him. Chechin, the mechanic, had just clambered into the cabin and Provarikhin took his place.

"Having informed the station that we were about to land, Ruchyov, the radio-operator, removed the aerial.

"Approaching Belushya Bay, the pilot throttled off and came down for the landing. The machine swayed and was about to touch when suddenly, at a height of only sixty feet, it unexpectedly bounced up. We felt something pushing it from below and pinning us to our seats.

"A few seconds later the pressure relaxed. For an instant the machine seemed to hover in mid air. Then it was hurled down, throwing us off our seats.

"The controls slackened. The pilot pulled back the lever but there was no response.

"Before we could collect our thoughts, the machine was low over the sea. There was a deafening report and that was all I could remember until I came to, wondering what had happened and where I was. I felt no pain and raising my head I saw the nose of the plane dipped in the sea. The engines were gone and the surrounding sea was splashed with oil.

"From the wreckage Chechin crawled out.

"Then there was a cry from near the cabin. Chechin dashed forward trying to reach out to the second mechanic, who was in the sea.

"I held out my hand and Chechin grasped it and bent over the side. Then, with my help, he pulled our wet and shivering companion to safety.

"The sun was setting and we were at least half a mile from shore. We couldn't swim the distance; besides the water was very cold, the temperature being below zero.

"The machine was gradually sinking. We were surprised that it was not being carried out to sea by the waves and wind but later we learned that the engines, wrenched from the framework by the impact, had fallen on a reef; and the control cables which were intact held the plane in place like an anchor.

"We had to make for the shore. In the tail section was a rubber dinghy. Chechin got the boat and found the valve bent. I don't know where he got the strength, but he righted the damage with his teeth. Blood gushed from his gums but his teeth withstood the strain.

"In moving into the dinghy we lost an oar. Chechin was in a frenzy and wanted to dive into the sea for it, but I restrained him—we could get to the shore with one oar.

"In the boat I realized that I was badly hurt in the leg and back. Progress was slow for Chechin was doing the rowing alone. He had suffered less than we had and was undoubtedly the strongest.

"The shore was rough and steep, and, afraid of damaging our rubber dinghy, we spent a long time looking for a suitable mooring place.

"The air was escaping from the dinghy. It had begun to crumple up and was letting in water. We discovered a fairly good mooring place but were swept past it. A minute later we spotted another. In case we should miss it again, I took the end of the rope in my teeth, jumped into the water and, despite the pain in my leg, clambered on to the first boulder within sight.

"I didn't have the strength to pull the boat ashore and so I held on to the rope, while Chechin pulled it in.

"That was how we got ashore. As I could not walk, I asked the others to hurry off to the polar station for help. Provorikhin wanted to rest, but I would not let him.

"'You won't get up if you do,' I told him.

"The two went off and for nearly three hours I trudged on, weakening with every step. Finally, when I was about half-way to the station, help came."

"And what happened to the others?" I asked.

"They perished," said Shevelev sadly.

★　★　★

The storm did not abate; it seemed as if someone was hurling snow at the windows.

A silence fell. It was not the first time we had heard such stories, which put the arctic traveller on the alert, preparing him for the surprises which the North holds in store for him.

The storm raged for three days. The machines were buried in snow and it took two days of hard shovelling to release the skis and clear the cabins. We returned from the work with blazing cheeks, weary but cheerful from the physical effort and the cold, crisp air. We had excellent appetites and dropped off to sleep the moment our heads touched the pillow.

The station personnel gave us every possible assistance. After the storm repairs were started on Alexeyev's rudder which had been damaged.

The planes were all ready for the flight, and there was good flying weather at Matochkin Shar, but a storm had developed at Franz Josef Land. When that subsided, there was more snow and another storm where we were, but, fortunately, it did not last long.

On April 17 the reconnaissance plane took off for Franz Josef Land.

Having passed Novaya Zemlya, Golovin steered for the Barents Sea. However, not long afterwards the radio-operators received the alarming message that he had run into a monster cyclone which was too much even for his comparatively light plane.

He was instructed to steer for Cape Zhelaniya.

We had intended to leave the same day, but the failure of the reconnaissance forced us to put off the start.

The days dragged on drearily. Everything was ready and tried out, and yet we had to wait.

Before turning in for the night we would console one another: "Oh, we'll certainly get away tomorrow."

But afternoon followed morning and we were still at Matochkin Shar. Rudolph Island was enveloped in mist.

In the evening a message was received from Rudolph Island: "Clear, calm." And so in the slanting rays of a dipping sun four machines rose into the air.

We skirted the eastern shore of Novaya Zemlya. Over the mountains floated cumulus clouds like fantastically shaped cliffs.

Before us lay Cape Vodyanoi. We flew on, due north.

Ahead, far away on the horizon, we could see an impenetrable black wall. It was an approaching cyclone.

The machine rolled lightly from side to side. We climbed steadily. The bright disc of the sun appeared rarely.

The cloud bank came nearer and nearer and then was suddenly right in front of us.

I climbed to 6,500 feet. The upper layer of clouds was already quite near. Another six hundred feet or so and we would be above them.

I put on full power. The engines roared and smoked, the exhausts put out light-blue tongues of flame. I pulled back the controls, increasing the speed to ninety miles an hour. The nose went up, but the machine was still in the clouds.

Then I pushed the controls forward and, avoiding the clouds, swung round to the left, circled and climbed without losing sight of the other planes.

Finally we succeeded in getting above the clouds. Beneath stretched a puffy, white sheet. The sun had set.

A few minutes later Spirin gave me my course. Ivanov reported that he could hear the radio beacon on Rudolph Island. I put on my ear-phones and could distinctly hear both "A" and "N" code signals; this meant that we were on the right course.

The going was good. But for the noise of the engines carrying us northward, we might easily have imagined we were drifting in a sailing boat on a nice, quiet day.

In the north-west the sky was aglow.

Babushkin smiled, pointing ahead.

"Did you ever see the sun rising in the west?" he said. "It's because of the polar day on Franz Josef Land."

I steered straight for the rising sun. Its rays, at first cold and hesitant, gradually became brilliant, making piloting difficult. We were in the region of polar day where the sun does not dip beyond the horizon.

Sima Ivanov, busy adjusting his wireless, was the only one who paid no attention to the wonderful spectacle.

Spirin reached out for the sun compass. We have many instruments for verifying our position in the air: the magnetic compass, sun compass, radio compass and the radio beacon. The most unreliable instrument in the near-Pole region is the magnetic compass, for its needle becomes unbalanced and keeps swinging from side to side even when the plane is flying straight.

On the horizon was the dark sea, which meant that the clouds would soon end. Then against the inky background appeared a white patch. Babushkin took his field-glasses and looking ahead smiled happily.

"Island! Franz Josef Land!"

We passed over Vilchek Land, covered with eternal ice and snow. To the right of us was Graham Bell Island.

I called to Bassein.

"D'you remember how we were stranded here for five days in thirty-five degrees of frost? We had a pretty rough time then."

First one and then another of the innumerable islands flashed past beneath the wings of our machine.

Then we saw the familiar Rudolph Island. The visibility was fine. The machines alighted softly on the spacious airfield. In latitude 82° N. we were met by two caterpillar lorries. Nearby stood two tractors and water-and-oil heaters. The airfield was well equipped. In the distance several houses could be seen. The people here had made themselves quite comfortable.

We shook hands warmly with the station staff, who were worn out with waiting. The chief of the station said jokingly:

"We were beginning to fear that you'd head straight for the Pole without giving us a call."

The crews could hardly contain their excitement. We were at the most northern Soviet polar station, almost at our goal.

Another lap, even if it were the most difficult, and we would land at the Pole.

oon Golovin joined us. Having made the machines fast, we set out for the station in tractors and caterpillar lorries. Skiing enthusiasts rejected mechanical transport, preferring to slide down a thousand-foot slope, and quickly reached the station which was decorated with flags.

On the doorstep of the cottage where the staff lived stood a white bear with a red band around her waist, holding a loaf of bread and salt. From her right paw dangled a key with the inscription: "Key to the Pole."

The bear, killed a few days before we arrived, had been frozen and placed at the entrance. With her were two little cubs which had been soon domesticated.

I was beginning to think that I would more than keep my promise to my son and bring him two little bears instead of the promised one. But when I had had a better look at the animals, I decided it would be best to send them by boat to the Moscow Zoo. This was done. The little bears were dispatched to the Zoo and their mother eaten. The meat was delicious.

We slept soundly that first night on Rudolph Island and woke up in the best of spirits.

After lunch we all, including the ship's commanders, went to the aerodrome. The mechanics busied themselves with the engines while the others poured petrol into the tanks. It was hard work. The flight to the Pole and back, with a three hours' reserve supply, required 1,600 gallons of petrol for each machine.

Before refuelling, the petrol drums had to be dug out and hauled by tractors along the soft deep snow to the machines.

We had only taken up our shovels when a strong wind began to blow and a blizzard commenced. No sooner would a drum be dug up than the drift would hide it again.

We were wearing sheepskin coats lined with fox, and I must

187

confess that these expensive coats were of little use, for the snow got inside, making them unbearably heavy. We could not help envying the Chukchi, who wear leather blouses over their reindeer jackets.

We did not give up in spite of the fierce wind. Discarding our coats we worked in woollies and leather blouses.

All hands plunged into the job for we felt rested and strong after our enforced idleness on Matochkin Shar. And we needed all the strength we could muster: it was necessary to haul 35 petrol drums to each plane, establish two hand pumps and, taking turns, see who would finish first.

Towards evening the job was completed, and in another three days all was ready for the take-off. But again bad weather detained us.

I remember that Fridtjof Nansen once said, "Patience is the greatest polar virtue."

There were two runways on the island: one, on the dome, two miles from the station, and another down below. The latter was very small and could only be used by light craft. The runways were at different heights above sea level, and it often happened that the weather near the lower runway would be fine but a ring to the top one would bring the reply: "Impenetrable fog."

Meanwhile there was nothing we could do but make a careful study of Rudolph Island. We were awed by the inspiring spectacle of the four domes capped with old ice. Wherever the glacier sloped into the sea or the strait, crevasses were visible. If a ski had got caught in one, it would probably have meant a smash. These cracks are particularly dangerous in winter when they are hidden by the snow.

On the beach huge blocks, separated from the glacier, drift into the sea. Some of these ice cliffs are of tremendous size. From the air they look like islets.

Less than a mile south of our station stands a hut built by the Ziegler expedition. During my first visit to Rudolph Island I had looked inside the dilapidated structure and found it all iced up.

A few days ago navigator Akkuratov and some others had cleared it of ice. We could see that the wealthy American had spared no expense to gratify his vanity. He had brought to the island a machine repair shop, a lathe, a geophysical laboratory, large stocks of ammunition, explosives, all kinds of products, wine, alcohol and books, including eighteen Bibles.

There were also a typewriter, saddles, dog harnesses, top-hats, tail-coats, patent-leather shoes, shirt-fronts, neckties, combs and

A moonlit night on Rudolph Island

even gold-plated skis with which the "conquerors" intended to reach the Pole.

Recalling the utter failure of this expedition I thought:

"Gold-plated skis will not help to conquer the Pole. When men are inspired by vanity, when there is no real companionship, the finest equipment is worthless."

Evenings we worked on plans for landing the expedition in the Pole area. It was decided to start out in four big machines; the flagship would land first and the others would follow. Before the take-off Golovin would make a reconnaissance flight. On reaching 85—86° N. he would report on the weather and ice conditions along the route.

Dzerdzeyevsky daily collected information about weather conditions from almost all parts of the northern hemisphere and compiled weather charts. When weather permitted, he used to go up in a light plane and, at an altitude of 9,500 feet, study the clouds, the extent of the cyclone which he had plotted on the chart on the basis of the reports.

We believed his weather forecasts although at times we did hope he would be wrong.

Sometimes we would look at the clear sky and long to get away but our meteorologist would say: "Impossible. The weather'll be bad in three or four hours. There's a cyclone approaching from the direction of Greenland."

We would rebel: "It's fine on Rudolph Island and who can say what it's like at the Pole when there's no meteorological station there?"

Then Shmidt would calm us.

"Patience, patience," he'd say. "When the weather improves, we'll send Golovin out on a long reconnaissance flight and if it's fine along the route we'll follow in the big machines."

We did not want to take unnecessary risks. The aircraft were heavily overloaded despite our careful checking. Papanin, knowing that he could take a load of no more than nine tons, weighed all his cases and bags at the depot and labelled them: "Pole, so many lbs."

It turned out that the flying weight of each loaded machine was twenty-five and a quarter tons. This was dangerous since it left only a small margin of safety; in the event of rough weather the wings might not withstand the strain.

The mechanics' equipment was reduced to a minimum; some spare parts and tools had to be left behind. The upholstered seats were dispensed with and the extra space filled with cargo. The crews parted with many of their personal belongings. Our stay would be short whereas the Pole party would remain a year at the Pole, and it was better that they should live in comparative comfort.

After much checking and rechecking, the cargo of each plane was reduced by another 300 pounds. But that was not enough. We had to cut the all-in flying weight to about twenty-five tons.

And, although we disliked the idea, we had to dump some of our petrol and make another check of the expedition's cargo.

We spent our leisure time reading, playing chess or dominoes, or listening in to Moscow.

Spirin and Ivanov were testing the accuracy of the radio beacon— a very important instrument for the forthcoming flight. Once they took their hand-operated wireless and drove in a dog sledge for two miles due north. There they got in touch with the depot and tested the beacon. They could hear well and the signals were distinct, which meant that they were within the zone.

Such a test did not, of course, satisfy them. They wanted to drive or fly for thirty or sixty miles and repeat the test from there. But the way farther north was blocked by rugged ice divided by broad channels of open water. It would be impossible to sledge there and very difficult to find a suitable floe for landing, particularly one situated due north.

Spirin and Ivanov decided to fly south where a landing could safely be effected on one of the islands.

Shmidt approved the idea, but asked what plane they intended to use for the flight.

"A U-2," replied Spirin.

"And who'll go with you as pilot?"

"I'll pilot the plane myself."

Just before the start Spirin asked Fyodorov to accompany him. "You'd be very helpful as an astronomer," he said.

"Very well," said Fyodorov. "It's a three-seater, so you can count on me."

The flight was calculated to last three hours. But in case of an emergency they took with them five bars of chocolate and about a pound of rusks. They wanted to take a tent too, but there was no room for it.

"We'll have no use for a tent—we're not going to stay there," Spirin murmured with a wave of the hand.

Having circled round the radio beacon he turned south, keeping strictly within the zone.

The visibility was not too good. There was a mist in the air, and in the distance loomed the hazy contours of Karl-Alexander Island.

Flying over the mainland in such weather is easy enough, for below you are woodlands, fields, villages, railways and many other landmarks. But here, over the snow-swept expanses, you can barely make out the shapeless ridges and the shores of uninhabited islands.

The low hummocky ice and the drifts merge, giving the impression of a flat surface which would make an ideal landing field.

We saw them take off without any misgivings for they were experienced and the weather was not so very bad.

The U-2 did not have a two-way radio. The short-wave set could operate only on the ground; the dynamo had to be worked by hand. Spirin and Fyodorov listened to the beacon signals on a long-wave receiver, fed by an accumulator and a dry battery.

We were resting in a comfortable room, but when three hours had passed and then four, we began to get worried.

"They're a long time returning," remarked Shmidt, turning the pages of a book.

"They are," I agreed.

"And there has been no contact with them."

"No. Our radio-operators are listening in, but not a sound so far. The weather's getting worse—Karl-Alexander Island is blotted out completely."

"We'd better radio to Tikhaya Bay and tell Kruze to start out and on the way here make a survey of the islands and straits," said Shevelev.

"Yes. Hurry up and do that," nodded Shmidt.

Shevelev left us. For about five minutes not a word was said. Shmidt walked up and looked at me searchingly.

"What can have happened to them, Mikhail Vasilyevich?"

"They must have let the engine freeze and can't start it."

"Then why can't we get in touch with them? I confess I'm worried—suppose they crash-landed and smashed the machine and the radio?"

"I don't think so, Otto Yulyevich. Spirin is a splendid flyer and it's quite easy to land with a machine of that type."

192

While we talked, Shevelev had contacted Tikhaya Bay. Hearing my reply, he supported me.

"I quite agree with Mikhail Vasilyevich. We've heard nothing because they can't get through. The emergency transmitter is weak. Let's hope they'll soon be here. There's a fog in Tikhaya Bay but as soon as the weather improves Kruze will start the search."

"That isn't enough," said Shmidt. "Let the mechanics get a big machine ready just in case we need it."

About two hours later a blizzard began. During the night it got worse and Shmidt gathered the ships' commanders to discuss search operations. It was decided to send a sledging party consisting of radio mechanic Storozhko and air-mechanic Latygin both of whom had plenty of polar experience.

Relentlessly the minutes ticked away. We were now thoroughly alarmed wondering where our comrades were and what had befallen them. Several days passed before we learned what had happened.

Spirin was to have landed and taken his bearings about sixty miles from Rudolph Island. But all around were channels of open water and not a single suitable landing-place.

Finally, sighting a small flat floe, he came down but didn't risk a landing because of the surrounding water.

Spirin realized that a faulty landing would mean a smash and that a relief plane would not be able to land on that floe. And yet he hesitated, reluctant to lose the opportunity.

"Land!" Fyodorov advised him.

But a voice seemed to whisper in Spirin's ear: "In such poor visibility you'll not see an ice block, and you'll smash the plane. Why take chances?"

He shook his head.

"Impossible, Yevgeny!"

Remembering that there were ice sheets in the strait, forty miles off Rudolph Island, he resolutely turned homeward.

Soon he spotted between the islets what he thought was a suitable place and, descending to about sixty feet, he circled round several times and then calmly came down.

But, having flattened out, he saw some big hummocks. The

machine touched the ice, raced along the snow and then suddenly bounced up.

Before the pilot could pull himself together another hummock appeared in front.

It was too late to circle again, for the machine lacked the necessary speed, but a crash was averted, thanks to Spirin's self-posssesion and flying skill.

Trying to prevent a pancake landing, he throttled out and, as pilots put it, held the machine in place by the engine.

Just then an ice block flashed under the skis. Despite full engine power, the plane could not keep the air and again "flopped" in the snow. It had lost its flying speed when another block appeared and this, obviously, could not be cleared.

Spirin swung around to the right, his left wing tip touching the snow.

"It's all right," declared the pilot. "The important thing is to land—it's always possible to get away. Sima, you get your 'organ' going while Yevgeny and I take the height of the sun."

He turned the machine against the wind, stopped the engine and covered it with fur to prevent it from cooling.

They plotted the sun's height on their chart and began the two-hour wait for the second reading, which would give them their bearings. A third reading would give them their exact position but that was not very important, for any deviation could be only slight.

"Well, is the radio ready, Sima?"

"It will be in a moment," replied Ivanov, connecting one end of the aerial to the transmitter.

"You get in touch with the depot while I examine the ice and choose a place for the take-off."

Spirin walked off. Ivanov asked Fyodorov to turn the dynamo and set about communicating with the depot. Rudolph did not respond.

Soon Spirin returned and asked:

"Make contact?"

"The radiation seems all right, but there's no response."

"You're tired," said Spirin to Fyodorov. "Let me try."

Taking off his coat, he began to turn the handle. The weather gradually deteriorated, clouds appeared and the sun was now and again lost behind them.

For two hours they vainly tried to contact Rudolph Island.

"Aren't they listening to us?" mumbled Spirin, putting on his coat.

"I don't think the waves penetrate," ventured Ivanov.

"Strange—to be so near and not get through."

"It isn't always possible to keep radio communication going in these places," intervened Fyodorov who had spent more than one winter in the Arctic.

Spirin meditated.

"Here, Sima. Dump your paraphernalia back into the machine," he said. "Fyodorov and I will determine our position while there's still a little sun, and get away."

Their findings showed that their course lay due south. Now, they could return to depot.

Having gathered the tools and uncovered the engine, Ivanov and Fyodorov took turns to swing the propeller.

"Contact?"

"Contact!" shouted back the pilot.

But the engine did not start.

"Must have cooled," cried Spirin from his cockpit. "Let's try the starter."

"But who'll do the pulling?"

"You'll have to do it alone, Sima. Fyodorov will hold the screw."

They applied the starter. Ivanov, knee-deep in the soft snow, pulled for all he was worth, but the engine showed no sign of life. They sweated in vain for three hours.

"Let's rest for a while," suggested Spirin, "and then we'll think of something."

Fyodorov for the third time took the height of the sun. This last reading showed that they had correctly determined their position. Ivanov clambered into his place and again tried to locate Rudolph.

The weather was getting worse. A strong wind was blowing.

Spirin removed the engine cowling to make sure that the coil to the booster magneto was in place. Having satisfied himself on this point, he said:

"If only we had something to warm the engine with!"

His glance accidentally fell on the hummock he had nearly hit in landing.

He must have had an idea for he walked up and carefully examined it.

He stood for a minute or two, looking in turn at the ice block and the machine, and then he cried out, "It must work!"

And he walked steadily towards the plane.

"Comrades!" he shouted. "Sima, Yevgeny!"

"Just a minute," retorted Ivanov looking out of the cabin. "Rudolph calling."

"Splendid," said Spirin, smiling happily, and told them his plan. "We must haul the machine up to that hummock and get the screw on a level with it. See what I mean?"

"Not quite," replied the astronomer coolly.

"Then listen carefully. Ivanov and I will take the rubber cord and stretch it around the hummock and you'll hold the screw. Then I'll rush for my seat in the machine. When I shout 'contact' you'll let go the screw."

"I understand."

"Comrades," interrupted Ivanov. "Rudolph's been listening in all the time."

"But alas, they can't hear us," said Spirin.

Ivanov told his companions that Kruze had received orders to go out in search of them.

"In this weather he won't find us," said Fyodorov. "We'll have to get out ourselves. Let's not argue but haul the machine into position."

And they set to work at once. Two held the wings and one the tail and by rocking the machine up and down and moving first one and then the other ski, they gradually inched their way forward.

It was hard work, and they often had to stop for a rest.

Finally they managed to pull the cord over the block. Stumbling, Spirin ran for his seat in the machine.

"Contact!"

Fyodorov released the screw. The impetus was good, but the engine remained dead.

This went on for nearly three hours, and all in vain. Then Spirin had a new idea. "Let's try a shorter cord," he suggested. The men worked with fresh hope, but the engine did not fire.

A blizzard developed, making a take-off impossible in any case. Ice began to form on the wings.

"Now I see what the Arctic's like," muttered Spirin clambering into the cabin.

Ivanov stood silently by the fuselage in his short fur-lined coat. He had put on some lighter clothing for the flight.

"You'll freeze, Sima, take that fur coat from the cowling," urged Fyodorov.

Ivanov obediently put on the coat and, swinging his arms, began jumping about.

Spirin and Fyodorov looked on, laughing.

"Who'd have thought Sima was such a good dancer? We've never seen such steps in all our lives!"

"Laugh, if you like," snorted Ivanov, "I'll wait till I see you dance."

The howling blizzard continued. The crew got into the machine, which trembled, but luckily it was facing the wind: the skis were kept in place by the snow-drift.

The hours dragged on slowly, as if time had come to a standstill.

Almost twenty-four hours had elapsed since the landing. The wind had subsided. Small horizontal openings began to appear in the whirling snow. Spirin suggested another attempt to start the engine.

"You never can tell—we may have better luck this time!"

"Hard to believe," said Ivanov with a grimace. "Besides, flying is impossible anyway."

"But the engine has to be warmed up."

"Is there enough petrol?"

"There ought to be. We only flew for an hour."

They tried their starter again. This time there was a spark, the first in twenty-four hours!

Now, there was hope. Spirin did not climb into the machine, but switched on from the wing and turned the booster magneto.

"Hurry—it may go!"

They applied the cord again. The jerk was followed by a spark, then another, a third ... and the engine barked, misfiring.

Spirin worked the booster magneto incessantly, afraid to touch the controls for fear of stopping the over-cooled engine. At times it knocked and snorted. Then the smile from the faces of Ivanov and Fyodorov would vanish and a despondent look take its place.

Soon the engine was warmed up and the machine made ready for flight. The weather, too, had cleared.

Spirin, followed by Ivanov and Fyodorov, got into the cabin, but then a blinding snow-fall began, and the take-off had to be postponed. The engine was stopped, but it was restarted every hour in anticipation of better weather.

Another twelve hours passed. The wind had abated. Conditions were not yet favourable, but there was a measure of horizontal visibility and the three companions, frozen and hungry, were prepared to fly in any weather. Spirin was an excellent pilot, which Ivanov and Fyodorov knew very well. Working with Finnish knives, they managed to free the skis. Spirin opened the throttle while his companions rocked the machine and with great difficulty moved it from its place. After a thirty-foot run it stopped and all got inside.

Then another obstacle. The skis had again stuck in the soft snow. The machine could not be moved. Ivanov once more rocked it. Although Spirin taxied slowly, it was difficult to get inside because of the deep snow and the propeller wash. Gasping for breath Ivanov barely managed to clamber in with Fyodorov's assistance.

Spirin put on full power and got under way. The snow was not only soft but wet and the machine was not picking up speed.

In front were ice blocks. Manoeuvring amidst them Spirin switched off and stopped.

"We'll taxi back to the old place," he shouted.

Fyodorov and Ivanov, taking hold of the wings, helped to tow the machine into position. When it was in its old place, they stepped aside and held a brief conference. When they returned, they surprised Spirin by advancing a new plan.

They insisted that he should go back alone to Rudolph, get a supply of petrol, provisions, and a tent and come back for them. Then together they would wait for the weather to improve.

Spirin heard them out but refused to go by himself.

"Let's have something to eat first and then we'll see," he said.

When they had each eaten a piece of chocolate and some rusks, Spirin checked his petrol supply and found that there was enough for only about forty minutes' flight.

"It won't take us to Rudolph," he said gloomily.

They had no choice but to build a snow house with their Finnish knives. But before starting on the job they had to have a good rest.

All climbed into the machine. They were cold and hungry and dying for a smoke.

Spirin never doubted that things would come right in the end, but he cursed himself for the fact that they had got into this scrape.

On the third day conditions improved. The shores of Karl-Alexander and Reiner islands were clearly visible.

The engine was soon started, some of the spare parts dumped and Spirin found a fairly good surface for the take-off. The weather began to deteriorate but they decided to go.

Applying the tried method, they moved the machine from its position and started the run. At first the going was bad, but then the plane began to bounce on the *zastrugi*—furrows formed on the snow by the wind.

Spirin decided not to hurry and let the machine gather speed. But when they had almost run the length of the field, and ice hummocks appeared in front of them, he pulled back the control lever gently and the machine was airborne.

About seven miles ahead they ran into a thick fog. The petrol supply was dwindling, but suddenly, on the left, the shores of

Karl-Alexander Island appeared. Spirin steered straight for the island but the mist hid it again.

Just as he was about to turn back, the shore appeared again. He brought the plane down to a height of about seventy feet and saw it again, but this time on the right. They were flying between Karl-Alexander and Reiner islands. Luckily their plane was small and manoeuvrable, and the pilot was able almost to turn it on its side to keep clear of the beach which would suddenly come at them from one side or the other. Spirin would have been happy to land but below him the surface was studded with ice blocks.

It was not long before black channels of open water appeared beneath the machine and a heavy snow-fall began. The plane was tossed from side to side. The fuel was liable to give out any moment.

Suddenly a huge black cliff arose in front.

An island? No. Maybe it's Cape Auk? Hardly ... it must be a black cloud, resembling a cliff.

Below were occasional floes. The machine was fifteen feet above the sea.

At last the long-desired cape was in sight. It would be easy enough to find the meteorological station, but would the petrol hold out?

Radio masts rose before them. Someone touched Spirin's shoulder, he turned apprehensively and saw a smiling Ivanov pointing to the ground where a huge white bear was craning its neck to watch the plane.

In the meantime, this is what was happening at the station.

It was April 30. The wind was lifting the snow in such whirls that it was difficult to understand which way it was blowing.

Molokov came in all white. Gloomily he took a broom and walked out again to sweep the snow.

"Tomorrow's May Day. Isn't the blizzard going to abate?" said Babushkin glancing up from a book. He rose from his bunk and went to the window.

"It's blowing hard. Storozhko and Latygin could easily have passed the plane without spotting it."

The uncertainty had affected everyone, especially Papanin.

"Why did we let them go? What if they've met with an accident, crashed? The expedition will end before it's properly begun, but that isn't the main thing. They're such splendid fellows!"

I did my best to cheer my companions, but I was desperately worried myself: they had gone out for three hours and now they had been away for three days.

I often recalled my last conversation with Spirin. Everybody had advised him to take provisions, but he scoffed and said, "What for? We'll be back by dinner-time."

Suddenly there was a muffled sound.

"Quiet!" muttered Babushkin, and we all listened.

"I thought I heard the drone of an engine," he whispered.

"An engine?" repeated Molokov. "No, it must have been a tractor or the wires buzzing. How could a machine fly in this weather?"

Then excited voices were heard from outside, "Look! Here they come!"

We jumped up. Behind a blanket of wet snow an aeroplane could be seen coming down.

"Here they are!"

"Hurrah!"

What a wonderful May Day present!

There were embraces and warm handshakes. Polar travellers are tough and unsentimental, but in the North, far from Moscow, they are linked by a special friendship.

The three men appeared surprisingly tanned and cheerful. But much of the "tan" disappeared as soon as they had washed and their good spirits gave way to tiredness when the excitement had passed.

"And where is the Arctic?" said someone, looking slyly at Spirin.

"Ah, the Arctic? I know now where it is."

At night the weather improved. It would have been pleasant to celebrate May Day at the Pole. But our weather man disappointed us: although it was fine on Rudolph Island, the weather on the route would be bad.

We had to reconcile ourselves to celebrating May Day on Rudolph Island.

It was a beautiful day. Knee-deep in snow, we marched with banners to the old depot. And in Moscow it was warm; people carried flowers and wore summer clothes.

At ten in the morning a meeting was held and Otto Yulyevich Shmidt made the opening speech. Spirin gave the order for three volleys to be fired into the air. Our small group, together with the whole country, sang the *Internationale*.

We returned to depot in the best of spirits. Only yesterday we had been despondent, worried about our comrades' fate. How wonderful to have them with us on the holiday.

Spirin, Fyodorov and Ivanov had already forgotten the hunger and cold which they had suffered on an ice-floe, in mid ocean.

* * *

"Friends," said *Pravda* correspondent Brontman during lunch, "I would like to read to you some excerpts from Spirin's diary which has accidentally fallen into our hands and which he intends to send to a girl friend in Moscow. The diary is in its original form, except that we have abridged it and slightly touched up the literary style. Now, listen carefully, please."

"Stop! Stop!" laughed Spirin. "I've never kept a diary and I've no intention of sending anything to anybody."

"Shut up," said Brontman. "You can't hide anything from us, old chap."

"Well, then, go on inventing things, if it amuses you," Spirin sighed resignedly.

Solemnly Brontman announced:

"Excerpts from the diary of chief navigator Spirin.

"'*March 1*. Appointed chief navigator of the North Pole expedition. In a way I'm pleased, for I'm sick and tired of flying to Afghanistan, the central black-earth regions and other hot and moderate zones. I want very much to fly in real frost. But on the other hand I am obsessed with doubt. Some of my well-informed friends, particularly Yevgeniya Sergeyevna,—'"

"I don't know any Yevgeniya Sergeyevna," protested Spirin.

"Don't interrupt," snapped Brontman.

"Go on."

"'—a girl friend of mine, said that the Arctic is an invention of Shmidt and his friends. Of course, there is such a place as the Arctic, but the stories they tell about it are monstrous exaggerations. It's an ordinary place with a normal climate . . . I really don't know whom to believe!

"'*March 4.* Have made a careful study of the subject. Read many books. According to Nansen and Amundsen the Arctic does exist. But my friends continue to say it's rubbish.

"'Judging by our outfits both are right. Bought a dozen body belts, just to make sure.

"'*March 5.* Went to the Arctic Café in Moscow. As the penguins, despite their clumsiness, have reached the Arctic without any trouble and stroll about gaily among the cosy ice-packs and bergs, the Arctic can't be so terrible, despite the polar classics.

"'*March 15.* Had no sleep for ten nights, wrestling with problem. Pale and pinched. My wife suggests going to Shmidt and asking him bluntly whether the Arctic exists.

"'Decided to go today. Shmidt ran his fingers through his handsome beard and said: "It's difficult for me to answer your question, Comrade Spirin. The Arctic exists, of course, but we've changed it since the days of Nansen. Conditions are easier there now, but . . . ."

"'And he said nothing after "but". So I am still in the dark.

"'*March 22.* In the Arctic at last! The so-called Arctic Gates have opened and they're exactly like Krasniye or Petrovka Gates in Moscow. In short, there aren't any gates at all, nothing but eating, resting and billiards.

"'*April 5.* Naryan Mar. Here we are now! The real thing! You'll not get away now. Deer, the Arctic Circle, aurora borealis, only bear flesh, walrus, seal, pelican, canned food, biscuits, and primus stoves.

"'Feeling fine. Standing up to the Arctic and the arctic cold very well. Here the frost runs into five below. Easily overcoming scurvy, successfully avoiding crevasses and leads we've read so much about.

"'*April 12.* At last! Novaya Zemlya! The Kara Sea! Ice! The Arctic! The real thing! Will soon land at Matochkin Shar! What a name! How it smells of the far-flung Arctic!

"'*April 13.* Very much disappointed. Neither bear flesh nor walrus. Fresh potatoes for dinner. However, Vodopyanov whispered to me that our crowd took fresh vegetables with them to spite me so that I don't get a real feel of the Arctic.

"'*April 18.* Today we'll be at the extreme point of the Soviet Union. There my doubts will end. We'll see who's right—Nansen or Yevgeniya Sergeyevna.

"'*April 19.* Just imagine, Yevgeniya Sergeyevna was right! There are cars and tractors here, telephone and electricity. The bears have been domesticated to such an extent that one even presented us with the key to the Pole.

"'For dinner fresh pork, apples and eggs. It's warm. The Pole is my last hope. If Peary has not lied, it is the only point on the globe where the glamour of the Arctic still lives.

"'*April 30.* Sent Yevgeniya Sergeyevna the following telegram:

"'Indignant at arctic slander stop suggest you visit Bok Strait Dik Island stop there you will get exhaustive information about the Arctic stop I got it stop so did Fyodorov and Ivanov stop best wishes.

"'*Spirin.*'"

It was an enjoyable evening. We listened to broadcasts from Moscow, Kiev and Leningrad.

Three days later Kruze arrived in a P-5 machine. He had seen Storozhko and Latygin, who were sent out in search of Spirin, and had informed them that the men had got safely back to Rudolph Island.

The days dragged on monotonously. We scrutinized the weather reports daily. Cyclones, apparently without end, were passing through Franz Josef Land.

Towards evening of May 4 the weather began to clear and Dzerdzeyevsky announced that a reconnaissance flight might be possible next day and if Golovin reported fine weather along the route, we should set out in the four big aircraft.

It was agreed that the flagship would land first. If the landing failed and the other machines could not come down before a good field was prepared, they would parachute provisions, return to their depot and wait until a field was made ready.

No one slept that night. Again and again we discussed the flight and a possible landing on the ice.

On the fifth, as Dzerdzeyevsky had predicted, the weather was fine—not a single cloud in the sky. We were all very eager to start, and Shmidt gave permission for a reconnaissance flight.

Just before he left Golovin took me aside and asked:

"If I reach the eighty-eighth degree and find I have enough fuel for a flight to the Pole and for the return trip, what should I do?"

I thought for a moment and said:

"If your petrol lasts and the chief doesn't order you back, make straight for the Pole."

"And suppose I land there?"

"That's your affair."

"What would you do?" insisted Golovin.

"Frankly speaking, if the ice on the Pole happened to be good I'd land without hesitation," I replied.

"And report the weather," he added.

"Yes, and report the weather. But remember, I know nothing about it."

He firmly gripped my hand and cheerfully went to his plane.

Finally, Golovin was ready for his long reconnaissance flight.

I alone knew the secret intentions of the fearless aviator—to reach the Pole and, weather permitting, to land there. A happy journey, and best of luck!

The sun shone brightly and he carefully checked his cargo. He was taking two months' food supply, guns, skis, sleeping-bags, a collapsible boat, two three-man tents, light sledges, an emergency radio and several petrol tins. In all he had petrol for thirteen hours' flight.

The pilot, navigator, two mechanics and the radio-operator took their seats. Golovin waved his hand and, having received the signal, he opened the engine and the N-166 went up into the air.

Immediately afterwards I gave the order for the engines to be warmed up on the big machines.

Every half hour Golovin radioed his position and weather conditions.

We read as the radio-operator jotted down:

"83⁰. Clear. Visibility good. Going ahead. Approaching 84⁰."

"Ask him what the ice is like, and if a landing is possible," I said to the radio-operator.

A few minutes later came the reply:

"Crossing 85⁰. Clear. Visibility good. Steering by sun compass and radio beacon. Ice rough but there are smooth surfaces for landing. Going ahead."

I at once telephoned the aerodrome. The mechanics replied that everything was ready and they could start the engines at a moment's notice.

When I returned Shevelev showed me a radiogram that had just arrived:

"Approaching 86⁰. Cirrus clouds on my left. Engines running smoothly. Calm. Everybody in excellent spirits."

The next radiogram read:

"88⁰. Facing a blanket of clouds. Decided to climb above them to find out their extent and nature."

Twenty minutes later there was another message:

"Flying over a thick cloud bank 7,000 feet high. 60–65 miles from the Pole. Going ahead."

"Ahead?" Spirin muttered in surprise. "He won't have enough petrol. Hadn't we better order him back?"

"He has enough petrol," I retorted. "Golovin has a head on his shoulders. And it's too late to order him back. Just try to get him to turn back with only sixty miles between him and the Pole. Personally, I wouldn't turn back."

"Vodopyanov is right," said Shmidt. "It would be almost impossible to make him come back."

Iceberg in latitude 88° N.

And smiling he added, "I wouldn't turn back either. I don't like knocking at a door without going in."

We talked, but our thoughts were with the valiant five who were nearing the Pole. Everybody was restless: had Golovin calculated correctly? Would his petrol last for the return journey?

Just then Dzerdzeyevsky entered. Asked if the weather might not change before Golovin's return, he shrugged his shoulders:

"The weather is deteriorating, but it's difficult to say if the dome here will remain visible. There's a high bank of clouds moving from the west. That's nothing, but it may be followed by low clouds. It's clear in the north—the clouds extend for only about twelve miles northward."

The information was at once conveyed to the crew who at once replied:

"Flying over the North Pole. Proud to have reached the top of the world in our orange bird. But unfortunately the Pole is obscured. Impossible to break through. Returning. Not worried about the weather on Rudolph Island. Petrol will more than suffice."

So, on May 5, 1937, at twenty-three minutes past four in the afternoon, Soviet aviators, flying a Soviet plane, reached the North Pole for the first time.

Everyone applauded and Shmidt sent a radio message, congratulating the courageous crew.

When the aerodrome staff was told that our start was postponed, the mechanics growled:

"Golovin got to the Pole, so why can't we?"

"Golovin in a twin-engined plane did not risk going down for fear of icing and you want us to take the risk in our big machines," I said soothingly.

"Now, we've got to wait again. It makes you fed up. We've already wasted two weeks here...."

Reluctantly they went to cover the planes they had prepared for the take-off.

A low cloud bank almost concealed the dome on Rudolph Island. Two airfields were made ready to receive Golovin; at each corner bonfires were lit. If he failed to land on the main airfield, the smaller one could, at a pinch, take his machine.

Four hours had passed since Golovin left the North Pole. The main airfield was now enveloped in mist and a landing there was out of the question.

In the north a gap was visible. I took off in a U-2 to see how far the mist stretched from Rudolph Island, and discovered that six miles ahead there was clear sky, which meant that Golovin would easily find the station.

Visibility beneath the clouds was quite satisfactory; from Rudolph Island the steep shores of Jackson and Karl-Alexander islands could easily be seen.

Hoping to spot Golovin, I circled at the edge of the cloud bank for about twenty minutes and then returned.

We refuelled and Mazuruk went up.

A radio message sent to Golovin warned him not to fly above the clouds but to keep beneath them.

Mazuruk came back. Golovin frequently asked for his bearings. He had evidently deviated from his course. Our queries remained unanswered.

Six hours passed and then a radio message came:

"Keeping under the clouds. Cannot see Rudolph. Running out of fuel. Broken ice and leads beneath us."

We kept our eyes on the north. The excitement was at its height, when the whir of an engine was heard, but from the opposite side of the island.

"There they are!"

"Look, over there!"

"Can you see it?"

From the south-west a tiny speck approached rapidly. Golovin came down; the machine touched the snow gently at the letter "T" and raced along the airfield.

Then it disappeared beyond a snow-drift and slid towards the old depot. Everyone ran after the plane wondering if it would stop or go over the cliff into the sea.

My heart was in my mouth, but the machine came to a halt at the very edge of the cliff.

Shmidt embraced Golovin and congratulated the valiant Soviet flyers—the first Soviet people to fly over the Pole.

"I did get nervous when we drifted off our course," said Golovin discarding his fur hat and lighting a cigarette. "The mist, too, was a bit of a shock, and your radio message was very disturbing. You told us we'd see the station seven miles beyond the clouds and we flew twenty-five miles and saw nothing but icebergs, broken ice and open water. Besides our petrol was almost gone. The mechanics had two sackfuls of provisions ready in case of a forced landing in the sea. It was touch and go—we even had to pump the last of the petrol with a hand pump." At this Golovin smiled happily and then went on:

"Suddenly a steep beach rose in front of us. An island! I didn't care what island it was, for I was overjoyed at the sight of land. Volkov, who was scanning the map, said: 'It's Karl-Alexander, not Rudolph Island. We've missed the depot. Turn back!' There was nothing else to do. I admit I was worried at the end, fearing to run out of fuel. Then I saw Rudolph Island—but we had to come down without circling."

fter Golovin's flight the weather grew worse, and was bad for a long time, fog alternating with blizzards.

We passed the time as best we could, playing jokes on one another. Bassein, assisted by Golovin, was especially active. Once Bassein smeared his high leather boots with grease. When he brought them into the room, Golovin, seeing the white on the seams and welt, asked:

"Is it good to rub boots with condensed milk, Flegont?"

"Didn't you know?" replied Flegont, playing up. "It's the only way to keep your feet dry. But more important, you'll never get frost-bite. Look," he said, handing the boots to Golovin, who examined them carefully and began to feel the leather.

"See how soft they are? That's with condensed milk."

"They are soft," agreed Golovin, turning to his companions.

One of them took a tin of condensed milk and promptly covered his boots with it.

"Put it on thick, Vanya," urged Golovin, helpfully.

Vanya tried hard, using the milk unsparingly. Then he spent all day cleaning his boots—and cursing.

The snow-storm raged for two days. The only human being at the aerodrome, where no one went, of course, was Melnikov, the commandant. To keep him company we regularly phoned him, joking and entertaining him as best we could. On the third day the wind became less violent, but a heavy mist enveloped the dome. We got ready to dig out the planes.

When we reached the dome, we found the commandant's small hut almost buried in snow. The door was snowed up, and so was the window. Melnikov, peering through a small hole in the top pane, was very glad to see us.

"I got fed up sitting here alone," he complained. "When I went to bed the other day there was very little wind. I decided that in the morning I'd go and see the machines and check the moorings.

But the door was blocked by snow and I couldn't get it to budge."

"Why didn't you let us know?"

"I did ring, but they wouldn't believe me, thought I was pulling their legs."

Heaps of snow had formed around the planes. The airscrews were almost touching the snow and there was ice on the wings. It was impossible to sweep them with ordinary brooms, special scrapers and hard brushes had to be devised.

On the eleventh of May it began to clear, and sunshine gleamed through occasional holes in the clouds.

As Golovin's machine was being overhauled after the Pole flight, Kruze was told to carry out reconnaissance in his one-engined P-5 machine. Generally, he never went beyond the eighty-fourth or eighty-fifth degree during reconnaissance and took petrol for an eight or ten hours' flight.

Dzerdzeyevsky went with him and they had Rubinstein as navigator and radio-operator. They were provided with everything in case of a forced landing. The machine was soon ready and an hour later was in the air.

Between Rudolph and Karl-Alexander islands there was a big opening and through this gap, avoiding the clouds, went Kruze.

We heard the roar of the engine as the plane passed overhead, steering for the north. Soon their reports began to come in:

"Flying at 4,700 feet over thick clouds. Visibility above the clouds very good."

We hoped that the cloud bank would end at the eighty-second or eighty-third degree and the reconnaissance pilots, having reached the eighty-fifth, or perhaps the eighty-sixth degree, would find a suitable spot and land. But the clouds continued and Kruze was forced to turn back.

At this point they met thick layers of clouds; it was a cyclone which our weather expert had predicted before the take-off.

As during Golovin's flight the weather unexpectedly grew much worse. The occasional holes in the clouds had disappeared and a light snow-fall began.

Kruze had only reached the eighty-fourth degree and was expected back in three hours at the most. But four hours had passed and there was no sight of the machine. He was still in the air, now and again asking us to direct him.

We knew that he had fuel for another hour's flight and that made us anxious, for in such weather it was difficult to find a suitable landing-place in the neighbourhood of Franz Josef Land.

A radio message from the crew increased our anxiety. Kruze reported:

"Petrol all but exhausted. Landing."

"What? Going to land? Where?" I cried involuntarily. "They'll not only smash the machine, but get killed."

Dead silence greeted my remark. Kruze's message had depressed everyone.

"We can do nothing at the moment," said Shevelev quietly. "Flying is impossible in such weather."

"We shouldn't know where to look for them," added Molokov.

The radio-operators put on their ear-phones, but all they heard was an incomprehensible squeak and the call signs of some polar station. Kruze was silent.

"Since we left Moscow everything has gone well, notwithstanding the difficulties," I thought. "Spirin had us worried and Golovin gave us a scare, but that's all over and done with. Kruze is in a much more dangerous plight. Where can they have landed? They probably need help?" I was terribly upset.

"Kruze can be relied on to make a safe landing. At worst he'll break the undercarriage," said Shevelev, throwing away a cigarette and lighting another.

"Have they got a boat?" asked a member of the winter station.

"They have, and a good supply of provisions. They also took a sledge," came the reply.

"If they have a boat with them, they're safe," he declared. "They must have landed somewhere not far away and they can make it on foot. Albanov* had a worse time. He was travelling south from the eighty-third degree, and the drift carried him back north—but he made it."

"Yes, but of eleven men only two survived," I remarked. "It's true that Albanov had only a makeshift sledge with narrow runners and wooden kayaks with a canvas covering, whereas our boys have a fine sledge and a collapsible dinghy...."

"And they didn't have a three-man silk tent. Their ten-man tarpaulin tent was heavy and cumbersome."

"Sh!" muttered Stromilov.

"What?"

"A plane?"

"Kruze calling?"

"Yes, but keep quiet, please, I can hardly hear him." Stromilov snatched a pencil and began to write:

"Shevelev, Rudolph. Bad weather and fuel shortage forced landing. Machine undamaged. Do not yet know our whereabouts. Will determine position with first rays of the sun. Meantime give us your bearings. Require 45 gallons of petrol. Kruze."

We seemed to have thrown off a terrible burden and everyone sighed with relief. The surprising thing was that the crew had found an ice sheet and landed without breaking the machine.

In the wake of the first message came another from our dauntless weather expert:

"Flight to the Pole impossible. Cyclone passing between the Pole and eighty-fourth degree. Dzerdzeyevsky."

As if nothing had happened!

Later we learned the details of a flight which had almost ended in disaster.

---

* V. I. Albanov (1881-1919) was navigator of a Russian polar expedition which sailed in the schooner *St. Ann* and was shipwrecked in latitude 83° N.

The pilot had to roam about the clouds for a long time. Flying blind he glided down reckoning that at about 2,000 feet he would emerge from the clouds and sight floating ice or islands. But at 1,300 and then at 1,000 feet there was still no gap in the clouds. Afraid of running into an elevation, Kruze began to go carefully. Suddenly, the dome of an island appeared in front of him. He automatically put on full power; the engine roared and the machine again climbed above the clouds. Then he tried again to break through and this time, at a height of 1,500 feet, he saw leads and ice and a wide expanse of open water. Believing that the plane had passed Franz Josef Land, the pilot turned back, thinking not so much about his direction as of getting away from the water.

When Kruze radioed that he was about to land, his machine was west of Rudolph Island. Passing over the water, he saw ice-floes and then a long strip of flat ice, where he decided to land. He made one circuit, but could not find the strip. He came upon several suitable ice sheets, but immediately lost them.

Descending to about thirty feet the pilot spotted a flat stretch of ice ahead, throttled down his engine and decided to risk a landing.

The machine touched the snow softly. At first it ran smoothly, then struck some small mounds and bounced up. After several sharp jerks it came to rest.

Kruze saw snow touching the wings and thought that the undercarriage was smashed.

After a thorough inspection the plane was found to be undamaged, thanks to Kruze's skill in steering clear of the mounds.

The men were in the best of spirits. They were not worried as to how they would get out of the place. Their radio was intact and as there were five big aircraft on Rudolph Island, they knew that sooner or later they would be rescued.

While Kruze and Dzerdzeyevsky pitched the tent and got some food ready, Rubinstein contacted Rudolph, arranging the time of his next report and promising to send their bearings.

Rubinstein was a navigator. When he arrived at Franz Josef Land a year ago he was unfamiliar with the technique of radio communication, but during the long polar night he had become an expert and was now regarded as the best radio-operator among the navigators.

The tent was pegged down, the primus stove was burning merrily and water was spurting from the boiling teapot. But the main item was the omelette—the work of Dzerdzeyevsky, who prided himself on being an excellent cook.

After they had eaten, the flyers took stock of their surroundings. There was only enough fuel for cooking, provided they were rigidly economical. Fortunately, the cold was not severe—only six below zero.

Their ice sheet was cracked and inspired little confidence. There were lanes of open water nearby and the ice was no more than three feet thick.

It would be out of the question to land another plane, although they might be able to take off at great risk. But they could not delay, for a single ice-pressure would leave no trace of the floe.

Twenty-four hours later Rubinstein, with the help of the sun and radio direction-finder, took his bearings. They had landed 75 miles north-west of Rudolph. The information was followed by another message from the tireless Dzerdzeyevsky, who continued to study the weather:

"Fog. Visibility poor. Flight to our camp and the Pole impossible. Dzerdzeyevsky."

Gradually life on the ice became a matter of routine. The men set up an eight-hour watch. And one night when the meteorologist was on duty, he suddenly saw a hummock move from its place and advance towards him.

In a moment he realized that it was a white bear. He at once raised his rifle and fired. The bear bounded away. Dzerdzeyevsky fired again and gave chase. The animal hobbled away behind a pile of ice blocks.

Dzerdzeyevsky ran to the place where he had first noticed the bear and saw the tracks and blood. Thinking he would find the animal dead, he followed its trail which led to the edge of the floe.

There he found fresh traces of blood. The bear had obviously plunged into the sea.

It is said that a wounded bear will always try to escape in the ice-pack. First it makes for the cold water to try to soothe its pain, but the salt sea-water only aggravates it and, roaring, the animal bounds back on to the ice.

Dzerdzeyevsky examined the floe but could see no traces of the bear which must have been so seriously wounded that it was drowned.

He turned back, following the trail to see where the bear had come from. To his consternation he discovered that before coming to meet him the bear had been actually a few steps behind him. Luckily bears are not hungry at this time of the year or our expedition might have been seriously handicapped, for the bear could hardly be expected to take into consideration the fact that we had only one meteorologist.

On May 14 we got another message from Dzerdzeyevsky:

"Weather here fine. Visibility good, particularly in north. Suggest you immediately set out for Pole. Do not worry about us. Our floe quite safe meantime. Dzerdzeyevsky."

We were astounded. Here was a man on an ice-floe which might break up at any moment, but instead of worrying about his own safety he was preoccupied with our flight to the Pole.

We could not start out for the Pole because the weather was bad at Rudolph Island. But even if conditions had been favourable, we would not have abandoned our comrades.

Knowing that a landing on the floe was impossible, Alexeyev's co-pilot Moshkovsky was instructed to get parachutes and rubber containers ready and as soon as the weather permitted to go out with Golovin and drop petrol to the stranded crew.

On May 15 the weather cleared and Golovin and Moshkovsky began their journey. Soon the marooned men sighted the plane. Golovin was about ten miles to the right of them and did not see them. Rubinstein had only indirect contact with Golovin—through Rudolph Island.

We at once radioed to Golovin:

"Kruze can see you, but you have passed to the right of him. Steer about sixty degrees leftwards."

Then Golovin saw the camp. Without the radio to guide him he would have had great difficulty in finding their small machine among the many cracks in the ice.

Moshkovsky is a parachute expert. He worked out everything perfectly so that the three parachutes came down whithin a few yards of the plane. Having delivered the petrol, picks and spades, Golovin returned to his base, and a few hours later Kruze landed safely on Rudolph Island.

To accustom themselves to polar conditions the mechanics abandoned their warm quarters and settled down in a tent which they pitched at the aerodrome.

"The air here is better than at any health resort," they assured everybody, "and it is not so noisy as at the station. But more important, we're always near the planes so that we can get them ready for flight at a moment's notice."

The real reason was that they were keen skiers. Skiing was very popular among the men; but Papanin disliked it. One day, seeing Shirshov sliding down a mound, he categorically forbade him to ski even on a flat surface.

"Nothing will happen to me!" objected Shirshov. "Why shouldn't I ski?"

Papanin who had obviously been waiting for just such an opportunity said angrily:

"Who d'you think you are? Isn't Mazuruk as good a skier as you are, and there he is laid up with a strained muscle. Akkuratov isn't a bad skier either, and I've seen him almost collide with a stone."

Not so long ago, when the wind was blowing from the station towards the dome, our skiers would attach a long rope to the parachute lines and, holding on to it, rise to the aerodrome at wind speed.

Once Papanin got on to me.

"These circus shows should be forbidden," he cried, pointing to some men unfolding a parachute for a ride. "Isn't that asking for trouble? The wind may drive them heaven knows where!"

"They're having a good time—why spoil their pleasure?" I said, but in fact I quite agreed with him. Afterwards Shmidt strictly forbade this needless and dangerous sport.

Not only the weather but the nature of the snow changed frequently at Rudolph Island. One day the skis would slide easily and you would shoot down a small slope, barely able to brake with the sticks, and the next day you could hardly move your feet.

At a temperature ranging from three to six below zero the snow became soft and skiing was difficult. After a snow-fall conditions became even worse. Then the skiers would say, "It's impossible to get under way in our heavy machines." But when the surface was warmed up by the sun's rays, the snow would settle, and then after a frost of ten to fifteen degrees it was difficult to keep one's balance.

"Just the weather for flying," our skiers would say delightedly.

At daybreak on the seventeenth of May the sky began to clear. Wasting no time Golovin set out on a reconnaissance flight.

That day the snow was unusually soft and the pilot had to repeat the run before he was airborne. That was disturbing, and we wondered how the heavily loaded planes would get away.

After about forty minutes Golovin radioed:

"High cloud bank ahead. Shall I climb it or return?"

As we conferred, weather conditions on the island grew worse. Shevelev ordered an immediate return. "Turned back, see land," radioed Golovin.

Melnikov laid out the landing "T" and lit a bonfire.

An hour passed, but Golovin was still away. We asked him for his bearings. Suddenly our radio-operator was interrupted by Stromilov, Golovin's radio-operator, who first asked for the zone and two or three minutes later for his course.

"It's beginning," I thought. "Lost their bearings. Must have mistaken Belaya Zemlya for Rudolph."

The weather continued to deteriorate. A mist hung over the sea. The dome was obscured. We got ready the small airfield.

A thick, grey cloud descended upon us as if intent on pressing us to the ground.

Four dreary hours passed. Shevelev and I were sitting in the radio room. Golovin did not answer our calls.

Suddenly Dzerdzeyevsky ran in. "He's coming!"

We ran out and heard the drone of an engine from the direction of Jackson Island. I climbed up the pole of our meteorological station to try to get a glimpse of the plane. But the sea was enveloped in mist and I could see nothing.

The noise grew louder and louder, the plane was heading straight for us and we expected it to emerge from the fog at any moment.

Then suddenly the whir of the engines declined to the left and grew dimmer.

"Radio immediately that he is gone off west of Rudolph," stormed Shevelev. "Tell him to turn 180 degrees and come towards us."

But the plane went on its way till we could no longer hear it.

"Why doesn't he reply?" cried Shevelev.

Staring into the grey murk I was beginning to imagine all sorts of things when Stromilov radioed:

"Landing, listen to us on the six-hundred-metre wave and on short waves."

"Mark Ivanovich," I cried gripping Shevelev by the arm, "if only it's nothing worse than a crippled machine ...."

Life at the station was at a standstill. We all walked on tiptoe and talked in whispers.

The radio-operators' room was crowded with men gazing silently at the loud speaker and scarcely daring to hope for another message from Golovin. I tried not to look at my neighbour for fear of betraying my harrowing thoughts.

Only Bogdanov, the radio-operator, was wholly absorbed in his work. We watched his hands, deftly setting the radio, and every twitch of his face.

At times it seemed that the walls must move apart under his

keen gaze, that he could see the whole world and the floe where Golovin was stranded. A faint rustle in the loud speaker made everybody jump.

"It's Cape Chelyuskin calling Dikson Island," said Bogdanov laconically.

Then all of a sudden he turned a knob and stopped dead. In a few seconds, which seemed like an eternity, he raised his hand and whispered, "Stromilov calling!"

For an instant we were stunned. Then we all jumped to our feet and rushed to the radio-operator.

"Have they landed?"

"How?"

"Safely?"

"Quiet, please!" Bogdanov checked the flow of questions. "Stromilov's only calling. He hasn't said anything about a landing. Wants to know if we can hear him."

But we persisted.

"Find out how they landed."

"Is everyone safe?"

"How's the machine?"

Bogdanov told Stromilov that he could hear him well, and passed on our questions.

A minute passed, then another and another . . . .

"Well?" we tormented the radio-operator. "How did they land?" Bogdanov shrugged:

"Stromilov wants to know our wave-length."

"To hell with the wave-length! Ask him if everybody's all right."

"Anybody hurt?" tapped the radio-operator.

With growing impatience we waited for the answer, but instead there came another query:

"How's the tone?"

This composure was getting on our nerves. We insisted that Bogdanov ask again about the landing.

Stromilov replied:

"Ship's commander Pavel Golovin is sitting astride an ice block and writing a message. Wait, he's finishing."

We were thoroughly indignant. They must be all alive and well or Stromilov would not have been so calm. That, of course, was the main thing, but why should they try the patience of their colleagues!

Finally, a long message came. Golovin reported that, fearing to run into an elevation, he had decided to alight, but for some time that was impossible because of broken ice. Finally, seeing a suitable floe, he had come down without any damage. According to our radio messages, which Golovin hadn't had time to read during the flight, they were near Rudolph. They had enough petrol, and so, as soon as the weather permitted, he hoped to return to the depot.

I vividly imagined the plane pressed to the ground by the mist and skimming the ice blocks and leads at a breathless pace. It was natural, therefore, that the pilot, afraid of colliding with some unknown island, gave all his attention to the instruments and had no time to answer radio messages.

When I met Golovin I found I had been right. While we persisted with our messages, he had been flying through impenetrable clouds at a height of ten-thirteen feet.

Golovin's message brought the station back to life.

Again we waited for favourable weather, but the forecasts were the same: fog, low clouds, the risk of icing.

Meanwhile Alexeyev and Babushkin put forward a new plan for the Pole flight.

They suggested that the flight should be made first by one plane since that would obviate the danger of a collision in mid air and so increase its manoeuvrability. Besides, in case of failure it would be easier to equip it for another flight, and less fuel would be required. Petrol was becoming scarce and we couldn't afford to waste it.

That same evening the matter was discussed at one of our regular conferences and a decision taken to send the flagship first; the other machines would follow as soon as the flagship landed.

This plane was to carry the chief of the expedition, two pilots, three mechanics, a navigator, a radio-operator, the Pole party of four and a cinema-operator.

The cargo was rearranged. The flagship took more provisions and implements to prepare a landing-place. The polar party's equipment was transferred to the other planes.

It was May 19 and we had been a month on the island.

Large masses of dark clouds hovered over the ground. The runway was enveloped in mist and there was nothing we could do but wait.

After supper I went out for a breath of fresh air. Looking up, I saw ragged clouds and open spaces with a blue sky gleaming through. The holes became more frequent, then a shimmer of light appeared and finally the sun.

I hurried off to see Shmidt and found the whole company gathered. Dzerdzeyevsky had brought the weather chart with the latest information; the weather was expected to be fine in the morning.

Seeing me he raised a hand in greeting.

"Get ready for the flight, Mikhail Vasilyevich," he said.

Later at night we drove to the aerodrome. The polar sun shone brightly from a cloudless sky.

Everyone helped to get the plane ready for the take-off. Some shovelled the snow from the skis, and others attached a line from the undercarriage to a tractor which would pull the plane free.

By four in the morning the plane was ready.

Dzerdzeyevsky hurried up with the latest weather report. From the look of the "weather boss" the news was not reassuring.

"There are thick clouds ahead," he said.

After a brief conference it was decided to fly.

"Keep the planes ready," said Shmidt to Molokov, "and look after them. If the weather at the Pole is fine, I shall call you at once."

We shook hands.

Molokov's eyes had a warm glow as he walked up and embraced me. Mazuruk came with set lips. He gazed into the distance where the sparkling surface of the ice merged with the sky.

"Soon we too . . .," he muttered, pressing my hand.

I understood.

The sun was still bright, but far away on the horizon translucent clouds floated. Would they grow into thick dark masses before our plane reached its destination?

We had to hurry. I took my seat at the control stick. Good-bye, Rudolph! Good-bye, friends! Until we meet again!

The whirling screws rent the air. In another second the roaring engines forced the machine forward.

The plane gathered speed, hopped once, twice, three times....
In twenty-four seconds we were airborne.

Down below, near the station depot, our delighted colleagues waved their hands, and tossed hats into the air.

Then the station disappeared.

At first we flew over an immense conglomeration of bergs and ice blocks, over vast ice sheets with huge ravines running through them. But the farther north we went the smoother became the surface.

I was so glad to be heading for the Pole that I almost forgot about the course in my excitement.

We climbed gradually to a height of three thousand feet. The temperature was twenty-three degrees below zero. A steady head wind was blowing. Our ground speed was insignificant. The machine was behaving well; there was no pitch which might prove dangerous for our overloaded plane.

The sun shone brightly, the horizon was clear. I followed closely the indications of the sun compass. In my ear-phones I heard the regular signals of the radio beacon. We were within the zone.

After twenty minutes' flight dark patches were sighted. Babushkin looked through his binoculars, then bent over to me and shouted, "Looks like fog!"

"That's nothing, so long as the Pole's open," I thought.

Soon we were able clearly to discern the ragged clouds. Farther north they were thicker. Gradually a mist hid the ice. Feather clouds hovered above.

We maintained an altitude of 4,500 feet. The weather was getting perceptibly worse. We were now flying between two layers of clouds.

Shmidt came up and, pointing to the bank of clouds, asked, "What d'you think of it?"

"We can go on," I replied.

We decided to forge ahead and turn back only if the upper and lower clouds merged and icing began.

The regular hum of the engines gave free rein to my thoughts and I imagined myself gliding down on the ice. I did not suspect that at that very moment my air-mechanics were having a troublesome time. Morozov had noticed steam rising from the left inside engine, and he and Bassein began to examine it.

Thinking the drain-pipe was to blame, Bassein plugged it with his hand but the steam continued to escape. Finally, Morozov discovered that the steam issued from under the wing. Passing a hand over the wing seam, he found it wet and then they realized what the trouble was: the anti-freeze was escaping from the radiator.

Bassein went up to Shmidt and, stooping so that no one should hear him, said:

"Within an hour or maybe less, one of the engines will go out of commission. There's a damaged line—the anti-freeze is dripping from the engine. We'll have to make a forced landing."

"A forced landing? Look at the thick clouds. How can we land?"

After a pause, Shmidt asked, "Have you reported to Vodopyanov?"

"Not yet, but I know what he'll say: 'We'll manage with three engines.'"

"I too think that we can go on. If we must land, let it be nearer the Pole. Anyway, you'd better report to your commander."

Bassein approached me:

"In an hour or so one of our engines will go out of commission."

I did not get the meaning of what he said, for my thoughts were far away at the Pole.

"What engine? Why?"

"The left inside one," replied Bassein. "It's losing its anti-freeze somewhere under the wing. The radiator has probably sprung a leak."

"Have you mentioned this to anyone?"

"Only to Otto Yulyevich."

"And what did he say?"

"He told me to report to you."

I thought for a while and then said firmly:

"We'll go ahead on three engines, Flegont! Then we'll see."

"Quite right. Otto Yulyevich thinks the same."

"Excellent. But, Flegont, not a word to anybody else."

Otto Yulyevich watched us closely. He must have guessed my decision, for when our eyes met he smiled. And I thought his smile expressed approval.

When Bassein left, Otto Yulyevich walked up.

"Well, what have you decided?" he asked.

"We'll go ahead on three," I told the chief. "Just listen to the roar of the engines. Don't you think the left inside one, the one that will stop within the next hour, is running better than the others?"

Otto Yulyevich put an arm gently round my shoulder:

"Keep calm! We're flying alone and we can afford to take some risk."

On his way back to the left wing Bassein was stopped by Papanin, who had been watching the mechanics for some time. He thought it strange that they should crawl into the wing and then hurry off to the reserve tanks or for some gear.

Taking the mechanic's arm, he asked quietly, "What's happened?"

"Where?"

"There, in the wing."

"In the wing? Nothing," replied Flegont, shrugging his shoulders.

"Anything wrong?" persisted Papanin, looking searchingly into Bassein's eyes.

But he read in them nothing but serene composure and mild surprise.

I steered through the clouds. The instruments took all my attention, but from time to time I would listen to the orderly whir of the engines. There was not the slightest indication of any irregularity in their mighty roar. All four engines seemed in excellent trim.

"If one engine did go out of commission, would it really mean we should have to come down?" I wondered, unwilling to believe it. I wished the clouds would end, so that if the worst came to the worst, it would be easier to find a suitable landing-place.

Spirin came up, looked at all the instruments and checked the course. I sat quietly at the controls. He looked round suspiciously and, bending, said, "Beastly weather!"

"Oh, that's nothing. It's a long way to the Pole and we'll have some good weather yet," I replied in a matter-of-fact tone.

"Shall we?" he drawled doubtfully.

"Of course, we shall! Where are we now?"

"Approaching the eighty-fifth degree, about four hundred miles from the Pole."

Spirin was watching me closely and I thought: "You don't know the engine may stop any moment. Shall I tell you? No, there's no use upsetting you."

However, it turned out that Spirin had known before I did that the engine was losing its anti-freeze and he, too, had decided to say nothing.

The weather got worse and worse. The clouds looked as if they were about to merge and we seemed to be tearing straight into the jaws of a huge monster.

I glanced at Babushkin who was sitting at the second control column and really suspected nothing.

I nodded towards the window as if to say, "Pretty bad, isn't it?" Babushkin shouted back, "Never mind, Misha—we'll make it."

While Babushkin and I piloted the machine, Bassein, Morozov and Petenin were not idle. They pierced the metal sheeting of the lower part of the wing, found a leakage in the piping of the radiator and bound it with insulating tape and braid. But the loss of the anti-freeze mixture continued. Drop by drop the precious liquid was escaping from the engine.

It is difficult to say which of the mechanics first thought of a way of stopping the leakage. The idea probably occurred to all three at once. At any rate they all worked with a will. Removing the tape, they applied dry flannel to the crack in the piping and when it became soaked with the mixture, wrung it out into a bucket and then pumped it back into the engine.

For this seemingly simple operation the mechanics had to discard their mittens and, in twenty degrees of frost, with a strong wind blowing, expose their bare hands to the outside cold. Very soon the skin came off their frost-bitten fingers and blisters appeared on their hands from the scalding liquid.

The corridor between the clouds was narrowing. Finally, the two banks came together, and we found ourselves in a milky haze.

I gave all my attention to the instruments. We were flying blind. I had lost the count of time. The thought that the engine would soon give out lingered in my weary mind.

All of a sudden I heard Bassein say, "Don't worry, Commander—the engine won't fail!"

I was overwhelmed with joy. Without turning, I nodded: "Thanks, old man!"

We continued to fly blind, keeping a straight course along the meridian. Noisily the propeller blades cut through the clouds.

Shmidt came up and asked:

"How d'you feel? The mechanics say the engine will not fail us."

"Everything's all right, Chief. We'll get there now."

The signals from the radio beacon constantly reminded us that we were within the zone. The clouds were thinning. Through the haze glimmered the faint rays of the sun.

At the eighty-eighth degree a bright sun appeared, as if someone had drawn aside a huge cloud-spun blind. Its rays slid across the sheeting, setting off a myriad of gay little sparks.

We fleeted past boundless snowy deserts. From a height of 5,500 feet the ice seemed very smooth, as if we could land wherever we liked.

The four engines were running perfectly but one was maintained by human effort. The three mechanics, despite the tormenting pain, worked in turn, pouring the precious liquid back into the engine.

We all felt sure that the weather would be fine at the Pole, too. However, we had another shock when we met more clouds. We might have flown beneath them but we should have lost sight of the sun and made it very difficult for Spirin to determine our position.

We had sixty miles to go. It was decided that if a landing at the Pole proved impossible we would return to the eighty-eighth degree and alight there. As soon as the weather cleared we could go on to the Pole.

At intervals of ten minutes Spirin measured the height of the sun. "We'll be at the Pole in twenty minutes!" he said.

I nodded, looking for a hole in the clouds and wondering whether the mist reached the very surface of the ice.

The twenty minutes dragged on endlessly. From the navigator's cabin Spirin walked out leisurely, took measurements of the sun's height and went back to make his calculations.

Everyone in the plane knew that we were approaching our goal and waited expectantly.

Spirin appeared again. Solemnly he declared:

"We're over the Pole!"

I felt like shouting at the top of my voice for the whole country to hear me! My joy was boundless.

The Pole! For centuries men had striven to reach it. They had sacrificed their lives, trying to force a passage to the roof of the world.

And here was I—once a simple village lad, now an aviator, trained by the Communist Party—over the Pole! In a few minutes I would land at a place where no plane had ever alighted.

The news that we had reached the Pole spread like wildfire. I saw the exultant faces of my comrades and Shmidt appeared from the navigator's cabin. He made straight for me, evidently about to say something, but I forestalled him.

"Otto Yulyevich, we're over the Pole! May I glide down?" I asked in wild excitement.

"Just a minute," he said gently. "Don't hurry—Spirin's checking his readings."

"I'm in no hurry. I simply want to save the fuel," I replied, justifying myself.

"I see," he laughed.

Spirin came up and confirmed that we were over the Pole. "But I suggest we go a little farther," he said.

"What for?"

"To make sure."

"Right," agreed Shmidt. "It's best to fly beyond a target rather than stop short of it."

"The Pole's beneath us," says Spirin

At first I protested.

"Spirin couldn't have made a mistake—the Pole is under us!"

But after a moment's thought I agreed: it was better to overfulfil an assignment than to underfulfil it.

Otto Yulyevich wrote out a radio message that we were over the Pole and Ivanov began transmitting it to Moscow. But when he had tapped out one or two words, the radio went out of commission. Communication with the outside world was cut.

For another ten minutes I flew on the other side of the Pole until finally I was given permission to break through the clouds.

"Now, do as you like!" said Otto Yulyevich Shmidt, hiding a smile in his beard.

First I swung round at an angle of a hundred and eighty degrees: at least we would be nearer the Pole. Then I throttled down and, from an altitude of 5,500 feet the plane plunged into the clouds as if it were diving off a monster tower.

The sun vanished. Every face was pressed against a window.

I wondered anxiously if there would be any flat ice down below, and if the clouds were right down to sea level.

Three thousand feet—I couldn't see anything. 2,700 ... 2,400 ... 2,100 ...

All at once, through the clouds, ice flashed and disappeared again before we could get a good look at it. And then there was again gloom.

1,800 feet ... At last! As if relenting, the cloud bank opened up. Before our eyes lay the panorama of the roof of the world. Boundless sparkling ice-fields were seamed with blue lanes of open water, and the vast ocean looked as if it had been paved with slabs of varying shape and size, like irregular geometrical figures drawn by a child's unsteady hand.

"We'll soon know who was right," I thought. "I or my opponents, who held that a landing on the Pole was impossible."

The next few seconds would give the answer.

I circuited, looking for a suitable ice-field. The machine continued the descent. The engines were running at half power.

"Mikhail Vasilyevich, here's an excellent field!" someone shouted frantically.

"Land on mine, Commander, look at it!" cried another.

"Wait, there are plenty of them," I said.

Then I saw a long stretch of ice and decided that as we had been flying against the wind, it would be blowing along the floe and therefore a landing would be possible.

Otto Yulyevich came up. "Found one?"

"Yes." I swung round and indicated the sheet with my eyes. "This one'll receive us hospitably, I think."

"A beauty!" agreed Mikhail Sergeyevich.

Shmidt looked intently at it. Then Spirin came and suggested that I come down to about sixty feet and fly over it.

All eyes were on the ice below. Even the mechanics had stopped collecting the anti-freeze mixture: it was no longer necessary, for we had reached our destination.

Sima Ivanov alone did not bother about any ice-floe. He was too busy repairing his radio which had gone wrong at the worst possible moment. He heard Moscow calling, he heard Rudolph—but could not answer. He could not let them know that we had reached the Pole.

Understanding Ivanov's feelings, Papanin tried to distract Sima's attention, but in vain.

I descended to about 150 feet, trying not to go too far in case I should lose sight of my ice-field. Guided by the dark narrow cracks running through the field, I glided down for about another sixty feet.

In front towered formidable ice blocks and beyond them was my chosen field.

"Here she is!" I shouted to Spirin and Babushkin. "Look!"

The field with a chaos of jumbled ice blocks round it reminded one of an ancient fortress within a towering wall.

Here and there it was dotted with little mounds, but in the centre was a smooth stretch of ice about seven hundred yards long and four hundred yards across.

Flying over the field we noticed *zastrugi* like those on Franz Josef Land or in the tundra. Judging by the ice blocks, the ice was thick and old.

Turning, I passed over the field once more. Spirin opened the hatch, ready, at my signal, to release a smoke-box. This box would burn for only a minute and a half; during this time I had to turn, determine the direction of the wind by the smoke, and land.

Spirin released the box on the spot where the machine was to touch.

Quickly swinging around, I turned into the wind (as I had anticipated, it was blowing along the field) and came down another thirty feet.

The machine raced forward barely clearing the ice blocks. In front lay a strip of flat ice. A stream of black smoke drifted towards us along the white snow. I asked Babushkin, the moment the skis touched snow, to pull the rip-cord handle and open the parachute which served as an air-break.

I gently eased the engines, flattening out to make the landing; the tail dropped and for a second or two the machine travelled

Flagship at the North Pole

about three feet above the ice. Then I pulled the control lever and the skis softly touched the virgin snow. I cut off the engines just in case the ice should not sustain its weight.

Babushkin pulled the rip-cord, opening the parachute. The machine slid forward and did not sink, and so I switched on again, deciding to land with the engines running.

After a run of 250 yards the machine stopped.

May 21, 11.35 a. m.

Before we had realized it, we were in each other's arms.

A few minutes later we were standing at the Pole.

The North Pole was ours!

Within ten minutes of landing everyone was busy working.

Spirin and Fyodorov were making astronomical observations and recording them. They caught glimpses of the sun as it appeared for an instant through a break in the clouds, and tried more accurately to determine their position. The mechanics were fussing about the machine, covering the engines with tarpaulin. Ivanov and Krenkel were arranging the radio while everybody else was helping to put up the mast.

Soon it was in position, but then the radio-operators reported that the wireless was dead. We at once began unpacking Krenkel's.

Within an hour a tent was pitched for the wireless station and an aerial secured to the mast. But then there was another delay: the accumulators had run down in the frost and had to be recharged.

Meanwhile in Moscow and Rudolph dozens of radio stations were searching the air for our signals. Shevelev was instructed by radio to get the other three machines ready and take the very first opportunity of setting out in search of U.S.S.R. N-170.

The three machines were standing ready but bad weather delayed the start.

Bogdanov and Stromilov put on their ear-phones and listened intently on two sets. The radio room was packed. Shevelev smoked continuously, puffing nervously at his cigarette. At times the silence was broken by a faint whisper as one person and then another spoke his thoughts aloud.

"What's happened?" wondered Mazuruk. "They were transmitting a message and then, in the middle of a word—silence. The machine couldn't have fallen to pieces in mid air."

In a few minutes the silence was broken by a hoarse whisper from Alexeyev:

"The radio must have failed. But they have another."

"Stop this guess-work," begged Shevelev. "You're disturbing the radio-operators."

But himself tormented by misgivings, he soon began to make his own guesses.

"Why couldn't the radio have gone wrong?" he asked. "Slight damage to the converter and the thing's dead."

Zhukov, navigator and radio–operator, objected:

"The transformer or a valve would be more likely to give trouble. The converter can't fail."

"Haven't they got a spare one?" asked Orlov, a pilot.

"No," replied Shevelev. "Converters are very reliable, but the winding may have burnt. I wired Moscow that I thought communication was cut owing to the failure of the converter."

"But can they hear us?" asked someone.

"They can," replied Alexeyev.

"Anyhow, there's no need to worry yet," remarked Shevelev, opening another package of cigarettes. "They'll land. And if Ivanov's radio really has failed, they'll use Krenkel's."

Thus passed eight dreary hours. Nobody left the room. Shevelev tried to induce the others to get some sleep.

"You've stayed up for twenty-four hours," he argued. "Supposing the weather improves and we have to start? Go and rest!"

"How can we?" they protested, unwillingly leaving the room. Bogdanov was dispatched to bed along with the others. Only Stromilov remained on duty.

* * *

Sima Ivanov did not leave the plane. He tinkered with the radio but he could not repair the converter. As I was leaving the tent where the accumulators were being recharged, I saw Babushkin pitching our sleeping-tent.

"Hi, there!" he called to me. "You want to live at the Pole, but others have got to build a house for you—is that it?"

I joined them. Near by Shmidt was walking backwards and forwards, hands behind his back. When we began building a snow wall round the tent, he joined in and the four of us soon completed the job. Then we pumped air into the collapsible mattresses, spread them out on the snowy floor, and brought four sleeping-bags. Our tent began to look snug and comfortable.

"I wonder if the foundations are strong?" I asked.

"They're strong enough to hold you and me," replied Babushkin. And they began to argue. One said the ice was no more than six feet thick, and the other said ten.

Shmidt looked at his watch: "Nine thirty-five p. m."

Ten hours had already passed. It was difficult to make conversation, everybody was too much upset at the absence of communication with home stations and the anxiety our silence must be causing. I tried to make jokes but they fell flat.

Sima scrambled out of the plane.

"I've been listening to Rudolph," he said. "They're calling incessantly."

"Don't listen and you won't worry," I advised and, putting an arm round him, added, "Krenkel'll soon have his wireless going."

But twenty hours passed and still there was no communication.

In his radio room Stromilov worked tirelessly, calling the N-170 and Krenkel on all wave-lengths. He knew the wave-lengths of both Ivanov and Krenkel. Besides he had made the transmitter for Krenkel and was to stay on at Rudolph to consult the North Pole radio-operator if necessary.

Overcoming his drowsiness Stromilov listened to every sound in the air and now and then called himself without getting any answer.

It was very quiet in the room. Everyone had retired for the night. All at once he was on the alert: he heard familiar sounds in his ear-phones.

He turned up the condenser and listened breathlessly. Then he shouted so loudly that in the next room everyone jumped out of bed.

"Calling, calling," he went on shouting.

He began to tap out something, and then suddenly he took off his ear-phones and ran out of the room.

None had ever known Stromilov get so excited. He was usually very composed, but now he seemed to have gone out of his mind. He ran into the adjoining hut, calling, "Mark Ivanovich, get up! They've landed!"

"What? Who's landed?"

"It's the accumulators! They've landed! I got in touch with them! They're at the Pole!" Stromilov blurted out and rushed back to his room.

In another minute the population of the island had gathered there. Stromilov was taking down the first radio message from the Pole.

All eyes were on his pencil. Finally, the message was handed to Shevelev who glanced over it and then read aloud:

"All well and plane intact. Sima's converter is gone. If communication is cut, call at midnight. Otto Yulyevich is writing a message. Ice first class."

Perched on a sealed food case, Shmidt was writing in a note-book on his knees. We surrounded Krenkel, asking him to send our greetings.

Otto Yulyevich finished writing and walked up to us. Then in his usual calm voice he dictated a message to Moscow and Rudolph:

"At 11.10 a.m. the U.S.S.R. N-170 under Vodopyanov, Babushkin, Spirin and Senior Mechanic Bassein passed over the North Pole.

"We went a little farther to make sure there was no mistake. Then Vodopyanov glided down from 5,500 to 600 feet and, breaking through a thick cloud bank, began looking for a strip of ice where to land and establish a scientific station.

"At 11,35 Vodopyanov effected a brilliant landing. Unfortunately, when the news was being transmitted a short circuit occurred. The converter went out of action and communication has only been possible now, when the radio has been set up on the new polar station. Our ice-floe is situated about twelve miles on the far side of the Pole and west of the Rudolph meridian. We shall define our position more accurately. The ice is suitable for the establishment of a scientific station to drift in the centre of the polar basin. An excellent runway can be built here for the remaining machines which will bring the station's cargo.

"We feel that we must have unwittingly caused you great anxiety when communication was interrupted. Very sorry. Hearty greetings.

"Please inform the Party and the Government that the first part of the assignment has been fulfilled.

"Shmidt, Chief of Expedition."

It was more than twenty-four hours since we had slept and there was still a lot to be done, so we had to get some sleep.

Amid the boundless snowy expanses, on a floe fringed by ice blocks, stood a big orange plane. Near it were the silk tents, also orange-coloured, where thirteen Soviet citizens were calmly sleeping.

We were quite comfortable in our sleeping-bags and did not feel the cold at all.

Papanin wakened us. He had already done lots of useful things and had now brought us tea and biscuits.

"Here, have some tea," he invited us hospitably. "In about ten minutes I'll have an omelette ready for you."

"What's the weather like?" asked Shmidt.

"Bad. Fog. Visibility poor."

Babushkin lit the primus stove, and in two or three minutes it was so warm in the tent that we were able to struggle out of the sleeping-bags in our underclothes and dress.

"What's the time?" I asked.

"Ten," replied Spirin confidently.

"Morning or night?"

"Morning, I believe," he said a little uncertainly now.

"I think it's night. We must have slept at least twenty hours."

Then Babushkin intervened. "The sun here circles over us at the same altitude. Of course, we can't see it at the moment, but that does not matter. It's difficult to judge by the sun anyway for our floe spins too."

"You just tell me whether it's day or night now," I interrupted.

"I think it's day," replied Babushkin.

But it was impossible to decide the question for the correct time could only be ascertained by means of the radio or chronometer.

Having folded our sleeping-bags, we placed a big sheet of plywood in the middle and, using it as a table, drank our tea squatting or lying down.

"We have to thank the chief of the North Pole station," remarked Mikhail Sergeyevich, pouring out another mug for himself. "I love tea!"

First day at the Pole

"Papanin likes entertaining his guests. And we are his guests now," smiled Otto Yulyevich.

Outside, the sound of approaching steps was heard.

"You're not asleep, Otto Yulyevich?" asked Krenkel.

"No."

"Here's a message," announced Krenkel coming into the tent.

Guessing where it came from, we all felt excited. Otto Yulyevich glanced through it and then said to Krenkel, "Would you mind calling the others, please?"

And there and then the first thirteen residents of the North Pole gathered for their first conference. Hats in hand, we stood quietly so that we should not miss a word of the message which Shmidt was reading to us.

"*O. Y. Shmidt*, Chief of the North Pole expedition

"*M. V. Vodopyanov*, Commander of the air group

"All participants in the North Pole expedition.

"The Party and the Government warmly greet the glorious participants in the North Pole expedition and congratulate them on the completion of their assignment—the conquest of the North Pole.

"This victory of the Soviet Air Force and science is the climax of the brilliant work carried out for the mastery of the Arctic and the northern sea routes so essential to the Soviet Union.

"The first stage has been accomplished, and enormous difficulties have been overcome. We feel confident that the valiant winter party, remaining at the Pole, will nobly fulfil their task of studying the North Pole.

"Bolshevik greetings to the valiant conquerors of the North Pole!

"*J. Stalin, V. Molotov,*	*M. Kalinin, A. Mikoyan,*
K. Voroshilov, L. Kaganovich	*A. Andreyev, A. Zhdanov.*"

As he finished reading, there was a cheer in honour of the Communist Party, the Soviet Government and our country.

Notwithstanding the vast distance between us and the mainland, we did not feel torn away from home. Every day wires reached us from all parts of our great country. Collective farmers and factory workers, Red Army men and officers, pioneers and scientists sent us congratulations.

These warm fraternal greetings were extremely encouraging.

* * *

We cut holes in the ice, made soundings and measured the thickness of the ice.

We worked and argued. Some said the ice was five feet thick, some—seven feet. Papanin insisted that it was over eight feet thick. He was right: it was ten feet.

In the middle of our argument Krenkel came over and announced, "Comrades, I saw a snow bunting!"

"Trying to be funny," I said, going on with my work. "How come this little sparrow here?"

"I don't know how it got here," he said, shrugging his shoulders,

"but I saw it with my own eyes on the food tent. I almost caught it."
We scoffed at the idea, making a fool of Krenkel.

This was our fourth day at the Pole. Time hung on our hands

The men of the North Pole station. Left to right: E. T. Krenkel, I. D. Papanin, Y. K. Fyodorov and P. P. Shirshov

for there was little we could do since the bulk of the equipment was to arrive with the other three planes, for which we waited impatiently.

After we landed the weather had changed for the worse. Heavy fog, wind, snow and blizzards delayed the start of the other machines.

On the evening of the twenty-fifth of May there was a clear sky and no wind.

"Otto Yulyevich, there's hope of better weather, so we may be able to receive the machines," I said.

"You think so? And what does Fyodorov say? He is our chief meteorologist now."

"Fyodorov says the weather ought to be good. I suggest we instruct them to get ready at Rudolph. If it does clear here in about two hours, they can get under way."

Shmidt agreed.

In an hour the mechanics on Rudolph Island had the machines ready. The weather on the island was not very good; low clouds hung over the ground, but horizontal visibility was fair.

On Shevelev's instructions Kruze went out at once on a reconnaissance flight.

The weather at the Pole had improved immensely; there was not a single cloud above us, and as the clouds moved from north to south it ought to clear soon on Rudolph Island, too. Kruze made a flight and found that the mist stopped at 83° N., which he at once reported to the winter party.

Mark Ivanovich Shevelev was in charge of the second group's flight to the Pole. Vasily Sergeyevich Molokov commanded the flagship.

At 11.15 p. m. Molokov's heavy machine with great difficulty took the air. The pilots had agreed to fly in the zone of the radio beacon and to meet at the edge of the cloud bank.

Without circling Molokov flew a little to one side, towards the radio beacon, entered the zone and set the course north.

The first stage was not easy. Visibility was practically nil, but fine weather was coming and soon Molokov emerged from the clouds and began circuiting, waiting for the other planes. In a few minutes Alexeyev's machine dived out of the clouds. Now only Mazuruk was missing.

The planes circled for some time, but there was no sign of Mazuruk. The time agreed on had long passed. It was dangerous to return to Rudolph, and Shevelev, who was on the flagship, ordered the pilots to steer for the Pole and inform Rudolph that they had gone.

When about half the way had been covered, Alexeyev began to fall behind Molokov, who reduced speed, but Alexeyev continued to lag behind and soon his machine disappeared. This was probably because Molokov was flying at a higher altitude than Alexeyev and the speed of the wind was less above than it was below.

And so all three planes flew solo. The weather was favourable and the machines reliable; the only risk was that they might not find our floe.

Stromilov, Molokov's radio-operator, was in regular contact with the island and with us. We received the first message about the start from the chief of the polar station on Rudolph Island.

At 0 hours 30 minutes we heard from Shevelev:

"Passed latitude 83°50′ N., longitude 58° W."

And at 5 hours 48 minutes there was another message:

"Reached the Pole. Happy and proud. Turning above the Pole. Coming your direction. Will be with you soon."

Babushkin and the mechanics got a runway ready. We all left our tents and peered into the deep blue sky, waiting to see the three black specks.

I put on my skis and climbed a big ice block to get a better view.
"Here they come," called somebody.

Bending forward, I lost my balance and rolled down the slope. Far on the horizon appeared a tiny dot.

"It'll pass to the right of us," I said. "Radio that they should turn left."

Krenkel at once did so and the dot changed its course, making straight for us.

The plane was rapidly coming nearer. We could see its outlines.
"Sima," I shouted to Ivanov. "Rejoice! It's Molokov and he has a spare converter for you, so you'll soon have your radio going."

In three minutes the orange plane was circling overhead. On its wings we could clearly read: U.S.S.R. N-171.

It circled twice and landed. Molokov taxied up and switched

off the engines. We embraced and congratulated the new residents of the North Pole.

"Well done, Ritsland!" I said gripping the navigator's hand. "Must have been pretty difficult to find us without a radio beacon, eh?"

"It was just luck." Ritsland was modest as usual. "I swung round over the Pole and set the course along the meridian where you are now. That's how I found you."

Throwing an arm round Stromilov, Sima asked, "Have you brought the converter?"

"Yes, of course."

Sima beamed.

"Have some tea, friends. Embraces won't satisfy your hunger," said Papanin. The arrival of the second plane meant that he now had twenty-two mouths to feed.

Just then a message was received from Alexeyev asking us to make the flares give off more smoke. He was circling somewhere near and Shevelev at once radioed:

"Molokov landed alongside Vodopyanov. If you think you cannot find us, land at once, take your bearings and then fly here."

On receiving this message Alexeyev decided to land rather than waste more petrol. Making one circuit he chose a floe and came down safely.

Zhukov, the navigator, was making astronomical computations. Twenty minutes later he traced the first line on the chart; it passed over the Pole. In another two or three hours he would be able to plot the second line.

The mechanics covered the engines to prevent their over-cooling, and Alexeyev surveyed the ice, to see if he could take off without special preparations.

Three hours afterwards Alexeyev wired his co-ordinates. It appeared that he was on the right course and that it was only a desire to save fuel which had prompted him to land ten miles from the Pole. He could not start out for our camp at once because the weather was bad.

We were worried about the fate of the third plane. We did not know where Mazuruk was and the only message from him had been in the early stage of the flight when he had radioed that everything was all right.

Ivanov had repaired his radio and was vainly trying to get in touch with him.

Towards evening a blizzard developed. Night set in, but no one slept.

A radio from Dikson informed us that Mazuruk had landed safely near the Pole and was now preparing a runway. He sent the crew's greetings.

We breathed freely.

Next day Dikson radioed Mazuruk's co-ordinates. He was no more than thirty miles from us.

It seemed a shame that Mazuruk, although he was so near, could get in touch with us only through Dikson, and we puzzled over the impassability of the radio waves.

Apart from food and scientific gear, Molokov had brought a windmill and dynamo for charging the accumulators. That same day, the "mill," as we called it, was put into operation.

When I heard its ear-splitting howl I pitied the group who would remain at the Pole. The only consolation was that Krenkel's accumulators would always be charged.

By morning the blizzard had abated, but low clouds covered the camp.

Towards midday we saw a narrow strip spread along the horizon and gradually widen. We at once informed Alexeyev that the clouds were rising and the weather was likely to improve.

In the next two hours conditions were so much better that a take-off was possible. Zhukov asked for his direction and said they were about to start.

Alexeyev turned into the wind, opened the engine, and the plane rolled forward. But before it had gathered flying speed they were near the ice blocks, which the pilot had just managed to clear when the plane flopped on the ice. Then it bounced up again and came down heavily. It was amazing how it withstood the shock.

The runway was obviously too short for Alexeyev to get up the necessary flying speed and so they all turned to, levelling out the hummocks with spades, picks and hacks.

Then they cut up a canvas cover into strips to serve as flags which they placed at regular intervals of sixty-seventy yards. Between the seventh and eighth flags Alexeyev had to rise into the air.

The men all took their seats, Alexeyev taxied to the starting point, and opened the throttle. The machine rolled forward till the fifth, sixth and seventh flags were left behind, but still it was not airborne. Before it reached the eighth, the pilot virtually forced it into the air and twenty-three minutes later he effected a safe landing on our runway. He was just in time, for a minute later the clouds had again settled over the camp.

Alexeyev brought supplies of food, a thousand litres of petrol in rubber containers and a big black tent with the inscription: "*U.S.S.R. Drifting Station of Northern Sea Route Administration.*"

With Alexeyev's arrival there were now twenty-nine men on the floe; housing was obviously lagging behind the growth of population.

Papanin, naturally, took it upon himself to plan the settlement. He set up three streets—Aircraft, Soviet and Warehouse streets—and the space in the centre was called Red Square.

One fine sunny day Ritsland, standing near Molokov's machine, cried, "I've caught it!"

"Caught what?"

He came forward holding a tin from which he produced a small live bird.

"A snow bunting!" we cried in chorus.

So Krenkel was right when he said he had seen one.

Our radio-operators worked tirelessly, trying to pick up Mazuruk's signals. At the Pole the first radio-operator to contact Mazuruk was promised a prize, but of course that was not what prompted them to sit day and night at their wireless sets.

On the 29th of May Molokov was sent out in search of Mazuruk. He circled the snowy plains for nearly an hour and returned without sighting the machine. But just as he was landing, Stromilov intercepted a message from Mazuruk.

"Everything all right. Can hear Molokov. Main set broken. Shall be on the air at twenty hours on the 625-metre band."

At the arranged time Akkuratov, the navigator, radioed that the men were in good health, that they would finish clearing the runway next day and as soon as weather permitted set out for our ice-floe.

The Arctic kept us on tenterhooks for another six days. Only on the fourth of June did blue holes appear in the grey sky.

Throughout the night of June 5 Shmidt, Spirin, Shevelev and I talked on the radio telephone with Mazuruk and his crew. We gave instructions, reported our co-ordinates and the speed and direction of the wind.

By morning the weather was fairly good and Otto Yulyevich advised Mazuruk to start.

The whole camp gathered at the runway which we marked out with flags. Sleeping-bags were laid out in the shape of the landing "T". The men were posted fan-like, each with field-glasses and with orders to watch a certain part of the horizon. The radio-operators were busy at their sets.

Far away in the clouds a black speck appeared.

Without lowering his field-glasses Spirin called to the radio-operators, "Tell him to steer ten degrees left."

The message was conveyed and the speck turned left. Soon we could discern the outlines of a plane.

"Tell him to turn six degrees to the right," called Spirin again.

This was passed on and the plane turned to the right. It was coming closer and closer making straight for us.

The drone of engines grew and in a few minutes the N-169 was circling over the camp.

Anxiously we watched Mazuruk come down. He had to land between my machine and the ice hummocks. The runway was 450 feet wide. In case he might not notice the flat blocks, we posted men on each of them to show that a landing there was dangerous.

Mazuruk took note of everything, and, carefully approaching the "T", made a brilliant landing.

Hats flew up in the air.

Petenin waved his flags to indicate the place for Mazuruk's machine. "Like a real airport," I thought.

The first to leave the plane was the four-legged passenger, Vesyoly. The dog ran up to its master, Papanin, and barking gaily, jumped on his chest. Patting the dog he said:

"You and I will have a good time here."

"Everything's fine," said Mazuruk as he came out of the machine. "We broke up sixty-eight hummocks."

After him came the rest of the crew—Kozlov, the co-pilot, Akkuratov, the navigator, Shekurov and Timofeyev, the mechanics.

When their first excitement had passed, the newcomers glanced round in astonishment. The camp was like a big construction site with its thirteen tents, including the main living quarters of the Pole party, the radio tent, galley, stores, meteorological box and the windmill.

During breakfast we heard about the crew's life on the floe. They had had a trying time. The floe on which they had landed was dotted with ice blocks, and only skilled piloting had saved the machine from damage.

It was some time before they could establish communication. They were not worried about themselves, but wondered anxiously whether Molokov and Alexeyev had reached the camp and landed safely. The crew at once set about clearing a runway. In ten days it was ready, and as soon as Otto Yulyevich told them that flight was possible, they came on.

The members of the expedition were all gathered. And the mechanics unloaded the last of the equipment.

Mazuruk had brought the long awaited winch with the sounding-line for hydraulic observations and depth measurements. The polar party lost no time in setting it up for we all wanted to know the depth of the water. There was a good deal of argument: some said the sea was 1,000 fathoms, and others argued that the 2,500-fathom line would not reach the bottom.

Eventually we learned that the depth of the ocean at the North Pole was 2,150 fathoms. When the cargo was fully unloaded, we began to calculate how much we had brought. It turned out that although Papanin was entitled to only eight and a quarter tons he had managed to squeeze in over ten tons.

We all stared at him and he smiled slyly, if rather guiltily:

"I can't think how it happened. But don't let it worry you, friends—it'll all come in handy."

The loads included a typewriter, chess, scientific gear, books, pots and pans, guns, textiles, collapsible boats, sledges, chairs.

Papanin had even brought a rubber stamp to the Pole. He said, "My office must function in proper form," and he stamped all the letters to be sent to Moscow.

The crews began to prepare the machines for the return journey. A petrol check showed that Alexeyev and Mazuruk were both short of fuel.

"Well, one machine will have to be left behind. Papanin will know what to do with it," I said airily.

I got the answer I expected.

"No," said Alexeyev calmly. "Ilya Pavlovich and I have already agreed to fly as long as our petrol lasts. The machines are light now and we'll be able to go as far as the eighty-third degree, find a suitable floe there and land. Then someone can bring petrol. If we leave a plane at the Pole we'll lose it."

The suggestion was adopted.

On June 6, at two in the morning, when all the planes were ready for the take-off, we gathered in the Red Square.

Otto Yulyevich stepped on to a sledge, which served as platform, and we got round him.

He spoke of the establishment of a drifting scientific station at the North Pole, his voice trembling with excitement.

"... We would not have done it if our Communist Party had not inspired us with faith in our country, steadfastness and confidence," he said. "We would not have done it without brilliant technique, without the initiative and effort of a splendid team. Our pilots, navigators and mechanics, all members of the expedition, have displayed amazing mental and physical ingenuity.

"We are leaving the Pole. Leaving it with regret because the

Pole for our Soviet expedition has not been a nightmare, but hospitable and kind.

"We are leaving, but four of our comrades will remain at the Pole. We know they will cherish the banner we now give into their care. We know that their efforts will find a place in the annals of world science and will open a new page of socialist victories in the history of our country.

"I congratulate the Pole party on the great task which our country has entrusted to them."

Papanin on behalf of the Pole party sent assurances to the Government that they would accomplish their task and prove worthy of the confidence placed in them.

Then Otto Yulyevich said:

"I declare the North Pole drifting station open. Hoist the flag."

Within a few seconds the flag of the U.S.S.R. waved from an aluminium pole.

Then a report to the Communist Party and the Soviet Government on the fulfilment of the assignment was read.

The sky was dark and there were showers of flaky snow, but the weather did not bother us for the planes had no cargo and it would be easy to climb above the clouds.

Latest reports showed that the weather at Rudolph Island was satisfactory. Kruze, who had landed at the eighty-fifth degree and would report weather conditions on the route, radioed:

"Heavy mist. Elevation 1,800 feet. Visibility thirteen miles."

"Otto Yulyevich," I said to Shmidt, "we must hurry before the weather gets bad at Rudolph."

"If flying is possible in this weather, go ahead," he said. "I'm ready."

I ordered the crews to their machines and ten minutes later all sixteen engines barked. First the mechanics, then the navigators and pilots, and finally Otto Yulyevich said good-bye to the Pole party.

"Don't worry,—we'll keep an eye on you," said Shmidt, "and if need be we'll be here in no time."

I sat at the controls. Bassein reported that everything was ready for the take-off, but just then there was another spell of blinding snow which made visibility almost nil. I pushed open the canopy and said a few parting words to Papanin, Krenkel, Fyodorov and Shirshov.

The snow stopped and the machines rose: four planes in the sky and four men on the ice.

From above I clearly saw the "settlement." In the centre were the main tents, and on all sides around them, loaded sledges with food stocks and equipment.

The windmill turned rhythmically. From the mast flew the red flag.

A s soon as we were in the air a heavy mist enveloped us. I began to climb. At a height of nine hundred feet there was a bright sun. Far on my left appeared Alexeyev's machine and behind him, farther to the left, Molokov's.

"Where is Mazuruk?"

Babushkin looked to the right, and nodded towards the plane.

We were making for a point where the fifty-eighth meridian and the eighty-eighth line of latitude cross and from there we would fly straight to Rudolph.

I could turn my head and see three machines at equal distances from each other, the sun glinting on their whirling screws. Through holes in the clouds the ice gleamed, the hummocks looking like small snow mounds.

I steered by the sun compass. We had to emerge at exactly the fifty-eighth meridian and this was possible only by a special system of navigation, for the meridians in the Pole are very close to one another.

I heard the beacon signals. The tone of the letter "N" was weak, which meant that we were not yet within the zone. The wind was favourable, and the ground speed was over 125 miles per hour.

Soon we were in the zone.

Spirin checked the course and said, "We're on the Rudolph meridian—in three or four hours we'll be there."

There was regular communication between all the machines; each navigator determined his own bearings by the sun and reported to Spirin.

Below us were rough snowy plains; the blinding sunshine forced us to wear glasses.

Ivanov brought a message from the men on the ice-floe wishing us a happy journey.

At the eighty-fourth degree Alexeyev informed the chief of the expedition that his petrol was nearly gone. He asked for permission to go down and look for a suitable landing-place as had been arranged. Otto Yulyevich agreed.

Meanwhile Mazuruk reported that at our present speed his petrol would last till Rudolph and asked if he might go with us.

As Otto Yulyevich and I were discussing this Alexeyev began to go down from an altitude of 4,500 feet. Soon he disappeared in the ragged clouds.

Mazuruk had begun to follow, when he got instructions from Shmidt to go on with us. His machine leapt out of the clouds, caught up with us and took its place in the formation.

"There's discipline for you," I thought. "Well done, Mazuruk!"

When we reached Rudolph a thick cloud was gathering over the island. Fortunately the three planes landed before the mist completely hid the runway.

I stayed on at the aerodrome to take charge of arrangements for the flight to Alexeyev's landing-place on the eighty-third degree.

Meanwhile Alexeyev's crew had begun to level out the ice, and soon a runway was ready.

It was agreed that Golovin would take the petrol in his reconnaissance plane, and to avoid any delay the crew settled down in the little bungalow at the aerodrome.

The weather was dreadful. It was two days before a north-easterly wind lifted the mist and chased the clouds across the island.

From the polar station Dzerdzeyevsky phoned to say that the weather was clearing and Golovin's crew should get ready for the flight.

A message from Alexeyev said the weather there was fine.

The mechanics warmed up the engines and Golovin set off.

Simultaneously, Kruze was instructed to return to Rudolph. On his way, seeing the N-172 plane, he circled, waggled his wings and went on.

Alexeyev informed us that we should get ready to receive Kruze. We replied that Golovin had set out for his camp.

Kruze was flying strictly within the zone, just under the clouds.

The going was good with no air-pockets or anything else to disturb the pilot, when all at once an orange-winged plane dashed from the clouds. It was Golovin, who was also keeping strictly within the zone. Kruze climbed sharply to avoid him.

Spirin was the first to see the approaching machine. All ran out to meet him. After a smooth circle over the airfield, Kruze landed at Rudolph. Just then we heard the cheerful voice of Zhukov:

"Golovin circling over us! Coming down for the landing. Going out to meet him."

A few minutes later Shevelev was heard on the loud speaker:

"Filling the tanks. Must be a special kind of petrol for it smells wonderful. Will be ready in two hours."

We waited in the radio room. Now and then Shevelev or Zhukov radioed to say how things were going. When Alexeyev's mechanics were warming up the engines Golovin set out on his way back.

The radio beacon was directing the plane to the island.

Golovin was on his way back. From the loud speaker came Alexeyev's final message:

"Hallo, hallo..., Coming in. Can see the shore. Get ready supper, embraces and hot bath. Greetings. Removing the aerial."

When the plane appeared overhead, Shmidt, Molokov, Spirin, Babushkin and I hurried off in a caterpillar lorry to meet our friends.

We felt years younger. The expedition was again fully assembled. Shmidt sent a radiogram to Moscow:

"At 0 hours 45 minutes Golovin returned to Rudolph Island, having brilliantly fulfilled the assignment of carrying petrol to Alexeyev. Alexeyev took off from the ice-floe and at 2 hours 10 minutes landed on Rudolph Island. All the planes of the expedition are at the base. The polar operation completed."

Every six hours Dzerdzeyevsky made up weather reports and this time not for the Pole, but for Moscow.

It was already the middle of June and we all wondered uneasily whether we could land on skis at Novaya Zemlya or Amderma.

Amderma radioed that a ski landing was possible only at a place about a mile from the settlement.

"Do not delay. In two days the snow will thaw completely," they warned us.

We could not change over to wheels at Rudolph because there were none there. And we did not want to wait—we were in a hurry to get to Moscow and report to the Party and the Government.

The pilots and mechanics maintained a constant watch at the airfield, ready to take off at a moment's notice. The people at Amderma urged us to hurry: daily they brought tractor-loads of snow to fill up depressions but under the bright merciless sun the snow thawed rapidly.

Finally, Dzerdzeyevsky announced that the weather at Novaya Zemlya and Amderma was good and we must get away at once. Just then a damp mist passed over the island. The snow on the runway was soft and the skis did not slide smoothly, but taking off was easier because the machines were underloaded.

The planes were ready to rise the moment the sky cleared.

It had been agreed that four machines would fly to Moscow: three four-engined and one two-engined plane. Mazuruk was to remain on Rudolph Island and be prepared at any moment to fly to the Pole.

Alexeyev picked the most favourable direction for the take-off, from a small incline, and placed red flags at hundred-yard intervals. By noon the sea opened up in the north-east, the mist lifted slightly and visibility improved.

I gave the order to get ready for the take-off. With the help of a tractor my plane started the run. One by one the flags rushed past beneath the left wing, but I did not gain speed. Here was the last flag beyond which was the slope. Then the air-speed indicator went up and in another second we were in the air.

It had been agreed that the machines would meet above the clouds, over Rudolph Island.

Flying low over the station, I saw a big bright spot between Rudolph and Karl-Alexander islands; this was the sun gleaming through a break in the clouds. To avoid icing I took advantage of this opening and began to climb.

From above I had a good view of Cape Auk. Using it as a landmark I circled at a height of 3,700 feet, waiting for the others. Sima Ivanov had told them about the hole in the clouds and our rallying point.

An hour and a half passed without any sign of the planes. After a consultation with Otto Yulyevich I dashed through the same loop-hole and began to descend.

The visibility had become decidedly worse. Obstructed by low-hanging shaggy clouds, I passed over the station, and, turning towards the runway, saw three dots in different parts of the aerodrome. They were aircraft. I glided down cautiously. Ahead lay a strip of smooth snow and on my left was the aerodrome. I had just cut off my engines when Mazuruk's machine suddenly appeared ahead.

I at once put on full power and eased back the controls. All four engines roared, holding the machine in the air. Like a trained horse, it cleared the hurdle and, having circled again, I effected a safe landing.

As I had expected the other machines could not get off on the soggy snow. A great deal of time and effort were required to tow them into position by tractors. This time we chose another place for the take-off, where there was a steeper slope. It was decided that Molokov would rise first, followed by Golovin and Alexeyev, and then myself.

The mist floated in waves over the airfield. Whenever the sea opened up the engines were started, but before Molokov could get ready to take off the dome was again lost in clouds.

Soon it was hidden completely. Feeling very tired, I went into the bungalow, dropped on a bed and fell fast asleep. I was wakened by an excited voice and someone shaking me by the shoulder:

"Wake up, Commander—the weather's clearing."

I dashed out, expecting to see the sun, but the mist had not yet lifted, although visibility had improved a bit. Meanwhile, Otto Yulyevich was resting in the wing of my machine, and unwilling to disturb him I gave the order to start.

Molokov rose first, followed by Golovin. They went up towards the west; from the east a dense fog was descending on the machines. Worried in case Alexeyev would be too late, I kept saying to myself, "Hurry, hurry, before the clouds get you ...." He was well aware of the danger and with the sea still in sight he quickly took the air.

The dome was now closed on all sides. Awakened by the roar of engines, Shmidt clambered out of the wing and Spirin told him that the other planes were in the air.

Otto Yulyevich looked around.

"How can we go up?" he asked. "Look at the clouds."

I could not take the same direction as my companions for without seeing the sea I could not keep a straight line.

Looking in the direction we had already taken off the first time, I faintly saw three flags.

"Otto Yulyevich," I said, "the flags are visible—I'll try to get away. You and everybody else go to the tail just in case. D'you think it can be done?" I asked Babushkin.

"We can try," he replied.

I opened the engine but the machine would not budge—the skis had stuck in the snow. Petenin, the mechanic, leapt down and tried to free them with a wooden hammer, while the station staff rocked the plane by the tail.

The machine rolled forward and, although I taxied slowly, Petenin, with snow sagging under him, could not get in and had to be dragged through the hatch. The engines roared, but the machine made little headway. We neared the last flags but had not yet attained any speed. Automatically steering straight, I pushed the controls forward, raised the tail and eased back the controls. When I had almost given up hope, something seemed to whip the machine from behind and it bounced up and leapt forward.

The air-speed indicator went on rising, showing a reading of a hundred ... a hundred and ten. I eased back the controls and the plane went into the air, on the very edge of the precipice.

Using the instruments for blind flight, I began to climb. At 1,900 feet the sun appeared. Three machines were circling above us and within a few minutes we were in formation, flying south.

The Barents Sea was completely hidden by clouds, but the Kara Sea was clear of both clouds and ice.

Six and a half hours later we sighted Amderma.

I looked for the aerodrome. There was land everywhere and we were on skis. Spirin, standing beside me, pointed down.

"Here it is."

Below us was a narrow white strip about 150 feet across and 2,000 feet long.

I swung round; gliding down, I saw Golovin's small plane make a good landing, and wondered how we would fare.

There was a side wind and I had to be careful not to run into any of the planes on the ground. Fortunately that did not happen.

Three days later the ice-breaker *Sadko* brought us the wheels. We quickly replaced the skis but had to postpone our take-off. We did not grumble about this unexpected delay for the reason was that all radio stations were busy intercepting signals from Chkalov, Baidukov and Belyakov, whose red-winged machine was taking them from Moscow, across the North Pole, to the U.S.A.

Eagerly we followed their progress.

Chkalov had already passed over the Pole and after a flight of sixty-three hours and twenty-five minutes landed on an airfield near Portland.

Another splendid victory for our airmen!

We left Amderma in high spirits, taking off from the airfield on which we had landed on skis only a few days before.

We rose easily from the sandy spit, setting the course for Arkhangelsk. As we sailed over the green tundra, the snow in valleys and ravines looked like white paint daubed on a green background by a careless painter. With such vivid landmarks flying was easy even in bad weather. I recalled all our difficulties when the tundra was completely covered in white.

As we approached Naryan Mar the white spots gradually disappeared. Instead there was a smooth green carpet. Later shrubbery appeared. Here and there were small lakes—evidence of recent

Moscow welcomes its heroes

floods. The farther we got the greener became the landscape, the tundra ended and the forests began.

Arkhangelsk greeted us with a clear sky, sunshine and flowers. We had left Amderma with the thermometer showing five degrees above zero, and now it was twenty-five.

We spent two days in the city. After the silence of the Arctic, Arkhangelsk seemed a noisy, bustling place.

We were given a very warm reception. To repay the city for its kind hospitality we agreed to lecture on the flight to the Pole.

On June 25 the planes took off for Moscow.

It was hard to believe that we would soon be home. Only three months had passed since the cold March morning, when the flagship had set the course north. But for us it had been a long bitter struggle against the elements.

We were returning in the best of health and spirits. The North Pole had been conquered without loss of life or damage to the planes.

Punctually at five in the afternoon the four ships, flying ·in formation, sailed over Moscow and alighted at the aerodrome. We had an overwhelming reception and with huge bunches of flowers in our hands we made our way to the platform.

After greetings had been conveyed on behalf of the Party and the Government, Shmidt spoke.

"The North Pole," he said, "will serve humanity. This victory would have been impossible if the Soviet Union had not been so strong and mighty, if we had not had such a magnificent industry. We can feel proud of our machines which were designed so skilfully, so well. Even the North Pole had to treat them with respect.

"And the men of our expedition? Of course, we picked them for the job, but all—and there are more than forty—are counterparts of thousands of our country's sons.

"We are ordinary Soviet people, devoted to our country, disciples of the Communist Party which developed in us the characteristics needed to conquer the forces of nature. The Party gave us a clear understanding of our aims, gave us strength, confidence in victory and devotion to the spirit of our assignment...."

Overwhelmed, I listened to Shmidt and watched the smiling faces of the leaders of the Party and the Government. Did we deserve such a welcome, I wondered.

Asked to speak, I walked up to the microphone, but I didn't know how to begin although I had so much to tell about the arctic wilderness.

I could not believe it was I who was speaking, though the words were familiar for I had repeated them so many times as I pictured myself back among my own people. But now I was speaking from a platform and thousands were listening to me.

"Before the flight I was asked: 'How will you fly to the Pole? How will you land there? Suppose you damage the machine, and have to come back all the way on foot?' I replied that I would land and if I smashed the machine I would not have to tramp back because I had the backing of a vast force—our great country."

I was filled with pride in our country and with the desire to give myself wholly to the service of the people. Turning to Comrade Voroshilov, I said:

"In such planes and with such men and pilots, Comrade Voroshilov, we can fly anywhere, wherever the country calls us."

I don't remember how I stepped down from the platform.

Adorned with flowers, our cars raced along the gaily decorated streets of Moscow. It did not seem so long ago that our planes had broken through the blinding snow-storm. And here we were again in Moscow, our cars breaking through a "snow-fall" of congratulatory leaflets.

My children greedily caught the flying "snow-flakes."

"Daddy, Daddy! Look! There's something here about you!" they cried happily.

Vera and Vova could not take their eyes off me. Misha nestled close to me, having already forgiven me for not keeping my promise to bring him a little bear.

In the evening the members of the expedition and their families attended a reception in the Kremlin.

nly a month after the establishment of the North Pole station the first Soviet plane flew over the wide vistas of the Central Arctic and opened the shortest air route between the Soviet Union and America.

Soviet pilots had become quite familiar with the Far North. They carried freight and passengers, flew doctors to the sick, reconnoitred ice conditions, took up scientists and instruments, surveyed and set up new mail and passenger services. Airlines linked the more important points in the polar circle with each other and with the centre.

Flights in the Arctic were now routine. The task at present was to learn to fly *across* the Arctic.

For a long time this was impossible for lack of aircraft able to cover long distances in the varying temperatures and meteorological conditions, able to fly across the whole of the Arctic.

The word Arctic has several meanings. We shall follow the example of Soviet polar explorers and take it that "Arctic" means all the land and sea lying north of the Arctic Circle. The diameter of the polar circle crosses the North Pole and measures more than 3,150 miles. Theoretically, therefore, a machine was required which could fly at great heights over clouds and fogs for 3,150 miles non-stop. Also the plane had to be equipped with instruments which would enable the pilot to fly a set course irrespective of the magnetic pole, for an ordinary compass is very unreliable in the high latitudes.

The brilliant flight of Heroes of the Soviet Union Chkalov, Baidukov and Belyakov from Moscow to Udd Island (now Chkalov Island), undertaken in the summer of 1936, showed that we had such a plane. Under extreme arctic conditions the NO-25 flew non-stop not 3,150, but close on six thousand miles. It was a test of the quality of aircraft, built entirely at Soviet plants and from

Soviet materials: a practical solution to the problem of trans-arctic flights.

Valery Pavlovich Chkalov, Georgi Filippovich Baidukov and Alexander Vasilyevich Belyakov were newcomers to arctic exploration. Their daring venture was, to some extent, a surprise for polar aviation.

Their route from Moscow lay across the northern regions of our country to the grim Barents Sea, across it to Franz Josef Archipelago, across the Barents Sea again in a different direction, across the Kara Sea to Severnaya Zemlya and finally over the little-known territories of our mainland—the lofty mountains of Yakutia, Stanovoy Mountain Range, the rich but wild Kolyma territory—to the city of Petropavlovsk-on-Kamchatka. The intrepid crew exceeded their assignment, landing not at Petropavlovsk, but six hundred-odd miles beyond it, in the area of Nikolaevsk-on-Amur—having covered a distance of 5,858 miles.

The very fact that the plane covered such a distance, despite the difficulties, was further proof of the leading position held by Soviet aviation in world aeronautics.

The valiant crew met with enormous difficulties which I could well understand from my own experience in the same area.

The most troublesome part of the flight began far beyond the polar circle. The Arctic and adjacent regions are notorious for lightning weather changes. For years past the Arctic has been known as the "factory of fogs." The reader may well imagine the meteorological surprises which beset the flyers in the course of almost six thousand miles. From the Barents Sea, for example, they had to fly blind, seeing neither land nor water. They survived many cloud belts and were caught in a cyclone. When the wings of their machine became iced up, they sent their famous radiogram:

"This day convinces us of the perfidy of the Arctic and the hardships it brings. We are not afraid of difficulties."

So many hours of blind flying in a head wind of forty-five miles an hour would be too much for most people.

On their last lap the treacherous Arctic used its most formidable weapon against them—icing. At that time there were no efficient means of combating this dread foe of aviation. Icing nearly always necessitated a forced landing, which often resulted in a crash.

Chkalov, Baidukov and Belyakov brought their splendid machine through blizzards and gales, impenetrable polar fog and icing.

In the space of several weeks the age-long dream of humanity had come true. The Pole was conquered. A Soviet expedition had landed on the dreary arctic wastes, established the North Pole drifting station and made possible trans-arctic flights via the Pole.

This of course did not mean that the North Pole was fully mastered. The expedition had just begun its work but the mere fact that weather reports from the Pole were available was an important factor in the heroic flight of the NO-25.

Chkalov, Baidukov and Belyakov wrote in an article:

"Some people ask what our country stands to gain from a study of the heart of the Arctic. Science expects and will obtain priceless data from the wintering party which has settled on an ice-floe in the polar basin. A message from the Pole, sent by navigator Spirin, provided us with some very valuable information on the influence of the magnetic pole on the radio beacon and gyro-compass. Now we know exactly how this will affect the readings of our air navigation instruments because we know the extent of the magnetic variations. Now we know exactly what the ice is like in the polar basin.

"We received meteorological data which enabled us to draw definite conclusions if only for a brief period. In short, the polar expedition did undoubtedly help to solve the problems connected with our North Pole-U.S.A. flight."

After months of detailed preparation, the machine started out on its trans-arctic flight from Shchelkovo Aerodrome, near Moscow, at daybreak on June 18, 1937.

For more than sixty hours world attention was focused on the splendid red-winged plane in which three Soviet flyers were blazing a trail from one hemisphere to the other across unexplored space.

The hundreds of miles between the silent arctic wastes of the North Pole and Rudolph Island could now be regarded as a "familiar"

A. V. Belyakov, V. P. Chkalov and G. F. Baidukov

route, but the remaining thousands of miles had to be covered through space where no plane had ever appeared, and over land where man had never set foot.

Apart from the pole of relative inaccessibility, about which geographers knew little, the land bordering the North American coastline—Prince Patrick Islands, Banks Land and other areas, including part of Canada—was a wilderness about which information was extremely limited, where weather conditions were difficult and a landing on wheels was impossible without the risk of a smash.

At ten minutes past four on the afternoon of the 18th of June the plane, steering for Rudolph Island, reached the seventy-sixth parallel, when icing began.

"A crust of ice began to form on the wing surface, producing quivering and vibration," recalled G. Baidukov in his reminiscences. "Valery urged me to use the anti-icer and when I opened the tap the knocking of the screw stopped. But the wings, stabilizer and the aerial were iced up and there was nothing we could do about it."

A pilot, knowing that soon his machine will become iced up and he will have to bend to the blind force of nature, feels both infuriated and afraid.

But, climbing steadily, the plane finally broke through the clouds to the sun.

On June 19 the crew radioed:

"8 hours 15 minutes. All's well, Pole behind, wind fair, open white ice-fields with cracks and leads. In good spirits. Altitude 13,000 feet."

Then the machine passed near the pole of relative inaccessibility and land was sighted. The pilots flew over the southern extremity of Banks Land, over Cape Pearse-Point, reaching the Canadian shore.

Overhead cumulus clouds hovered, the weather had deteriorated and the plane began to roll and pitch. On the left the way of the plane was barred by an approaching cyclone. A decision was taken to turn towards the Pacific coast.

After many hours' flight at 10,000 or 15,000 feet they had to rise again. At 20,000 feet Chkalov's nose began to bleed. The oxygen supply was nearly gone.

They had a difficult time at night, flying over the ocean in a strong head wind which lessened the ground speed of the plane.

The petrol in the service tank was steadily diminishing. They had no choice but to come down.

On June 20 at 4.30 p. m. (Greenwich time) the NO-25 landed at Borax Aerodrome, near Portland, U.S.A. That was the end of the epoch-making trans-arctic flight of the intrepid pilots who stayed 63 hours 25 minutes in the air.

The flight by Chkalov, Baidukov and Belyakov laid the foundation for an air route between the two continents.

But even before that the Pole flights had enabled Soviet pilots to make a detailed survey of ice conditions between Franz Josef Land and the North Pole. The landing on the ice of heavy machines settled the question of runways on drifting ice-floes. There remained the question of ice conditions on the "other side of the Pole" and the answer was provided by the Chkalov crew who made observations of ice conditions between the Pole and Alaska. They observed enormous fields which would serve as landing grounds, channesl of open water and thaw pools. The flyers plotted the direction of the leads and hummocky formations. Though the observations of one flight could not be taken as conclusive they did widen our knowledge of ice conditions in the Arctic Ocean.

The flight of the Chkalov crew stands among the great accomplishments of our times as a model of unparalleled valour, as a great Soviet contribution to world science and progress.

"We're the first but not the last," said Chkalov, Baidukov and Belyakov before taking off on their famous flight.

And this proved true.

On June 13 Krenkel, the radio-operator of the drifting polar station, received a message from the plane which was then passing over the Pole: "Greetings to conquerors of the Arctic." He at once radioed back: "Greetings to Soviet eagles."

Fighting fogs and cyclones, Mikhail Mikhailovich Gromov, Hero of the Soviet Union and his crew, Yumashev and Danilin, flew from Moscow to America.

I was resting at the time in Lipetsk, my native town. I bathed and fished in the deep winding River Motyr and frequently entertained Pioneers from a nearby camp.

Often the youngsters would ask me about flights to the North, about the doings of our arctic flyers. One day they came to me with red, flushed cheeks. That was when Gromov began his flight. I told them all I knew about the wonderful aviator who was known abroad as our number one pilot.

Gromov holds the Gold Star of Hero of the Soviet Union, which he was awarded in 1934, soon after the seven pilots who took part in the *Chelyuskin* relief operations. He was decorated for his record endurance flight over a closed circuit, when he covered 7,752 miles.

Gromov had always dreamed of flying over the most inaccessible parts of the globe. But this was only possible after the courageous winter party had conquered the Pole.

On July 12, 1937, at 3 hours 21 minutes, Moscow's best pilots applauded the faultless take-off of the giant heavily laden plane in which Mikhail Mikhailovich Gromov, Sergey Alexeyevich Danilin, aircraft engineer, and Andrey Borisovich Yumashev, test-pilot, started out on their non-stop flight from Moscow to North America via the North Pole.

When the trans-arctic flight was over and two world records broken for non-stop flights over long distances and closed circuits, Gromov was asked what he thought was the most difficult stage. He promptly replied, "The start." That was true. At exactly fifteen minutes after the take-off the machine, weighing eleven and a half tons, ran into a cyclone. The obvious thing to do was to skirt the danger zone, but the flyers did not take the line of least resistance, and went straight ahead.

They flew in accordance with a prearranged schedule. Keeping strictly to the time limit for given points, Gromov would change his plans when he met unforeseen difficulties and then go back to the time-table. Except for slight variations, the plan was followed with clock-like precision.

The machine flew a straight course along the line charted before the flight. When danger threatened, the flyers did not turn right or left but climbed higher and kept to their course. With this in view, they took three times more oxygen than was carried by the Chkalov crew. Danilin, one of the best Soviet air navigators, kept the machine over the charted course. They flew over the North Pole, over ice and the open waters of the Arctic Ocean, over the pole of inaccessibility, over the desert zone of the Canadian north-western islands, over the Cordillera and the Rocky Mountains, keeping to a straight line. This brilliant piloting won admiration all over the world.

They crossed San Francisco with a good supply of petrol, and decided to go on.

At daybreak Gromov passed over San Jacinto and made for San Diego. As the Mexican border was near they could not go farther south; otherwise their flight might have been even longer.

After being sixty-two hours seventeen minutes in the air they landed safely three miles from San Jacinto. "It was a perfect flight, exceeding by far all the known long-distance record flights," said the Government commission responsible for organizing it.

M. M. Gromov, S. A. Danilin and A. B. Yumashev by their plane

The United States newspapers wrote that the record itself was of less importance than the precision with which the flight was made.

Many explorers abroad said after the brilliant flight of Gromov, Yumashev and Danilin that "the Arctic was no longer a big mystery spot on the globe."

Exactly a month later another machine—the giant four-engined N-209—left Moscow for the north. This was the third attempt to reach the U.S.A. from Moscow via the Pole. The machine chosen this time was a transport plane, capable of carrying passengers and freight over long distances.

I can clearly remember Shchelkovo Aerodrome on that sunny morning when we went to see off our friends on their long journey.

I vividly recall the tall upright figure of Levanevsky, Hero of the Soviet Union, a renowned pilot, well known to everyone in the polar air service. Levanevsky had already displayed his skill, courage and human sentiments when he rescued Mattern, a U.S. pilot, in 1933.

Flying a plane pretentiously named *The Age of Progress*, Mattern intended to make a round-the-world flight. Taking off from New York, he flew to Berlin and from there to the U.S.S.R. His travels over familiar places with a comparatively soft climate were quite successful.

In the Soviet Union the American pilot was warmly received and given every possible assistance. Starting from Khabarovsk, he wanted to fly non-stop to Nome, Alaska, but succumbed to the severe climate in the north-east of the U.S.S.R. The machine was forced down and Sigizmund Alexandrovich Levanevsky, accompanied by Levchenko, his navigator, went in search of it. Undeterred by fog, storms and cloud banks, they found Mattern and flew him to the city of Nome.

Levanevsky's crew for this trans-arctic flight included skilled and tried aviators. His co-pilot Nikolai Georgiyevich Kastanayev was a broad-shouldered, open-faced man whom we all knew as an outstanding pilot and who, along with Baidukov, had set up a world long-distance record with a load of five tons. Later he worked as a test-pilot.

Victor Ivanovich Levchenko, his navigator, was expert in guiding aircraft over unexplored territory.

Grigory Trofimovich Pobezhimov, the air-mechanic, was a very modest man. In this respect he was very much like his friend Vasily Sergeyevich Molokov, his flying companion since the Civil War. Pobezhimov went with Molokov on many of his arctic flights.

Levanevsky, Kastanayev, Levchenko and Pobezhimov were old acquaintances, but Nikolai Nikolayevich Godovikov, the air-mechanic, and radio-operator Nikolai Yakovlevich Galkovsky were practically strangers to me, although I had heard plenty about them.

They were gifted aviators and, like all the members of the expedition, were cool and confident, and glad to have been picked for such a responsible mission.

At first all went well. At 13 hours 40 minutes a message from the plane read:

"Passing over the North Pole. Had a difficult time getting through. From the middle of Barents Sea continual heavy clouds. Altitude 20,000 feet. Temperature 35°. Wind-shield frosted over. Head wind in places sixty miles an hour."

Soon communication with the plane was interrupted. At 17 hours 53 minutes the Cape Shmidt radio station intercepted the following message: "Can you hear me? Wait." Then nothing more was heard of the plane, which had evidently been forced down on the ice in the central polar basin.

Immediately afterwards Shmidt, Shevelev, Molokov, Spirin and I were called to the Kremlin, where a conference was held in the presence of Stalin, Molotov, Voroshilov and Kaganovich.

That day the crews were picked. It was decided to send out two search-parties: one in the west Arctic and another in the east.

The search-party detailed for operations in the west was to have Rudolph Island for its main depot, with an auxiliary base on Papanin's ice-floe, which was then at zero meridian, 87°20' northern latitude.

In the east, the *Krasin* was to sail to Cape Shmidt, take three aircraft on board with their crews and petrol, make for Cape Barrow in Alaska, and from there sail as far north as the ice would permit. The ship *Mikoyan*, which was then in the Bering Sea, was instructed to take on a full cargo of coal and deliver it to the *Krasin*. Zadkov was ordered to take his hydroplane, the U.S.S.R. N-2, from Nogaevo Bay to Uelen and from there fly to the *Krasin*.

Meanwhile, Golovin and A. N. Gratsiansky were to get two planes ready, fly to Dikson Island and await further orders.

In the space of two days Zadkov covered 1,553 miles flying over Okhotsk, Nogaevo, Penzhino, Markovo, Anadyr and Provideniya Bay. From there he went on to Uelen. The weather was unfavourable, but Zadkov went on and after covering another 700 miles reached Cape Barrow, where he made a brilliant landing in a lagoon. Altogether he covered 2,400 miles in a matter of three days.

Meanwhile Mattern offered his services in the search for the crew of the lost plane. This gesture of the American pilot to repay Levanevsky for saving his life proved to be a fake. At his request the Soviet Government purchased a Lockheed Electro plane in which Mattern leisurely took off from Fairbanks for the north. Flying along the 148th meridian he reached the 75th parallel ... and then returned to Fairbanks, having given up the search.

ur navigators were faced with the unprecedented difficulty of flying in arctic latitudes which had never been explored. Our flight and the search were further handicapped by the approaching polar night.

On the morning of the 24th of August the planes were ready for the take-off. Dzerdzeyevsky had a weather chart of the route from Moscow to Arkhangelsk. Conditions were bad and we had to wait till the following day. It was decided to try out the machines in the meantime. We took them up twice, testing their readiness for the flight and found everything—the engines, radio, electrical and navigation instruments—in splendid shape.

Next morning there was a clear sky with not a shadow of a cloud, and no wind.

At six forty the engines on all the planes were tested. They hummed perfectly, driving their three-blade propellers.

The latest weather reports, which Shevelev and I studied carefully, showed that we would run into a crossing of two fronts. The forecast was not very inviting. I looked at Shevelev, who was in charge of the expedition.

"Shall we go?"

"Yes."

The engines hummed again, and the plane quivered as the screws turned faster and faster.

Then came the final embraces and good-byes, which were drowned in the roar of the engines.

The crews took their seats. The gangways were withdrawn and the hatches closed. The people on the ground stepped aside.

One by one the planes taxied to the starting point.

I opened the throttle and the engines roared, forcing the plane forward. Gathering speed, it raced along the concrete runway and rose into the air.

In my wake came Molokov and after him the N-172, piloted by Alexeyev. Moscow was left behind in a thin mist which blurred the horizon.

Several days later our planes were flying over the Barents Sea. Glancing down, I thought that Bassein, Ivanov and I were passing over it for the fifth time.

We maintained regular communication with the polar stations. From Tikhaya Bay Mazuruk radioed that they could receive us at any time.

As we were nearing Rudolph we got a message that a fog was settling over the dome. We had expected to see the settlement within a few minutes, but it was behind a huge grey cliff of clouds.

Seeing floating ice near Karl-Alexander Island, I dived under the clouds and Molokov and Alexeyev followed suit. We were now flying at a height of three hundred feet, steering by compass.

It was snowing. Soon the steep shores of Rudolph appeared.

I tried to reach the station from the coast, but visibility was too bad and, using my instruments, I began to climb.

Rising to 2,500 feet I emerged from the clouds with Molokov and Alexeyev close on my heels.

We had to land quickly. I decided to fly over the island, hoping to find part of the dome still open. Beneath me were heavy clouds.

"Well?" asked Spirin, realizing that the situation was not too good.

"It's all right. We'll dive through a loop-hole, and find the airfield," I shouted without turning.

We skirted the island, flew over and under the clouds, but could not find a hole over the settlement. Rudolph radioed that they could hear our engines, but were unable to receive us because of the fog.

We had no choice but to swing round and steer by compass for Tikhaya Bay. We had hardly done so when a message came from Mazuruk:

"Make haste—the Tikhaya plateau is closing."

"That's wonderful," I cried. "Now where are we going to land?" Passing over Karl-Alexander Island I noticed that in the south-east it was still open. From above it looked flat and after conferring with Shevelev and Spirin I flew low over the part of the island which was still open.

The slope looked smooth. I radioed that I was coming down and, turning, saw cracks and holes under a thin coating of snow. They proved to be so wide and deep that the whole undercarriage would have sunk in them.

Near by was Reiner Island, round and white, looking like an overturned soup-plate. From the centre, even stretches of ice reached out to the sea on all sides. It was an excellent natural landing field. I at once eased off the engine and, despite the side wind, made a safe landing.

Bassein, Morozov and Petenin jumped out and, running to one side, flung themselves on the snow, forming a letter "T", but it was a "T" that kept moving lest Molokov and Alexeyev should alight on the landing sign.

A few minutes later three four-engined planes were stationed on the ice, transforming the uninhabited island into a busy airfield.

Reiner is only thirty miles from Rudolph, a quarter of an hour's flight. We decided not to rest but to fly to the polar station the moment the mist lifted. But hours passed, and darkness set in. Everybody was tired and drowsy. We made ourselves comfortable in the wings, but could not sleep because of the cold wind blowing through the seams of the metal sheeting.

At three in the morning the mist gradually lifted from Rudolph, but a grey haze enveloped our island. Then it cleared on Reiner and became foggy on Rudolph.

The Arctic was again playing tricks on us. And we had only thirty miles to go, a stone's throw!

We pitched our tents and spent the night in sleeping-bags. We cooked on primus stoves and had three hot meals a day. We had a large variety of choice foods, including Russian borsch, chocolate, cocoa and other luxuries.

The wind carried the appetizing smells far and wide, tempting even a bear, whose trail we saw on the snow near our plane.

The weather on Reiner Island improved. It was agreed that I would go up first and, if the weather at Rudolph was good, I would signal to the others.

I went up before sunrise and in the gloom of the polar dawn, slipped through to the sea between two islands; flying at six hundred feet, I reached Rudolph.

Looking down, I saw dark hazy figures and black smoke drifting across the runway; on my left flares burned and beyond them was grey monotony.

Having asked Mark Ivanovich to radio instructions to Reiner that they should take off at once, I glided down for the landing.

The machine touched softly and, after a short run, came to rest in the deep snow.

On Reiner Island there was clear ice and here was soft, deep snow which made taxiing almost impossible even with four engines running and no load.

It was quiet. A lonely little bear was lashed to the doorstep of the bungalow. The sun had risen in a clear sky. The outlook was bright.

That same day Mazuruk returned from Tikhaya Bay. The station staff bombarded us with questions. We talked, shared experiences and listened to an account of their work. We also learned that Mazuruk was planning to set up an aero-club for the winter party.

Two days later the machines were ready for the flight to the Pole.

We agreed that three planes would begin search operations while the fourth would be kept in reserve on Rudolph Island.

As soon as the weather permitted, Mazuruk and Dzerdzeyevsky went out on a reconnaissance flight. At the eighty-third degree they ran into a thick fog but they pushed on till a solid cloud bank forced them to return to Rudolph. Our take-off had to be postponed.

Days passed in an agony of suspense. The nights grew longer and darker. The sun peeped out rarely; soon it would go off into hiding for the long polar night.

And yet the start had to be put off. A flight to the Pole could be made only in good weather—we had had to wait nearly four days to make the quarter of an hour's trip from Reiner to Rudolph!

The machines were in full readiness. Notwithstanding the twenty degrees of frost, the blizzards and fogs, the pilots and mechanics worked tirelessly at their machines. Each had a petrol supply sufficient for eighteen or nineteen hours' flight and a six months' food supply. We knew that a forced landing at or near the Pole would mean spending the long polar night on a drifting ice-floe.

Gathered in the mess-room we spent hours discussing new plans to relieve the lost crew.

Finally it was decided that Mazuruk would remain in reserve at Rudolph while Molokov, Alexeyev and I would fly to the Pole, land on a suitable floe, set up a depot and from there explore every square mile on the other side of the Arctic where the N-209 might have landed.

If we failed to find a suitable ice sheet in the centre of the polar basin we would explore the zone as far as the American coastline.

It was a good plan, but for the soft snow on the runway. Could we break loose on wheels in the heavily loaded machines?

There was only one pair of skis at Rudolph, brought the year before by the ice-breaker *Rusanov*. We had no hope of getting any skis from the mainland, because the cold was already very severe and thick pack-ice blocked the way for ships.

I asked Alexeyev to taxi about the airfield to see if a take-off on wheels was possible.

The plane covered about a hundred yards with great difficulty, and only with the help of a tractor.

We had to alter our decision and send out only one plane in search of Levanevsky.

All hands worked hard to prepare the machine for the flight. First the wheels had to be replaced by skis. Before we began this difficult operation we had to empty the tanks. The plane was raised by means of jacks which required the construction of a special platform.

As the left wheel was being replaced the jack crumpled under the weight of the machine. "Look out!" shouted the mechanic lustily thereby averting an accident.

Suddenly the plane rolled back and great effort was required to save it from destruction. But there our troubles did not end: a hard crust of ice formed on the wings and propeller blades. First they were cleared with wooden spades and then with hot water and anti-freeze. Then we all set to work to clear the ship of snow.

With Shevelev's consent I got ready to start at the first signs of better weather, but the island was hidden all the time by either a milky haze or a heavy snow-fall.

I counted on a full moon, when the visibility would be thirty miles and flying would be easy. But the moon was seldom seen, except through breaks in the clouds.

Finally at midnight, on October 6, we looked into a cloudless sky. The stars twinkled brightly, and in the east was the fading moon.

We at once gathered in the mess-room to study the weather chart. A cyclone was coming from the west. Dzerdzeyevsky warned me that the weather was likely to get worse.

"A take-off is possible, but the way back to Rudolph will probably be closed."

Dzerdzeyevsky made me think. The sun shone for only four hours and we had to get under way now, at night, to return to Rudolph before nightfall. The first to speak was Molokov, who suggested postponement. Alexeyev and Mazuruk supported him.

"Why risk eight more lives?" said Mazuruk. "Where will you land if a mist hides the runway?"

"There are many islands here," I replied, "they can't all be closed by fog. If the worst comes to the worst, we'll land in Tıkhaya Bay or Karl-Alexander Island."

Spirin supported me, insisting that we get away at once. The final decision rested with the chief of the expedition.

Shevelev listened carefully to each of us, and then said:

"The job has to be done. If the plane commander and the navigator think the flight can be made, let them go."

A tractor hauled a huge sledge full of people. The dome of the island was clear. Bonfires lit the runway, the fluttering flames casting long shadows beside the four planes on the snow. On the roof of the bungalow a small searchlight was beamed on the flagship, the U.S.S.R. N-170.

All hands surrounded the plane, thickly coated with frost. Some were sweeping the snow from the metal sheeting while others dug up the skis. The mechanics warmed the engines. The work was done in silence, every face alert and anxious. Later, during World War II, I saw the same expression on the faces of many of my friends detailed for a dangerous bombing mission.

Dzerdzeyevsky kept looking up, for he was afraid the clouds would obscure the sky and hide the stars. Never had he longed so much for his forecast to prove wrong.

In the west the horizon was clear, and in the east the sky was slightly aglow.

Bassein said, "Are we going, Commander?"

"Yes, and be quick, for we have to be back before dark."

Our remaining friends shook our hands and peered into our faces as if trying to impress our images in their minds.

"Good-bye, for the present!" I shouted trying to seem cheerful and confident.

The take-off at night on an overloaded machine, weighing 25 tons, was a complicated affair. The plane ran down the slope gaining little speed. I made the run, steering straight for one of the many stars overhead.

The plane dashed forward, bounced, and was finally airborne. I made a long circuit of the island, testing the engines and instruments; a reddish flame issued from the exhausts.

Bright stars twinkled from the black sky. Electric light illumined the navigator's cabin and the pilot's cockpit.

But soon the stars disappeared behind a curtain of feather clouds, the mist became thicker and we were caught in a cyclone passing north of Rudolph.

At the eighty-fourth degree the clouds merged with the fog. There were breaks here and there, but soon we ran into an impenetrable black wall. To keep the ice in view we flew below the clouds.

The nearer we approached the Pole the more inaccurate was the magnetic compass. We had to steer by the gyro-compass and make the necessary adjustments in its readings every quarter of an hour. However, Spirin managed very well.

The mist and the clouds thickened. Visibility was bad. We were forced to fly low. Beneath the wings dark strips of open water and grey ice-fields fleeted past. The altimeter recorded 150 feet.

I could not help thinking that if I were forced to land there was not a suitable ice-floe anywhere.

Bassein shouted in my ear, "Look out! You'll hit the ice!"

I could not fly blind for long in an overloaded machine because of the danger of striking a hummock.

"What are we going to do?" I asked.

Shevelev and Spirin suggested that we should try to reach the Pole, but turn back if the clouds ahead were still low.

The ice surface reminded us of the tundra at night—grey, dreary and monotonous. But in a few minutes holes appeared in the clouds, the mist lifted and we were able to rise to the safe height of a thousand feet.

The machine forged ahead.

We reached the eighty-ninth parallel when the weather grew worse again. It was more than twenty below. A dense heavy fringe, which we continually had to penetrate, suspended from the clouds. I looked up questioningly at Alexander Nikolayevich Tyagunin, my co-pilot.

He replied to my mute question calmly and confidently:

"There's no danger of icing in such cold. This means we can go on. At the worst we'll break through over the clouds."

I nodded, thinking how good it was to have such a companion.

As we neared the Pole a scene of indescribable beauty opened before us.

The sky seemed to slide apart. A cherry and a light-blue strip merged overhead. The first, on our right, grew gradually brighter on its way to the horizon. Its distant boundaries, illumined by the rays of a dipping sun, seemed a flaming red. On the left the colours faded, assuming a dark-blue hue. A vanishing day on the one hand and an approaching night on the other.

At 8 hours 34 minutes I took off my mittens and warmly shook hands with Tyagunin. Under us was the Pole.

Maybe, somewhere near by was the N-209.

We all peered through the windows and hatches, carefully scanning the snowy wastes. Each of us knew what he was to do and where exactly to look. Every minute somebody's tired eyes seemed to see the silhouette of the plane, which on approaching proved to be cracks or jumbled ice.

Suddenly Morozov shouted, "A plane, I see a plane!"

My heart thumped.

"Where? Where is it?"

"Over there," he said pointing to the right wing. Turning the controls over to Tyagunin I rushed to the window.

What bitter disappointment. I saw leads in outline resembling an aircraft.

We continued the search, flying zigzag. Spirin changed the course every ten minutes. Soon a mist concealed the ice-bound ocean, and it became more and more difficult to distinguish the channels of open water and cracks in the darkness.

Hoping that the mist would soon lift, we kept on our course, diving under the clouds, scanning the ice and then climbing again.

Finally a wall of fog and clouds barred further progress and we had to follow a broken course. We turned ninety degrees to the right, but again clouds barred the way. We turned again. What if they were close by and could hear the drone of our engines?

We pushed on, but the clouds kept pressing us down lower and lower. The path ahead was blocked by a thick fog.

We left the region with a heavy heart, forced to yield to the Arctic, which threatened to ice up our plane.

On the way back dense clouds made the going very hard. I looked at the wings to see if any ice was forming on them. The beacon signals were very faint. No stars were visible.

At the eighty-fifth degree a pale sun appeared, shining faintly through the cloudy haze.

Near Rudolph the sun grew brighter. Suddenly we broke out of the clouds into a clear blue sky, leaving behind a vast black mist.

We landed on the Rudolph airfield at 13 hours 10 minutes after ten hours' flight. Preparing for new flights we again replaced the skis by wheels. But the situation was aggravated by fierce cyclones, fog and snow-storms.

Then the frosts began. Ice covered the lagoons. Gratsiansky, who had made six daring flights from the U.S.A. into the Arctic, was recalled.

He examined a total of 6,250 square miles in forty-two flying hours. Gratsiansky flew in extremely unfavourable conditions, at very low altitudes, when a slight inaccuracy threatened a crash.

However, neither the polar night nor the grim Arctic winter deterred the Soviet Government from continuing the search for the lost Levanevsky crew.

Our planes, based on Rudolph Island, were not adapted to night flights in the Arctic. Therefore, the Government decided to continue the search with specially equipped planes. Moscow plants soon had the craft ready, and early in October heavy machines piloted by Hero of the Soviet Union Babushkin, Moshkovsky and Chukhnovsky left Moscow for Rudolph. The co-pilot in each had special experience in night-flying. Apart from this two P-5 aircraft and three weather reconnaissance and liaison planes were shipped to Rudolph by sea.

We were ordered back to Moscow. The take-off on wheels from the snowy runway did not worry us much for we had thoroughly lightened the machines, taking petrol for only ten hours' flight and a two months' food supply.

A tractor packed the snow on the runway to facilitate the take-off. The machines rose in the air. We fell in and set the course for Amderma, but an intercepted weather report forced us to alter the course and steer for Cape Zhelaniya.

A short time after we had alighted a blizzard began.

While we waited for better weather I received a radiogram from my home town. Here, in latitude 77° N., my compatriots informed me I had been nominated to the Supreme Soviet of the U.S.S.R.

I replied at once:

"Thanks for the honour. Shall try to prove worthy of your trust. Shall soon be with you."

On the 29th of October the weather was fine. I was about to taxi up the runway when a deafening report occurred and my machine listed to starboard.

"What's happened?"

Spirin jumped out of his radio cabin and discovered that a tire had burst. We did not have a spare wheel.

I immediately radioed the chief of the expedition on Rudolph Island. Shevelev replied:

"Instructed ice-breaker *Rusanov* to deliver spare wheel from Tikhaya Bay."

Meanwhile the temperature on Franz Josef Land dropped sharply and *Rusanov* was locked fast in the ice. I consulted the mechanics. A splendid idea occurred to Sugrobov. He suggested removing the tire and tube from the wheel and winding some thick rope round the rim.

"I assure you," he said confidently, "we shall get away with this wheel and land on the sandy airfield without any trouble, especially as the machine is empty."

The proposal was adopted.

When under Sugrobov's supervision the tire was removed, the diameter of the wheel diminished from six to only three feet. We wound rope into place and fastened a wire net over the rim.

After this operation the plane looked as if it had just come out of an orthopaedic workshop.

The plane had carried a crew of nine as far as Cape Zhelaniya, where Dzerdzeyevsky, Tyagunin, Kistanov and Morozov were left behind to lighten the plane. The cargo was redistributed so that the main weight should fall on the undamaged wheel; from the right-wing tanks two tons of petrol were emptied into the left.

On November 2 weather at Cape Zhelaniya was again fine. Delay was dangerous. The sun had already dipped beyond the horizon. A weather report from Matochkin Shar read:

"Visibility three miles, clouds thousand feet. Amderma reports visibility satisfactory, but wind."

Amderma was the only place where we could land our crippled plane and get a new wheel which would be brought from

Arkhangelsk. I knew I could not return or alight anywhere en route for even if the machine did withstand the shock of landing I would not get away again on that makeshift wheel.

At first the plane made little headway; sparks issued from the metal rim as it struck stones on the runway. But gradually I gathered speed and, lifting the right wing, dashed forward on the left wheel. Meanwhile, the rope round the damaged wheel had been cut on the rough stones and become entangled round the struts. Finally, it got caught in the wheel which stopped turning, but we were already in the air.

"Well," said Spirin, walking out of his radio cabin, "the wheel's secured fast now."

Turning the controls over to him I glanced at the wheel. It really was tied fast to the strut, but I hoped the rope would break in landing.

Molokov and Alexeyev also rose and all three machines set their course south.

Spirin took the seat of the co-pilot. Navigation was unnecessary at the moment since the Novaya Zemlya coastline was a good landmark.

Gradually, the mist grew thicker and visibility worse. But at times we got glimpses of the precipitous cliffs.

We were approaching Matochkin Shar. Beneath us raged the sea and we could now clearly see the foaming crests of the waves. Vertical visibility was excellent but the horizon was heavily veiled.

A huge cliff suddenly rose from the fog. I put on full power, pulled the controls back, and the machine began to climb, losing speed. And just as we all expected a collision I managed to turn and miraculously skirt the very edge of the cliff. Spirin and I exchanged glances, well aware that only a second before we had stared death in the face.

The shore was on our right and I turned towards it. We were in a "stone pocket" with land on the right, left and in front of us.

"It's a bay," I thought.

The shore came upon us suddenly. Spirin put on full power and executed a vertical bank. The machine quivered.

"What are you doing?" I shouted.

I managed to flatten out almost on a level with the waves.

"You must be mad to turn a heavy machine like that, Ivan Timofeyevich," I said.

"What else could I do," he replied, "when we nearly hit the shore!"

I decided to steer clear of the dangerous shores and fly blind across the Kara Sea to Vaigach Island.

Under us was the raging sea which would now hide and then reappear in breaks in the clouds.

The crests of the waves faded. The sea and mist blended into grey and flying became very difficult.

Then we sighted what seemed to us to be the dark contours of the shore again but on approaching we found it was a sloping cape, which we managed to clear and break out to the sea.

Three hours had passed since our take-off from Cape Zhelaniya. The weather had improved. We felt as if we had emerged from a dark cellar into light and fresh air.

Meanwhile Sima Ivanov had received a message from Amderma: "Storm. Visibility nil."

We hoped to reach Amderma at dusk. Visibility was already poor, which meant that it would then be quite dark.

How were we to land in the dark on one wheel?

But we decided to go on.

Ahead appeared a black speck which looked like a plane.

I increased the speed and caught up with it. On the fuselage I clearly saw the sign—U.S.S.R. N-171; it was Molokov.

I wanted to get in touch with him on the radio telephone, but his operator was talking to Amderma and did not hear us.

"Since there's a storm at Amderma," I said to Spirin, "let's land in the tundra on Novaya Zemlya. They can bring the wheel there."

Spirin suggested that we push on a little more.

"We may be able to get as far as Cape Menshikov," he said. "I saw a little hut there. If we could land somewhere near it we would at least have some kind of shelter."

We skirted the coastline of Novaya Zemlya, to its southernmost point again.

285

Molokov did not see us. He went on, heading for Amderma.

The weather had grown worse. The machine leaped up and down. But there was Cape Menshikov. We saw the huge waves rush towards the shore and break up in thousands of sprinkles.

After one circuit I chose what seemed to be a flat strip of ground between two small lakes and turned into the wind. I switched off the engine and cried to Spirin, "I'm coming down!"

The plane touched on the good wheel and then gradually leaned over on the sick one. Then the rope snapped and the plane limped like a wounded bird.

The next minute some unknown force swung us around to the right and the machine had raised its tail and had begun to tip over on its nose. Then, as if uncertain what to do, it swung from side to side and obediently dropped on its tail. We gave a sigh of relief.

Spirin made a rush for the radio cabin and from there shouted, "It's all right, the machine's intact!"

We jumped out. The right wing was almost touching the ground. The sound wheel was resting on thin ice which covered the tundra. The rim of the sick wheel had broken through the thin crust of ice and was now half buried in the ground. The snow around was littered with bits of rope and wire with which we had so painstakingly fastened the wheel at Cape Zhelaniya.

A strong wind, blowing under the lifted wing, threatened to turn the machine over. To avert this danger we hacked a big hole near the good wheel and with a big pole we had found on the beach turned the tail until the wheel slid down into the hole. In this way we levelled out the machine and were now able calmly to await the arrival of the ship with the spare wheel.

We examined our surroundings. The deserted shore looked very uninviting. But we were glad to be on the ground and that no harm had come to the machine.

Ten minutes later we informed Amderma that we had safely landed on Cape Menshikov. I had asked for the whereabouts of Molokov and Alexeyev when suddenly communication was interrupted.

Not long afterwards Sima Ivanov overheard a conversation between Amderma and Moscow. Amderma radioed:

"Visibility poor. Molokov just appeared over the polar station and alighting. Landed well in storm."

The only thing to do now was to find Alexeyev. Sima listened in to all the stations but an hour passed before Dikson Island informed us that Alexeyev had landed in Blagopoluchiya Bay.

It was time for us to settle down too.

Bassein made his way to the lighthouse which twinkled at regular intervals. Near by stood a dilapidated hut which must have been the abode of the lighthouse builders.

I was informed by radio that dog sledges with provisions had left for Cape Menshikov. But they did not reach us for soon a blizzard broke out and the drivers, almost exhausted after three days' wandering in the tundra, returned to depot.

They wanted to send a motor launch but the captain did not dare make the trip in the raging storm.

We decided to pitch a tent, but then changed our minds for it would have been carried away by the gale. We had no choice but to make Ivanov's radio cabin our quarters. Slamming the door shut we spread our rubber mattresses on the floor, turned the sleeping-bags inside out and covered them with our fur coats. In spite of all these precautions the ice wind penetrated the walls of the plane. The howling wind and snow-storm kept us awake all night.

Day after day passed. It was already November 6, the eve of the 20th anniversary of the Great October Revolution.

At night we went to the beach, gathered some brushwood and made a big bonfire. We could not take our eyes off the bright flames and were reluctant to go back to the cold cabin in the plane. But there was an icy wind blowing and eventually we slowly and unwillingly trudged back to our crowded quarters.

We awoke in high spirits. It was the 7th of November, and we, five Soviet citizens, marooned in the wastelands of the polar region, celebrated the great historical date together with the whole country.

Our thoughts were in the Red Square where at that very moment troops marched and aircraft sailed across the sky. We seemed to see the Mausoleum and the familiar, smiling faces of the country's leaders, dear to the hearts of all Soviet citizens.

The blizzard abated only on the ninth day. Twenty-four hours later, in the dead of night, a radiogram came from the motor launch *Vikhr*, which was making for us. The captain radioed:

"See lighthouse. Approaching Cape Menshikov. Dark. Light flares on beach."

We at once rushed to the shore with rockets and a bucketful of petrol.

Soon lights gleamed in the dark. It was the *Vikhr* approaching. The lights drew closer and suddenly seemed to hang in mid air—the motor launch had dropped anchor.

We stood around the bonfire when the sound of voices reached us.

"A little more to the left!" somebody was saying.

It was our friends landing from a boat.

They brought us food, cigarettes and a wheel, which was the most important.

All hands plunged into work. The machine was hauled from the pit and the wheel replaced; now we were ready to take off.

I throttled out and rose into the air.

Amderma met us with a clear sky and a gentle breeze.

I flew from Amderma to Arkhangelsk with three passengers on board: husband, wife and child. I must confess I did not want to take them. But the young couple—students who had come here for practice and were now waiting for a return boat—pleaded with me so much that I had to give in. And I was not sorry I did. The infant felt fine, as if he had spent all his life in the air.

"Your son will grow up to be an excellent pilot," I told the young mother at Arkhangelsk Aerodrome.

On our first day in Arkhangelsk I noticed Sima Ivanov's eyes were strangely dim. I asked if there was anything wrong with him but, trying to seem cheerful, he replied, "Don't worry, Commander. I'm quite all right."

Throughout the day he looked glum; in the evening when we were getting ready to go to the theatre he said, "I don't feel very well. I'm a bit feverish. I think I'd best stay home."

We called a doctor at once.

"It's difficult to say as yet, but it's probably the flue," the doctor said.

Two days later we started out for Moscow. Ivanov was still feeling queer. He was running a temperature.

"I'll be all right in Moscow," he said going about his duties as usual.

We didn't reach Moscow so very soon. Near Vologda a thick fog and heavy snow-fall forced us to fly low over trees, buildings and a railway.

Ivanov intercepted a radiogram on weather conditions beyond Vologda: "Fog thickening, danger of icing."

In the Arctic we sometimes had to take risks, but here we had no right to do so.

We decided to land in Vologda.

Sima was getting worse. He could not move his right arm and tried to work with his left, but his condition was becoming grave.

Seeing that the weather might keep us long in Vologda, I sent Sima to Moscow in the company of a doctor.

Two days later we were in Moscow, and I went to see him at once.

Now that he was ill I felt the bonds of friendship especially keenly. Sima and I had had many harrowing experiences during our flights to the North.

I recall how Sima dreamed about the sun and vegetation when we were stranded at Cape Menshikov. . . .

"Mikhail Vasilyevich, take me to the sanatorium with you," he said. "Together we flew to the Pole, together we'll rest."

In a howling wind, shivering with cold, we built plans for a trip to Kislovodsk. And now he was in a hospital, feeling very bad and even unable to talk.

The doctor advised me not to go near him.

"The meeting may excite him and accelerate his death."

Two days later Sima died.

* * *

In the summer of 1937 the ice conditions in the Arctic were exceptionally bad. Several ice-breakers and ships were frozen in. The ice-breaker *Krasin* was wintering in the Laptev Sea, Kozhevnikov Bay. A convoy of ships was fast in the ice off the shores of Taimyr and another in Vilkitsky Channel. The ships *Sadko*, *Malygin* and

Ship locked in the ice

Sedov were beset by heavy ice off De Long Islands and the *Rusanov* in the Barents Sea, near Franz Josef Land.

Some of the ships wintering in the ice drifted with the winds and currents. The crews had always to be on the alert, for ice pressure threatened to crush and sink the ships. But the men on board went on with their arduous duties, conducting scientific observations and investigations. None of the captains ever asked for assistance. They knew that if necessary help would always be forthcoming.

At the close of February, 1938, three four-engined orange giants left Moscow. The three ships were piloted by Alexeyev and Golovin, Heroes of the Soviet Union, and by G. K. Orlov, who had already made one trip to the North Pole.

The route of the air group lay across Kazan, Sverdlovsk, Omsk, Novosibirsk, Krasnoyarsk, Yakutsk and farther north to Tiksi Bay, from where the planes were to fly to the drifting ships.

The crews, picked for the expedition, included some of the best pilots, navigators, mechanics and radio-operators with flying experience in the Arctic, many of whom had been to the North Pole. This was a new glorious page in the history of polar aviation.

The aircraft forged ahead through fog, snow and blizzards. The flyers, anxious to help their comrades, paid no attention to difficulties.

Soon the crews were all gathered at Tiksi Bay. On the third of April an "all-out attack" was launched. The crews under Alexeyev took off from Tiksi Bay to the relief of the ice-breakers *Sadko*, *Sedov* and *Malygin*. From then on they made regular flights to the ships.

No country in the world had ever undertaken such large-scale air operations in the polar regions.

By the first of May rescue operations were over. The planes took five hundred persons off the ships and flew them to the mainland; in addition they delivered more than four tons of cargo for those remaining on board.

This brilliant operation in the east of the Arctic was further evidence of the skill of Soviet flyers and the splendid quality of our polar aircraft.

★   ★   ★

That same year in the west of the Arctic another air expedition was engaged in taking Papanin, Shirshov, Krenkel and Fyodorov off the ice.

The ice-floe with the North Pole station was being carried south at a perilous pace. The party had envisaged the direction of the drift, but not the speed, which increased as they neared Greenland.

According to plan Papanin and his party were to have been taken off the ice in March. The operation was naturally less difficult than establishing a station at the Pole, in spite of the persisting fog in the Greenland Sea at this time of the year and of the fact that the relief operations had to be conducted with the help of ice-breakers without any land bases for the planes.

The expedition included the ice-breaker *Yermak*, the ice-resisting transport *Taimyr*, and an air group under Hero of the Soviet Union Spirin.

The *Murmanets*, a hydrographic ship, was detailed to keep watch over the edge of the ice-pack in the area of the drift.

At the end of January severe storms raged in the Greenland Sea for six days in succession. The drifting floe was tossed about and cracked.

At daybreak on February 1, the blizzard abated and the wintering party saw a strange picture. They did not recognize their floe: dark scars encircled their tent, while all around were cakes of ice, divided by channels of open water.

Two depots and their technical equipment were cut off. There were signs of a crack running under their tent. The party worked all day moving to a safer place. The size of their floe was diminishing catastrophically and by evening it was 30 by 50 yards. However, all the more valuable property was saved.

The crumbling of the floe seriously hampered relief operations for now it was obviously inadequate for the landing of a big plane.

The Government decided to send ice-resisting ships to the Greenland Sea without delay. On the third of February the *Taimyr* sailed out to sea taking on board a flight of light reconnaissance planes under Gennady Petrovich Vlasov.

The air group under Spirin was to have for its base the *Murman*, an ice-resisting ship, which was specially outfitted for the operation. The ship carried two planes on board: a P-5 on skis and a Sh-2 amphibian which would be piloted by Ivan Ivanovich Cherevichny. The *Murman* sailed on February 7.

Meanwhile the Leningrad workers were working hard repairing the ice-breaker *Yermak*. The ship was to sail under Captain Vladimir Ivanovich Voronin and was to carry Otto Yulyevich Shmidt, the chief of the expedition.

When the floe was broken up by the storm, the *Murmanets* was nearest to the drifting station and the Government instructed the ship's commander to make an attempt to break through and take the group off the ice. I. N. Ulyanov, the captain of the ship, was to radio his bearings to Moscow every six hours.

On her way to the floe, the *Murmanets* twice ran into fierce storms and was iced up. When only about forty miles from the station she was pressed in by the ice. Six days passed before the ship could break free and thread her way in the leads to the shores of Greenland.

Meanwhile the *Murman* and the *Taimyr* ploughed through a surging and boiling sea. The waves rose high over the ships, falling on deck in thousands of sprinkles and streams. The wind knocked the men off their feet, and they had to clutch at handrails, cables and slippery props.

On February 10, the *Taimyr* began to grind her way through heavy pack in the Greenland Sea. That same day, the *Taimyr*'s radio-operator managed at last to get in touch with Krenkel and to maintain regular communication with him.

The *Taimyr* slowly smashed her way through thick pack in the beams of three searchlights, one of which was installed on the captain's bridge.

The morning of February 12 brought good news: Krenkel radioed that they could see the beams of the searchlights. It was decided to check on this by exchanging signals. At the arranged time a spark flashed and disappeared far out on the horizon. That was Papanin and his men burning magnesium and everyone aboard the ship rejoiced.

Next day the *Taimyr* found herself amidst impassable ice. Forty miles north-east the *Murman* was forcing a passage through heavy ice. The *Murman* sailed long after the *Taimyr* but caught up with her at the edge of the pack and now the two ships were almost within sight of each other.

Heavy ice retarded the progress of both. Everything now depended on air reconnaissance, on the work of the pilots. On February 15 solid ice barred the way of both ships. That same day Cherevichny and Vlasov made reconnaissance flights.

Cherevichny took off in his Sh-2 from an ice sheet near the *Murman*. After being 45 minutes in the air he returned and landed alongside the ship. His survey of the ice showed that the drifting station could not possibly be in that area. Papanin's messages stated that their station was in pack-ice and jumbled blocks whereas the ship was surrounded by brash ice.

Some time afterwards Cherevichny flew again towards the camp but was caught in a blinding snow-storm and had to turn back owing to poor visibility. But by then a mist had enveloped the *Murman*.

Afraid of colliding with the ship, Cherevichny turned for the Greenland shore, found a suitable floe and landed, deciding to wait for better weather.

In the morning conditions improved and they began warming up the engines, when the torch burst into flame. Cherevichny threw it on the snow smothering the flames in a canvas cover. When he examined the torch he found it beyond repair. However, the *Murman* was near at hand, so he decided to wait for help.

On the same day, when the *Taimyr* turned, intending to join the *Murman*, a fifteen-foot ice cake fouled on the propeller, tearing off two blades. The ship was now at the mercy of the drifting ice. Mechanics, divers and electric welders worked on the repairs for almost twenty-four hours.

Despite all these misfortunes the day brought good news: Vlasov had located the Papanin camp.

The pilot reported the situation was quite satisfactory and the drifting station was surrounded by a five-mile belt of pack-ice. His observations showed that the ships could proceed in a westerly direction. The order was immediately given to go ahead.

Next morning Vlasov went out in search of Cherevichny whose machine had no radio. Dividing the search area into squares, he methodically explored each. In one he sighted a black speck which was Cherevichny's machine. A few minutes later Vlasov landed and offered to take Cherevichny with him, but the pilot refused to abandon his plane. However, Vlasov finally prevailed on him by pointing out that his refusal would hold up relief operations. Only then did the pilot agree to sacrifice his small machine. Removing everything of value, he returned with Vlasov to the *Murman*.

Vlasov flew four hours guiding the ships to the camp. Crushing the heavy ice under them, the *Taimyr* and the *Murman* made steady progress.

On February 18 the camp flying the flag of the U.S.S.R. was clearly visible through field-glasses.

At midnight a light was seen to twinkle in front. The long-awaited moment had arrived. The crews of the two ice-breakers gathered on deck or climbed up the shrouds. And there in the distance, on a tall hillock, stood the four members of the drifting station waving torchlights.

The station was now only about two miles away. The whistles of the *Taimyr* and the *Murman* cut through the cold winter night. Decorated with flags the ships greeted the polar party.

The *Murman* reached the camp first, with the *Taimyr* following. The members of the expedition walked down the ship's gangway on to the ice and forming in two columns marched to the camp.

From the opposite direction came the valiant four.

"Glad to see you, brothers," said Ivan Dmitriyevich Papanin with a catch in his voice.

A meeting was held on the ice. Papanin walked up a snow mound and made a brief, but moving speech:

"We, four Soviet citizens, greet the two glorious ships' crews. By their persistent effort they showed the world once again what the Soviet people can do.

"I can't help asking myself if it is possible for any Soviet citizen to get lost anywhere? The solicitude of our country for the people proves that it is impossible. We were sure that you would come for us in due time. And you have come."

In reply lusty cheers rang across the bleak arctic wastes.

After the meeting the seamen and the wintering party marched to the camp where all was ready to be transferred to the ships. Before the radio equipment was taken on board Krenkel radioed a report to the Party and the Government about the completion of the work of the North Pole drifting station.

When everything was transferred to the ice-breakers, the North Pole party bid a silent good-bye to the camp.

Soon the *Murman* and the *Taimyr* left the fringe of the pack. On the snowy surface remained human trails. In the wind, over the former drifting station, flapped the red flag.

On the way back the ships met the ice-breaker *Yermak*, and Papanin and his men boarded it.

On March 15 the *Yermak* moored at the Leningrad port.

Papanin, Krenkel, Shirshov and Fyodorov were back on Soviet soil.

The data collected by the North Pole drifting station aroused keen interest among all Soviet scientists and, particularly, at the Arctic Institute, where many more expeditions were being planned for the exploration of the high latitudes.

The scientists were most interested in where and when the drifting stations would be carried out to the open sea, the depth of the Arctic Ocean in different latitudes, the temperature and currents of the water at various depths, the passage of the Gulf Stream, magnetic declination and meteorological data.

All these purely theoretical interests of the Arctic Institute were known also to the polar flyers, and not one of them was indifferent to arctic exploration.

Cherevichny, the well-known aviator, had many plans for erasing the blank spots from the map of the Arctic. But he was not satisfied with the old methods of studying the polar basin for they required a lot of preparatory work and cut off the members of the expedition for long periods (up to three years) from the outside world. Besides, the explorers could only work where the drift carried them irrespective of the purpose of exploration.

Cherevichny's idea was to establish temporary scientific stations on drifting ice with the help of aircraft, equipped as laboratories. The idea occurred to him in the summer of 1939, when he was reconnoitring the ice in the Laptev Sea.

But only in March, 1941, was a high-latitude air expedition undertaken in the area of the pole of relative inaccessibility.

The duties of the crew of the big four-engined N-169 included assisting the scientific personnel and "keeping house." Thus, Akkuratov, the navigator, worked as meteorologist; Shekurov, the airmechanic, helped the hydrologist and Kaminsky, the co-pilot, was cook.

Cherevichny's machine was well adapted for flights beyond the air

297

bases and was provided with all the essential comforts, including even a kitchen. The expedition was only dependent on the mainland for petrol and oil for the engines.

The feature of the expedition was that it had no information about the places of intended landings.

Cherevichny and the members of the expedition were to make several flights from Wrangel Island far into the polar basin, land on drifting ice and make observations for several days.

By March 20, 1941, the expedition completed the first part of its assignment—the reconnaissance of ice conditions in the high latitudes (from Franz Josef Land to Wrangel Island). On Wrangel Island a storm kept them grounded for a fortnight.

The long-awaited fine weather came as suddenly as the storm. The white snowy surface had turned grey: the sand had mixed with the snow but the surface was still smooth, and they started preparations for the take-off.

I. I. Cherevichny on the ice in the area of the pole of inaccessibility

On April 2 Cherevichny took off from Wrangel Island and, flying north for almost a thousand miles, alighted on a big flat ice-field.

Three hours later ten Soviet polar explorers pitched tents in the area of the pole of inaccessibility, and from the main tent waved the flag of our great country.

The first two days on the ice were devoted to scientific work. But on the third they had to think about building a runway. This was hard work, although the surface was relatively level, the snow was soft, and the drift snow was easily shovelled away. In three days the floe drifted over thirty miles north. It was only about six and a half feet thick, whereas the ice of the North Pole drifting station was roughly ten feet.

They remained on the floe for four days.

The next two flights were similar to the first with the only difference that the crew now regarded them as routine work.

During the second flight they spent four days on the ice and during the third the observations continued for six days.

On April 23 the expedition completed its programme of scientific work and returned to Wrangel Island. Valuable meteorological observations had been made, currents determined, ice conditions explored and soundings taken in areas little known and difficult of access.

In 65 days the N-169 covered a distance of some 16,250 miles.

Cherevichny's flight proved that his flying laboratory was well adapted for exploring all "blank spots" in the polar basin. Cherevichny had penetrated to places where the eternal silence had never been broken by the drone of an engine.

* * *

In June 1941 I left Moscow with instructions to make an air survey of the Kara Sea. A few days later I landed on the Yenisei, near Igarka.

"How quickly our North is developing," I thought, viewing from above the straight streets of the polar town, which had risen before my eyes. Here was the well-appointed aerodrome and the stairway leading to the majestic Yenisei, where flying boats landed.

On the way to town we saw potato plants—formerly a rare thing in the North. On a distant island the buildings of the state farm were visible.

Cherevichny arrived a few days later.

"Let's see who'll make the longest flight," he suggested.

He and I started an emulation.

It should be mentioned that, not long before, Cherevichny had set a kind of 23-hour endurance flight record.

On June 21 we went out to reconnoitre the ice with our tanks full. My crew of six included: co-pilot Pusep, navigator Shtepenko, radio-operator Bogdanov, mechanics Sugrobov and Shcherbakov.

The flight was successful. We flew over the Kara Sea ice, I and Pusep taking turns at the wheel. Shtepenko was busy charting the ice conditions while Sugrobov watched the engines. Everybody was in the best of spirits.

We explored the whole of the Kara Sea, gathering valuable information. We also fulfilled another particularly pleasant assignment: parachuted parcels and letters to the polar personnel.

The non-stop twenty-five hours' flight was drawing to an end. We were steering south for the far-away Igarka. Bogdanov got in touch with Cherevichny who was then over the Laptev Sea.

"We've beaten your record!" radioed Bogdanov.

Cherevichny at once replied:

"I know it, congratulations! My radio-operator has been keeping an eye on you. But don't you be too pleased. I'll beat you in a few days."

"Very well, we'll go on competing," I said.

But our emulation was not destined to continue.

On our return to Igarka we learnt of the perfidious nazi attack on our country and the speech by Vyacheslav Mikhailovich Molotov.

I told my comrades there and then:

"No more ice reconnaissance. Let's go home to defend the country!"

The polar flyers fought staunchly at the war fronts. Their ability to fly in all kinds of weather, in fog and storms, came in very useful in air combat. And when the victory banner was hoisted over Berlin and the bloodiest of all wars had come to an end the flyers returned to their favourite occupations in the Far North.

Early in October, 1945, Soviet people made another visit to the North Pole. The pilot, Mikhail Alexeyevich Titlov, flew to the Pole in an ordinary two-engined transport plane—N-331. The crew consisted of navigator Akkuratov, air-mechanic Shekurov, radio-operator Namestnikov and Somov, a scientific worker.

In the ice

The chief aim of the flight was to survey ice conditions in the autumn post-navigation period and also in the central polar basin along the route—Severnaya Zemlya-North Pole-Novosibirskiye Islands.

Flying conditions were difficult. The flyers had to overcome snow-falls, impenetrable clouds which blotted out the sky, and, frequently, icing.

In the region of the Pole Titlov discovered vast fields of heavy pack-ice with numerous patches of unfrozen water, leads and channels. We steered towards Cape Anisy (Kotelny Island). At 83°30' the polar night latitudes were passed and the aviators beheld the sun. Soon big stretches of water appeared and then the sea. Finally the flyers saw Cape Anisy through breaks in the clouds.

During this flight Titlov collected some very interesting data on ice conditions in the autumn over a vast area of the central Arctic.

It was a spectacular arctic flight. And what about the routine flights of our polar flyers? Actually, no flights in the North are "routine" for every time the pilot takes his machine in the air he does not know what surprises await him.

I was reconnoitring ice conditions for ships sailing along the Northern Sea Route. Once, on returning to depot, I found everybody very much excited.

"What's up?"

"The ice-breaker couldn't reach Komsomolsky Island and is returning...."

Only those who knew the situation at the Komsomolsky polar station could fully appreciate its gravity.

Two years before, six young enthusiasts had graduated from higher school and had taken an appointment at a newly established polar station on a small rocky island surrounded by heavy ice. Storms were frequent on the island and sometimes their living quarters were snowed up and they had to dig their way out. In the spring the area was notorious for thick fogs.

In the North all were aware of the hardships endured by the young people and admired their courage. For two years they worked round the clock in all kinds of weather.

Every member of the party fulfilled his duties accurately and in good time, and, since all six were Komsomol members, the real name of the isle was soon forgotten and it was referred to simply as Komsomolsky.

All had a tender affection for the Komsomolsky staff. The polar parties in the near and distant stations had become very friendly with the young people. It was purely an arctic friendship born of radio talks and promoted chiefly by the radio-operators. Our depot radio-operator, for example, had become so attached to the Komsomolsky operator that they both decided to settle in Leningrad when their time expired.

Every man in our depot was familiar with the life of each of the Komsomolsky members, discussed their characters and even appearances. I recall a friendly cartoon of the young people in one of the mural papers. Although none of us had ever seen them it was generally agreed that the likeness was good.

You can imagine how eager we were to give them a grand reception when an ice-breaker set out to take them to the mainland.

The ship was carrying a fresh party and large stocks of provisions. On the way back she was to call at our depot and here we would at long last meet our correspondence friends.

But the ice-breaker did not reach the island, which meant that the party would have to spend another year at the station. This the young people did not mind, but the trouble was that they were short of vital food stocks, which were replenished annually. There was any amount of flour, cereals, tinned foods and concentrates on the island, but not a single onion, no garlic, potatoes, cabbage or any other vegetable. The young people were already suffering from scurvy and anxiously awaiting the arrival of the badly needed supplies.

The party had to be provided with vitamins but how this was to be done no one could say. It would, of course, have been very simple to send a plane to Komsomolsky. But it was always thought impossible to effect a landing on the rocky island, or on the nearby ice, which was a chaotic mass of ice with never a flat strip anywhere. That was why no flight to Komsomolsky had ever been attempted.

However, I was asked to give my view.

I suggested dropping boxes by parachute.

"That would have been easy enough if we had any," replied the chief of the depot. "We have to think of something else...."

The situation was ticklish. The obvious thing to do was to land on the island, and that seemed impossible. If we were to dump the cases in passing, they would break against the cliffs and everything would be lost.

"I think we ought to ask the boys again. Let them look for a landing-place. Maybe they'll find something suitable. I'll try and land on any little strip," I said.

A query was sent, but when the young people again set out to explore their territory, an accident occurred: their radio-operator fell through a crevice and broke a leg.

A few days later another message was received. This time the news was good. The party did not give up the search after meeting with misfortune.

"A long thaw pool has formed near the shore in old, crushed ice," they radioed. "This strip is now freezing, but the crust is still thin, only four inches thick. The field is flat and the cold severe, so it can be expected to grow rapidly. Hope to be able to prepare a runway there."

And we waited for the ice sheet to thicken.

Komsomolsky radioed daily:

"Eight inches.... Nine, eleven...."

Meanwhile, with the frost, approached our foe—the polar night.

"How d'you intend to light up the runway?" I inquired.

"We have only enough coal for heating," came the answer.

This was a pretty pass, if you like. What could we do?

The situation was alarming. The radio-operator was in a home-made splint. If improperly applied, the broken bone would not knit well. The hydrologist was so weak from scurvy that he was now "lying down," as his comrades put it. Indeed, it was obvious that they were all in a bad way. And here were we with a doctor, food and vitamins, and yet unable to get away until the runway was "ripe."

It was then that the young people displayed their mettle.

Once they radioed that the ice had grown eight inches in the space of one day. We were very glad.

"How come this fortune?" we inquired. "A sudden spell of frost or some arctic god?"

"Neither," they replied. "Simply a bit of rationalization. We decided to increase the thickness of the ice ourselves: we have a motor pump with which we are drawing water from under the ice. Now it is growing thick on both sides, and especially on the top."

"Well done, lads!" we radioed back. "And have you done anything about lighting?"

"We have. We've collected empty tins and filled them with all sorts of fuel—grease, oil and kerosene—but that does not matter, they burn well. When you start out we'll line them up along the edge of the floe. It'll be like daylight landing for you."

We began getting ready for the flight.

Two planes were to fly to Komsomolsky. Finally the day came when our big machines rose in the air and set the course for the far-flung island. But on the way another unpleasant surprise awaited us. A radio message from Komsomolsky read:

"A storm at night split the runway in two: one part is five hundred yards long, the other four hundred and fifty. The smaller one has lost a corner. In view of the serious risk entailed, go back. We can wait."

I did not have the heart to turn back from a flight I had looked forward to so much. Nor was I prepared to take upon myself the responsibility for the possible consequences, so I asked Moscow to advise me. The reply was that I should use my own discretion.

I don't remember ever being so undecided.

The safety of my passengers did not worry me, but I could not be so sure about the machine.

Then I thought of the party ill with scurvy and decided to go on to the island.

"Get your tins ready, we'll be with you in forty minutes," I radioed.

Finally, we saw beneath us a chain of flares fringing the runway. The landing "T", showing the direction of the wind, was also formed from the same flares.

Scanning the tiny field I made one, another and then a third circuit. My companion was to land immediately after me.

I can't tell you how glad I was when my plane and in its wake the second landed safely. We taxied up to the very edge of the runway, beyond which was the bottomless sea.

The little party ran up to meet us and we embraced and kissed them.

The doctor was at once taken to the radio-operator. We, too, had to hurry for there was a heavy swell at sea and the ice was not very reliable. We immediately unloaded our cargo. Every minute of delay might prevent us from getting away. I was so terribly excited that I began to hurry the two young men helping us:

305

"Come along, hurry up, lads! The landing is only half the job. We also have to get back!" I shouted.

They worked on in silence, breathing hard. Then I realized my mistake: the poor chaps were weak with scurvy, and here was I making them sweat.

"Stop!" I cried. "Leave those cases where they are. We'll unload them ourselves."

But they wouldn't listen to me, with the result that we nearly quarrelled. These things do happen in life: I was yearning to reach these fellows and when I met them the first thing I did was bawl them out.

The same thing was happening at the second machine, where two other members of the polar station were lending a hand.

In spite of all these little misunderstandings the cargo was dumped in about twenty minutes. We ought to get away at once. The engines were running. But how could we go without seeing the radio-operator, without looking into the little bungalow where this friendly Komsomol company lived? Besides, we had to know what the doctor said about the injury. And so we turned for the polar station. The young people did not want to delay us. First one and then another would say:

"Well, it's time. You really ought to hurry. But let's take your picture before you go. That's all! Make haste!"

The weather was really unreliable. From time to time we heard the treacherous reports of crunching ice and the din of colliding hummocks.

In the hut I wasn't at all sure who was Vanya, Petya or Sasha. All I remember was the sturdy radio-operator arguing heatedly with our doctor and stubbornly refusing to come with us.

"What difference does it make where I lie?" he said. "How can I leave my pals? We came here together and we'll leave together!"

"But what if some complication occurs?" objected the doctor. "You need medical care. A good hospital on the mainland will soon put you on your feet."

"But you yourself said the splint was good. And now that you've

306

put me in plaster all I have to do is stay in bed. Look! I can lie here, near the wireless, and go on with my job. And what will I do in a hospital? Whatever you say, I don't intend to leave my comrades."

And the radio-operator got his way. Frankly speaking we sympathized with him, and this scene made us wish we could stay a little longer with these splendid fellows to get to know them better and to talk to them without having to hurry. But that was out of the question.

We left the Komsomol party and went on our way. Apart from the radio-operator, they all came to see us off.

They lit their "fireworks" again. My machine was the first to taxi up for the start. It ran along the smooth surface. I expected it to rise any moment when suddenly I was pitched forward, hitting the framework with my head. The machine crawled on its belly. Blood streamed down my face. Then the plane stopped.

I put my handkerchief to my forehead and it was immediately soaked in blood. We all got out of the plane. The undercarriage was smashed. We found that the wheels had caught in a newly formed crack which we had not noticed. Our runway had diminished by another hundred and fifty yards. The rift continued to grow before our eyes. Towards us ran the Komsomol party and the crew of the second plane.

I confess that we were somewhat put out. The doctor alone remained imperturbed. Producing his bag he calmly bandaged my head. I could see that everybody was worried about my injury and that made me more anxious than any of them.

"What shall we do?" I mumbled to myself.

"I'll tell you what," replied the doctor. "Bend down and be quiet. Don't fidget or interfere with my work."

When my companions had somewhat calmed down and satisfied themselves that I was not in such a bad way after all, they began to think how best to get the second plane under way.

The first suggestion came from the Komsomol party.

"What if we fill in the depression with ice and pour water over it?" they said timidly. "Maybe the plane could then clear it at full speed? We could fetch the pump."

"Your pump gives me an excellent idea, boys!" I said. "Of course, we can fill in the depression, but we can also make a spring-board!"

"How's that?"

I explained what I meant. It was all very simple: we would build a snow mound in the edge of the crack and pump water over it. A spring-board would be formed and the plane could easily clear the rift at a run.

Even before I finished everybody was hard at work, and in a few hours all was ready for the take-off.

I was very sorry to have to board another plane and was leaving in low spirits. It was not my head wound that worried me so much as the necessity of abandoning my plane.

"That's the end of our beauty," I said sorrowfully to the mechanics who lingered near the machine as if they could help. While they conferred I was trying to decide whom to leave behind to remove the instruments. Suddenly both turned to me and said:

"Mikhail Vasilyevich, let us both stay. We can at least—"

I put my arms around them:

"Splendid, do! There'll be enough food now and a winter here won't hurt you. Try to save at least the instruments and if possible remove the engines. You'll hardly be able to do more, but even that will be good."

We shook hands.

Our faith in the spring-board was justified. Although the machine was carrying a full load, it easily cleared the crack and leaped over the second half of the floe for another seven metres. From there it broke away and we could see beneath the wings the disappearing lights. Soon everything was enveloped in the inky darkness of the polar night. We set the course for our depot.

Later I learnt the true worth of the splendid Komsomol party. They gave my mechanics such valuable help that within a week a radiogram from the island informed us:

"Machine dismantled and the parts hauled on shore. Stored them against the wall of our dump. Building the remaining three walls with snow. The machine will be in good shape. Greetings to Vodopyanov and tell him not to worry."

They were fine lads who wintered on Komsomolsky Island. If I had any say in the matter, I would certainly give it that glorious name and put it down on all the maps of the world.

* * *

The future of the Soviet Arctic depends upon our wonderful youth who in increasing numbers go to make up the personnel of the polar stations and to augment the ranks of the polar aviators. They are drawn to the Far North by the romanticism of the fight against grim nature, by the difficult but interesting work which is of great importance to the Soviet State.

Our young people like to brave difficulties and be in the forefront of socialist construction. They will be found in the Altai ploughing virgin land, or building a giant hydro-power plant on a great Siberian river.

I had the good fortune of visiting one big construction site and of talking to some of the young people there. A slim young fellow with deep blue eyes said to me:

"When I went to school I wanted to be a pilot. All other vocations seemed dull to me. But today I would not exchange my walking excavator for any aircraft. I've learnt to love my profession. I am taking a correspondence course and hope to become an electrical engineer."

"Well, that's how things ought to be," I said. "Each of us thinks his job is the best and most interesting. And our life is really good."

I spoke to the young builders about the arctic wilderness, which came to life under Soviet rule, and about the conquest of the North Pole. Then we talked about the present and the future. My companions told me they were all studying and that most of them hoped not only to work on the splendid machines already in existence but to design and build new ones.

I n 1954 I was detailed to inspect the polar stations on the shores of the Northern Sea Route and on the islands. I was also to make an early reconnaissance of ice conditions in the Chukchi, East Siberian and Laptev seas.

On April 11 we alighted at Cape Shmidt. What a coincidence! Exactly twenty years before, on April 11, 1934, I made my first flight to the extreme point of far-away Chukotka, which I reached with great difficulty. From there I made a hop to an ice-floe drifting in the Chukchi Sea, on which, in the foggy haze, the shipwrecked Chelyuskinites waited to be taken to safety.

Very few people believed in the success of our perilous air expedition. They knew our route lay across tall mountains, unexplored space, over places where no aircraft had yet flown. In 1934 the journey from Moscow to Chukotka took almost a month.

In 1954, taking off one early spring morning from an aerodrome near Moscow, we reached Arkhangelsk—the gateway of the Arctic, as polar explorers are wont to say—in two hours forty minutes, and were in Chukotka the next day.

It was not only that a fast plane in 1934 could do no more than 113 miles an hour compared with the 200-odd miles of a modern passenger plane. The treacherous Arctic is inhospitable to air travellers irrespective of the speed of their craft. The weather changes almost every hour, and you never can tell what surprises await you. But now we are able to fly in any weather. Therefore the Arctic is now much nearer Moscow.

We reached Cape Shmidt when the sun was only rising over the horizon. The arctic settlers were still asleep. Their day is very similar to that everywhere else. They begin their working day at nine in the morning. In Moscow at this hour the Kremlin clock chimes midnight. The man on duty at the airport took us to the aviators' quarters where we had a good rest.

I could hardly recognize these familiar places. When I first came here, there were only two or three tiny huts which housed the staff of the polar station, and four or five Chukchi tents. The polar station at the cape was established in 1932. The first arrivals did not have an easy time, having to live in tents or in the open air, although they had brought building materials with them. There were no carpenters or builders among them and yet they managed, in a relatively short time, to build tiny huts, a warehouse and a radio station.

Today there is a long street of two-storey wooden cottages on Cape Shmidt. I did not see a single tent, for the Chukchi natives had also moved into new houses. Each cottage has four roomy apartments with all comforts available in the North, including electricity. This arctic settlement has all that is necessary for a normal existence: a bath-house, club, hospital and shop. In this most northerly shop in our vast country I bought a box of Moscow cigarettes, chocolate and fresh lemons. Yes, bright yellow fragrant lemons—the fruit of the sunny South. Here scurvy—the much-dreaded disease of the North—has long been forgotten, for all the arctic settlements and far-flung polar stations have onions and garlic in abundance, fresh vegetables and nearly always lemons, which contain all the essential vitamins.

Here, I visited a seven-grade school. I was surrounded by Chukchi children, many of whom had come here from tundra settlements, situated one or two hundred miles away. They live in a comfortable boarding-house at state expense throughout the school year. The black-eyed little chaps and girls in neat blue suits and dresses, nearly all wearing red Pioneer ties, were very cheerful and curious. They asked very many questions, all of which I could not possibly answer. I told them about my flights to the Arctic, about Moscow and how school children on the mainland live and study. Finally it was my turn to put questions. I asked Zoya Kangalyavle, a Young Pioneer in the sixth grade, a strongly built little girl with thick black hair and broad Mongolian features, why she and her school friends did not go home for the winter vacations.

Zoya replied in good Russian, but with a slight accent, that her parents were deer breeders in the Lenin collective farm and frequently moved from place to place.

"I simply don't know where to look for them in the tundra," said the girl. "Even when somebody does come here from the collective farm, we don't go home for fear of being late for school. But when the summer comes we hurry off to the mountains or the tundra where the rivers flow."

The children of this boarding-school entertained us, dancing, singing and reciting in Russian and Chukchi.

Our plane left Cape Shmidt on a clear fine morning.

It's nice in the North on a quiet sunny day. The visibility here is incomparable with anything in any other place on the globe. We had only risen aloft when far ahead of us, in the Chukchi Sea, we saw the mountain tops of Wrangel Island, which was about 125 miles distant.

It must have been on such a clear spring morning that, several hundred years ago, the Chukchi first saw from their native shore the mysterious land rising from the waters of the cold and turbulent sea, which even in the summer w̄as covered with floating ice. Already in 1645 Mikhailo Stadukhin, the founder of the Nizhne-Kolymsk settlement, reported to his superiors that, according to some Kolyma woman, "there was on the yonder side of the Yana and Kolyma rivers an island visible from the mother shore...."

On the map of the polar region, charted in 1763 by the brilliant Russian scientist Mikhail Vasilyevich Lomonosov, north of the Chukchi Peninsula was the big Somnitelny Island, the position of which was very close to that of Wrangel Island.

Only in 1926 was the hitherto uninhabited Wrangel Island permanently settled. And these first settlers were Soviet people. The chief of the island was Georgi Alexeyevich Ushakov, who later became a leading Soviet explorer. The other settlers included two Russian hunters and several Eskimo families. From then on large-scale and important scientific work has been conducted on the island and large numbers of polar fox, walrus, white bear and seal hunted.

In 1936 the newspaper *Pravda* published a letter from the Eskimo hunters on Wrangel Island:

"Ten times in the winter the sun dipped and there were ten big nights. Ten times the sun in the summer remained for long in the sky and there were ten big days. Ten times in the summer walrus came and birds flew. That's how long we live on Wrangel Island.

"Sometimes we look back on our old life at the Chukchi Peninsula. We were all sorry to leave the land of our fathers for an unknown island. Now we know the island as our own tent. We also know the mountain passes, the rivers and gorges. We have learnt to hunt sea and fur animals. Formerly, before Soviet rule, there was darkness in our heads as during the big night in winter when there is no sun.

". . . We all see we have changed. We hunt better and live better. We now got to baths, wash our plates and dishes and bake bread. We like wearing underwear, and we wash it. We have European clothes and, when it's not too cold, wear them. We are no longer *inorodtsy* (aliens), as we were called before the Revolution. Now we are citizens, like all who live and work on Soviet soil."

The Eskimo hunters on Wrangel Island have now organized themselves into artels. A good many of them have been decorated for outstanding production achievements. The Eskimoes live in good, well-furnished houses. Many have radios.

The Eskimo hunters on Wrangel Island have big incomes and are big buyers of clothing, fabrics, dresses, underwear, layettes, watches and sewing-machines.

Not so very long ago the hunter would go to the shaman when he or one of his family were ill. Today they seek the advice of the doctor. If necessary the sick are evacuated to the mainland for further treatment. In February, 1954, Ainafak, a hunter, and Misha Nioko, a schoolboy, were thus flown to the mainland in an ambulance plane.

There are already several settlements on Wrangel Island, which have changed the landscape of the grim wilderness. Soviet people have also changed the fauna of the northern island. When flying over the island I saw about two hundred reindeer pasturing in different places.

Where had these animals come from?

As I learnt later, eight years ago, Kruze, the polar pilot, and his navigator Akkuratov made regular flights to the island, bringing food and ammunition for the polar party and the Eskimoes.

Once they arrived with an unusual cargo—seven young reindeer. "In an emergency the islanders can always slaughter the reindeer, which will give them the badly needed fresh meat and skins," thought the pilot.

The animals found more than enough feed on the island. There had been reindeer there many years ago. This was evident from the many antlers that were found on the island, though, of course, no one knew when and how they had disappeared. They may have succumbed to some disease or, driven by hunger during the snowy winters, when the winds pack the snow so tightly that the earth cannot be reached with an iron spade, they may have escaped across the ice to the Chukchi Peninsula. Some may have reached land or they may all have perished on the way.

The hunters chased the herd into the tundra. The animals appeared to have a good appetite after the flight and, digging up the snow with their hoofs, began to feed. Only one young mother did not graze. The hunters wondered whether she was affected by air sickness and had fallen ill. When the engine began to hum, she dashed towards the plane as if determined to go back.

Next day Kruze returned with eight more animals. And again the mother roamed about the beach. The hunters chased her to the tundra, but she invariably came back as if expecting the return of the plane.

The hunters decided to kill the stubborn mother, but the chief of the island stopped them.

One old Eskimo guessed what was the matter. The mother must have grieved the loss of her calf left behind on the mainland. Eventually she joined the herd.

The deer became acclimatized, multiplied and ran wild. At present males are even hunted.

★ ★ ★

The Soviet Arctic is being harnessed more and more. Our polar explorers abide sacredly by what M.V. Lomonosov had commanded them: "Everywhere to take note of the different places rich in fish and animals, or places where depots and shelters could be established for the good of future navigation.... To undertake physical experiments ... not only essential to science for the interpretation of nature, but also for the glory they will bring us and for the help they may be to future navigation."

The network of scientific polar stations is steadily growing.

Take, for example, Henrietta Island, the northernmost of the De Long string of islands. Before World War II a polar station functioned on this little islet. The three little bungalows are still there and now a new group of scientific workers has settled in them. Once again the polar station radioes its observations and another "blank spot" has disappeared from the weather chart.

Through the ages, by the efforts of various expeditions, sometimes at the price of heavy sacrifice, humanity has amassed true knowledge about the nature of the central basin of the Arctic Ocean. Gradually, the mysterious "blank spots," the fantastic islands and continents were erased from the maps. Many great explorers had pried into the secrets of the polar regions, but it was the Soviet explorers who by their daring penetration to the heart of the Arctic—the Pole— had ripped the veil of mystery from them. Their exploits have made it possible to travel in this icy wilderness as in places of habitation.

Soviet science has made tremendous progress in the study of the majestic and formidable Arctic Ocean. The various expeditions and the work of the drifting stations have made it possible thoroughly to survey previously unexplored regions in the central Arctic.

And here again aircraft has been of invaluable assistance to the polar explorers.

In 1937, soon after the establishment of the North Pole drifting station, Academician O.Y. Shmidt wrote:

"The experience of our expedition shows that the possibilities of aircraft as a means of exploration are much higher than was previously considered. Apart from the fact that a drifting station like Papanin's can be established on the Pole or in some other part of the central polar basin, aircraft can be used extensively for scientific work of several days' or several weeks' duration on chosen ice-floes. Such a flying laboratory will be able to work in different parts of the Arctic in one season. And now there is not the slightest doubt that aircraft will be able to alight anywhere. The new types of planes with a larger range and greater speed, which our country is now producing, will easily solve the problem."

I took part in several expeditions in the high latitudes, organized on this principle. On one occasion the air group was commanded by Cherevichny and Kotov. I flew with Cherevichny in the capacity of assistant chief of the expedition.

We took off from an aerodrome near Moscow and setting the course north, that same day reached Tiksi Bay, covering 2,500 miles. We established our depot on land and flew to the region of the pole of relative inaccessibility.

The panorama beneath our wing was monotonous—solid pack-ice, scarred by leads. There were also frequent chaotic accumulations of ice. Finally Vadim Petrovich Padalko, the navigator, reported to the ship's commander: "We are in latitude $80^0 30'$ N. and longitude 150^0 E." This was precisely the point where the first drifting base was planned.

The two planes circled in search of a suitable ice-field. Soon one was found and Cherevichny went down for the landing. I do not know about the ship's commander but, frankly, I was just as excited as when I made my first landing on the North Pole.

We landed well on the deep snow coating the big flat ice-floe. Kotov followed. Before long there was a big "settlement" on the floe. Our tents, designed by Shaposhnikov, covered with tarpaulin, closely resembled the Chukchi tents and had the same shape of a clipped cigar-end. It took but a few minutes to assemble the duralumin carcasses. Inside it was warm and cosy. Each had a two-ring gas-stove, so the crew lived in comparative comfort. The cooking was done in turns. We had a good variety of food. But

An assembled tent

in addition to the usual supplies we were provided with fresh reindeer meat and pork, frozen fish and sackfuls of meat dumplings. The sacks generally contained a moving note with greetings and best wishes. This was now a tradition. Like in the years of the war, when our young women invariably enclosed touching letters in parcels, sent to unknown soldiers at the front, the Siberian girls now sent messages to their "dear polar comrades" together with their delicious dumplings.

The tents for scientific work were pitched near the residential tents. The meteorologists, magnetologists and hydrobiologists all had their mobile "laboratories." The magnetologists also built square snow pavilions to keep the wind from disturbing their precision instruments. Observations continued day and night; readings of the instruments, of the force and pressure of the wind, and of the temperature and humidity of the air were taken every hour.

Another observation point, where scientific work was conducted, was established some 250 miles from the geographical pole. The

317

hydrologists took many soundings. Tents were pitched over holes drilled in the sea ice and primus stoves kept burning. It was warm inside and the men worked in their sweaters or fur blouses, while outside it was 30 or 35 degrees of cold.

For soundings automatic winches were used. Measurements were taken of currents at various depths as well as of the temperature and salinity of the water.

Each day the planes hopped from floe to floe where new "points" were set up. Generally, the first plane would choose a suitable floe. The pilot of that machine carried a drill for measuring the thickness of the ice, explosives with which to open the ice for hydraulic soundings, while the second machine delivered the tent, winch and scientific personnel. It took but a few minutes for the hydraulic station to begin to operate. The pilots and air-mechanics helped the hydrologists and meteorologists to unload, pitch the tents and set up the winch. The crews always worked in close contact with the scientific personnel. Their work done, the men would abandon their post and start out for another. ,

No soundings had yet been made of vast areas in the Arctic Ocean. There were still white blanks on the maps of the central polar basin which we tried to erase.

The depth altered sharply. One day, it would be 13,500 feet, and the next, when the floe was carried to another place, it would be different. In some places the line would only go down to 3,500 feet. This showed that the bed of the Arctic Ocean was very uneven.

The data gathered by our expeditions made it possible to draw up the first reliable chart of the depths in the central part of the Arctic Ocean. This helped to solve the question of subaqueous mountain chains in the central polar basin. Soviet polar explorers discovered and explored the huge subaqueous mountain chain, which rises to a height of ten or twelve thousand feet and runs across the Arctic Ocean from the Novosibirskiye Islands to Greenland and Elles- mere Land, as well as other elevations on the sea bottom, dividing the ocean into a number of deep hollows. The newly discovered subaqueous mountain chain has been named after the glorious

On a drifting floe

founder of arctic oceanography, the great Russian scientist, Mikhail Vasilyevich Lomonosov.

The observations of our scientists refuted the view of the extreme poverty of life in the central Arctic.

Once I was in the hydrobiological tent on a drifting floe when Yakov Yakovlevich Gakkel was taking samples of water. We saw a little fish with a blunt tail brought up from the sea. It was not particularly beautiful, grey, about four inches long, and very much like our gudgeon. This was our biggest catch in latitude 87° N. The North Pole is no place for fishermen, but hunters would have a busy time.

We saw the first polar "resident" in 1937, soon after the landing of the N-170 on the North Pole. It was a snow bunting. Then came sea-gulls, white bears and seals. We came across polar fox, wild ducks, sea hare. Unknown species of plankton organisms, including a number of crayfish with paddle-like legs, were also discovered in the arctic depths.

And so after many years three more planes went to the North Pole. Cherevichny came down first on a floe about seven hundred yards long.

We felt quite at home at the Pole. This was my third trip. Many were making their second Pole journey, among them cinema-operator Troyanovsky, navigator Akkuratov, pilot Mazuruk and air-mechanic Shmandin.

The first thing we did on landing at the Pole was to give three cheers for the Communist Party and the Soviet Government and to hoist the red flag on the tallest hummock. The machine piloted by Cherevichny soon turned back, Kotov and Maslennikov remained on the ice.

Tents were pitched, a hole made in the ice, and two and a half hours later the first sounding was made, following which samples of sea-water were taken from various depths. Step by step, without any fuss, observations were made: the sea-water was subjected to chemical analysis, thermometers registered the temperature of the water with the precision of up to one-hundredth of a degree, hydrometers recorded currents at various horizons.

Pavel Afanasyevich Gordiyenko, the hydrologist, suddenly discovered a narrow crack running across the ice. This seemingly innocent little crack, which passed near the tent covering the hole in the ice, was the forerunner of grim events.

The alert was sounded and the mechanics at once began starting the engines. That was not an easy task in the frost. Meanwhile, things happened fast. The crack, which first ran across the thin ice of the landing field, now stretched far beyond the old pack-ice, where the planes were stationed, and was growing wider and wider. After great effort the crevasse, which was now nearly a yard wide, was bridged with plywood, planks and ice. The engines already hummed and the machines were able safely to move on to a new floe where the tents and equipment were also shifted. This was done in good time. The red flag, proudly flying on the hummock, began slowly to drift aside. The airfield we had landed on and hoped to use for the take-off was also on the move. This was the only suitable runway in the vicinity.

Hydrologists establishing winch with the sounding-line

Soon a strong wind began to blow and the ice to break up. One of our companions graphically called this "threshing." Our old camp drifted past us at a speed of over a mile an hour. Our runway was split up, and the numerous ice cakes ran over one another during pressure and then parted as if they were playing leapfrog. And then in a newly formed rift the head of a seal would pop up. It was an unusual sight, for no one expected such a visitor at the northernmost point of the globe. The first to regain his composure was Piskaryov, co-pilot of one of the machines, who ran into his tent, grabbed a rifle and killed the seal.

The ice continued to break up. Our chances of getting under way diminished every minute. The old depot had drifted away. The red flag on the hummock was now barely visible.

The radio-operator reported the situation to the chief of the expedition. The latter took off at once and radioed that the nearest strip of flat ice was over thirty miles distant. But how could we hope to taxi thirty miles, threading our way amid huge hummocks and hopping over leads?

Two days later the wind abated and visibility improved.

Gordiyenko, Kotov and Maslennikov decided to go out and take stock of the surroundings. The picture they beheld was not very comforting. All around was a chaotic mass of jumbled ice, eight and ten yards high, with no sign of level ice anywhere. Nature seemed to have exerted every effort to prevent our leaving the place. All at once we came upon a small cake—the remains of our old runway—which had returned and, colliding with other floes, formed a winding strip about three hundred yards long. The sheet was scarred with cracks, and hummocks rose at the junction points.

We decided to turn this three-hundred-yard floe into a runway. That was our only chance. All hands immediately turned to, levelling out the rough spots and filling in the depressions with snow and ice. In about twelve hours the floe was made to look more pleasing, but it was still too short. A take-off seemed an impossible undertaking. It was, therefore, decided to lighten the plane to the limit; to empty all the tanks, leaving only enough petrol for an hour's flight.

Kotov taxied up the runway, put on full power, the machine dashed forward and rose into the air within only a few yards from the ice blocks. Even Kotov with all his skill and experience had never before taken the air from such a short and crooked runway. The feat was repeated just as skilfully by Hero of the Soviet Union, Vitaly Ivanovich Maslennikov.

Half an hour later the two machines landed on another floe.

★ ★ ★

A most interesting element in arctic science is the study of land magnetism in the central polar basin.

The first studies of land magnetism were made by ancient seafarers, who examined the phenomenon with the ways and means then available, seeking mainly to determine the magnetic declination, that is the angle between the true meridian and the magnetic meridian. The study of magnetic declination is of immense importance for both sea and air navigation.

Meteorologists on the floe

For a long time magnetic observations were mostly confined to the moderate latitudes. In the central Arctic the study of land magnetism is of recent standing. But even the scanty information that science was able to collect about the peculiarities of the geomagnetic field in the central Arctic was of outstanding interest.

Apart from the usual and calm fluctuations in land magnetism, there are sometimes sharp changes of several hours' and even of several days' duration, which spread over large areas of the earth's surface. These are the so-called magnetic storms most frequently observed in the polar regions. The observations made during the drift of the *Sedov* show that the magnetic storm which broke out on April 17, 1939, in latitude 86°16' N. and longitude 87°50' E. raged for several days. The amplitude modulation during this storm in the course of the day was over 52°, while in other areas the displacement of the magnetic needle did not exceed 10-15°.

The Soviet arctic expeditions and polar stations amassed extensive data on the variability of the earth's magnetism in the high latitudes.

A big contribution to the study of the central polar basin has been made by a group of scientists under Somov.

Mikhail Mikhailovich Somov, Doctor of Geography and Hero of the Soviet Union, is one of the best-known representatives of the younger generation of Soviet arctic explorers. I shall speak about him at greater length.

Fate brought Mikhail Somov, a young Muscovite, to the Far East where his father, an ichthyologist, had taken on an engagement. Somov worked as a turner in the workshops of the Pacific Ocean Institute of Oceanography with some young people who sailed the Pacific and were fascinated by the Far East.

Recalling his initial steps along the road of science Somov said he had felt sore when his companions returned from voyages with thrilling stories about Kamchatka, Sakhalin and battles with the storms while he worked at his lathe. Finally, in 1932, giving way to temptation, he set out with an expedition in the capacity of hydrologist. Somov was then twenty-four.

Two years later he was admitted to the Moscow Hydrometeorological Institute. There he studied under Professor Nikolai Nikolayevich Zubov, well-known polar explorer, who imbued in him love for and interest in the Arctic. Somov managed to complete the course in two and a half years with the degree of oceanographic engineer. The young graduate was sent to the Central Weather Institute and charged with setting up a marine department to compile weather charts for all Soviet seas.

Under Zubov's supervision Somov and his companions made a detailed forecast of ice conditions for 1938 along the entire Northern Sea Route from Bering Strait to the Barents Sea. It was the first forecast based on the findings of a scientific institution rather than on the personal views of one explorer. Ice-condition forecasts for given regions had formerly been made by individual explorers and later discussed by the inter-departmental ice-forecasting bureau.

That same year it was decided to put a hydrologist on aircraft reconnoitring ice conditions; this work had formerly been done by the navigators. The first man appointed to the job was Somov.

From 1939 Somov worked in the system of the Northern Sea

Route Administration. He participated in many expeditions, was hydrologist during many sea voyages and stayed in the Arctic for years at a stretch.

I made Somov's acquaintance at a drifting station. The supplies of the station had to be replenished and I was charged with the operation. All the cargo had to be brought from Cape Shmidt.

The expedition disposed of two twin-engined planes under the command of the well-known polar flyers Titlov and Osipov, and our invariable four-engined "arctic lorry," piloted by Zadkov.

Somov told me that a narrow runway was ready on the drifting floe.

"All's well," I thought.

The long polar night was drawing near. Strong winds and snow-storms prevented regular flights, though the pilots were not very much worried about the weather as long as landing conditions were adequate.

Approaching the station we saw the "T" lights, indicating the direction of the landing, and the flares lining the runway.

We delivered part of the provisions, a caterpillar lorry GAZ-67, letters and newspapers. Needless to say the valiant wintering party gave us a hearty welcome.

Somov's companions were splendid. Much could be said about Nikitin, M.Sc., a veteran of the Arctic Institute, and about the youngest of the group, Gudkovich.

Gudkovich was the hydrologist and meteorologist as well as the ice-surveyor. In addition to these duties he was the driver of a dog team.

The young man learned to drive a dog team in a few days. True, he had quite a lot of trouble with one obstinate dog which bit through the harness and ran away. This was when the dogs' "psychology" manifested itself. The nine other members of the team were very angry with the "idler," which ran around them refusing to do any work. At the sight of it they would pull at their lashings, upset the sledge and Gudkovich would lose control. He was inclined to shoot the ungovernable hound, but Somov would not permit it.

All our attempts to capture the idler were useless for it fed on leavings, which were plentiful, and was not even tempted by a luscious chunk of beef. Next day the dog was cornered by its harness mates which would have torn it to bits if we had not come to the rescue. We tried to get it into harness but the team would not let it near the sledge. Somebody suggested giving it a sound thrashing in front of all the dogs or they would kill it. The idea was adopted. There was a lot of squealing, but when the stubborn hound was again harnessed, it was left alone and there was no more trouble.

We were getting ready to repeat the flight when a message from Somov stated: "Cracks running across our floe, cannot receive the plane. Wait until we prepare another."

Meanwhile instructions from Moscow arrived, urging us to deliver the cargo with all speed. Then I decided to drop such loads as butter, meat dumplings, beef carcasses and other unbreakable goods.

When our aircraft appeared over the camp in the middle of the night and began to "bomb" it, Somov radioed in panic to Cape Shmidt and Moscow: "Stop this barbarous waste of food."

The experiment was obviously a failure. The sackfuls of beef bumped against the ice: nothing remained but the bones and a reddish meat powder over an area of about 20 or 30 yards. The dumplings flew on all sides like bomb fragments which the party later gathered like mushrooms. The cigarettes were packed in sealed containers. Many of the Kazbek cigarette boxes were in perfect condition, but inside there was not a single cigarette intact.

A few days afterwards I was able to make another flight to the drifting station. We took with us Dr. Volovich, who was an ardent arctic enthusiast.

Volovich volunteered to be also the cook of the drifting station. The party eagerly awaited his arrival. But the doctor proved to be no expert on the job and although he had an excellently bound cookery-book with him he was rarely able to produce a dish without burning it. Once Volovich decided to treat us to a mushroom soup. He put some dried mushrooms into the water and let it boil until it turned into a brownish mess. Volovich cooked for over six months, but I don't think any decent restaurant would employ him even as a kitchen-boy. He worked under very trying conditions, but never complained.

Finally a runway was prepared and Zadkov arrived in his heavy plane with the remaining cargo; the station was now supplied with all necessities.

Warmly taking leave of the polar party, we started out for the return journey.

In the spring, when the polar day set in, Mazuruk took the Somov group off the ice.

Reconnoitring ice conditions about four years later, Maslennikov saw broken cases and a ragged tent on a floe in the ocean. Flying low he satisfied himself that it really was the remains of the camp of the Somov group. Somov and his men left the floe in latitude 82^0 N. and Maslennikov found it at 75^0. How did the remains of Somov's floe come to be 440 miles south?

An article by V. Burkhanov, published in *Pravda* on May 16, 1954, shows that the abandoned ice-floe with the empty cases and ragged tent had traversed a long path. First it drifted north, northeast, then east and south, finally it skirted the Canadian arctic archipelago in the direction of Cape Barrow, and from there returned to the meridian of Wrangel Island. It follows that this ice-floe made a full circle clockwise and continued on its former drift.

* * *

Never before had such large-scale exploration been undertaken in the Arctic, and with such first-class equipment, as in recent years. The country supplies Soviet explorers of the high latitudes with all they need.

With the new technology came new men, and the explorers now working in the Arctic are usually men with extensive knowledge. The Arctic appealed to them and they went there well prepared for the struggle against the grim nature and for the big and vital work which the country entrusted to them. Let me mention some of them.

Alexey Fyodorovich Treshnikov is a young scientist who was

awarded the title of Hero of Socialist Labour for his extensive scientific exploration with expeditions in the high latitudes.

Treshnikov ranks among the leading Soviet scientists who have made vital contributions to arctic study. He is the author of an outstanding work, which provides new data on the ice in the central Arctic, data which refutes the former view that the Arctic Ocean is a solid mass of pack-ice.

Hardy, persevering and cheerful, Treshnikov continues the glorious traditions laid down by the pioneers of Russian scientific exploration—Makarov, Rusanov, Sibiryakov, Vize, Zubov, and others.

Yevgeny Ivanovich Tolstikov, Master of Geography, is an aerometeorologist by profession. He was graduated from the Moscow Hydrometeorological Institute in 1937, and has since devoted himself to arctic studies.

Tolstikov was chief of the first meteorological bureau in the eastern Arctic on Cape Shmidt. His first papers devoted to meteorological conditions in the Chukchi and East-Siberian seas are valuable contributions to arctic research.

Tolstikov is particularly well known for his splendid work during extremely difficult arctic operations. He participated in the most important expeditions in the high latitudes and wintered in various parts of the Arctic. Tolstikov's wife is also a polar explorer and considered to be one of the best meteorologists in the Soviet Arctic. Their children were born beyond the polar circle.

Pavel Afanasyevich Gordiyenko, a hydrologist, is also well known among arctic explorers. He began preparing himself for work in the Far North when studying under Professor Zubov at the institute. He strove not only to acquire special knowledge, but also to steel his body, which is so essential for the polar explorer. Gordiyenko was one of the first mountain climbers to ascend the Elbrus in winter. He also devoted a lot of time to yachting. All this helped him in his experimental work on oceanography, conducted under very trying conditions in the vicinity of Dikson Island, Long Channel and other places.

Gordiyenko was the initiator of extensive use of aircraft for ice reconnaissance. His more than 30 scientific papers are devoted to methods of reconnoitring and forecasting ice conditions. Gordiyenko carried out a series of daring operations in escorting ships through ice, participated in many expeditions in the high latitudes and flew several thousand hours observing ice conditions and covering almost a million miles over arctic seas.

Nikolai Alexandrovich Volkov, another outstanding hydrologist, has as many flying hours to his credit. I might mention that, like Somov, Tolstikov and Gordiyenko, Volkov had been a skilled turner. The youthful turner from Kimry had read the books of Amundsen, Nansen, and other polar explorers and then entered the faculty of geography at Leningrad University. He acquired his first arctic experience with an expedition which was sailing to the Kara Gates. The ship *Lomonosov*, with Volkov on board, was caught in a hurricane which wrecked the radio room. The storm drove the unnavigable ship to the Norwegian shores.

Volkov spent many winters in the Arctic and took part in many polar expeditions.

Thanks to the endeavours of our hydrologists who participated in ice reconnaissance, navigation in the ice is now safe. The days of errors which the ships' captains could not possibly avoid have now passed. Had the *Chelyuskin*, for example, not skirted the edge of the ice, keeping close to the shore, but turned twenty miles north she would have reached open water and sailed to the Bering Sea.

Having made a study of the ice-drift, our hydrologists can now determine beforehand where and what course to follow, find leads and channels and escort the ships under most difficult ice conditions.

The efforts of the Soviet people to master the Arctic are already bearing fruit. The Northern Sea Route has become fully navigable. The arctic seas can be sailed only with the aid of powerful ice-breakers and an excellent air reconnaissance service, based on a network of hydrometeorological stations, which make systematic surveys of the atmosphere and provide navigators with the latest data on ice conditions. We have all this. All this had been created by our polar explorers.

Our Far North has become a highway connecting Europe and the Far East. Today our arctic seamen are working to prolong the navigation season in the Arctic. Ships sailing from Tıksi and Nordvik east and west in the late autumn are no exception nowadays.

The work of our Soviet polar explorers—scientific personnel, wintering parties, pilots and seamen, engaged in the study of the arctic vistas and the Northern Sea Route—is part of the general endeavour of the great Soviet people, building communism.